Secrets from the Lost Bible

SECRETS
FROM THE
LOST BIBLE

KENNETH HANSON, PH.D.

Council Oak Books

San Francisco / Tulsa

Publishers have generously given permission to use extended quotations
from the following copyrighted works:

From "Imagine," by John Lennon, © 1971 by EMI Blackwood Music, Inc.
(BMI Work #713414). Used by permission.

From "Mrs. Robinson" by Paul Simon and Art Garfunkel,
© 1967 by Paul Simon Music (BMI Work #1021471). Used by permission.

From "Superman," by John Ondrasik, © 2000 by EMI Blackwood Music, Inc.
(BMI Work #5291886). Used by permission.

From "Teach Your Children," by Crosby, Stills, Nash and Young,
© 1970 by Sony ATV Tunes (Title Code: 500201703). Used by permission.

From "Tin Man," by Dewey Bunnell, © 1974 WB Music Corp., Warner Bros., Inc. (Title Code:
500229774). Used by permission.

Etchings by the famed nineteenth century illustrator Gustav Doré appear on the following pages:

Page 1: Illustration from John Milton's *Paradise Lost*, "So numberless were those bad
Angels seen, / Hovering on wing, under the cope of Hell (I. 344, 345)

Page 7: Illustration from the 1865 "Doré Bible" (*La Sainte Bible*),
"Adam and Eve Driven out of Eden" (Genesis 3:24)

Page 53: Illustration from the 1865 "Doré Bible" (*La Sainte Bible*),
"Elijah Taken up to Heaven in a Chariot of Fire" (II Kings 2: 11, 12)

Page 123: Illustration from the 1865 "Doré Bible" (*La Sainte Bible*), "Baruch," (Baruch 3:14)

Page 171: Illustration from the 1865 "Doré Bible" (*La Sainte Bible*),
"Judith Showing the Head of Holofernes" (Judith 13:14)

ISBN 0-7394-6039-0

To my wife, Elena
and my sons, Jonathan and Pieter

C⊕N+EN+S

PREFACE

Secrets from the Lost Bible is a new approach to what is literally the wisdom of the ages. While few people even know that these texts exist, they have survived for thousands of years, ready to be mined for the wealth of secret knowledge they contain. The lessons and parables of the ancients have as much relevance to our own lives today as they did when these pages were written, for they offer us the means to realize our full potential.

The tangled history of the books themselves—how they came to be written and preserved—is almost as fascinating as the wisdom they convey. For centuries, these manuscripts were systematically suppressed, because their liberating messages of individual power challenged the authority of political and religious leaders.

This little-known library illuminates the path of personal redemption and contains the secrets of how we can realize our individual creative potential. Some of these lost books turned up among the ancient library of the Dead Sea Scrolls. They include assorted mystical teachings which later developed into an entire esoteric discipline called Kabbalah, Others include a host of books that never made it into the Bible, called the Apocrypha (which means hidden) and the Pseudepigrapha (called false writings by those who suppressed them). Additionally, there are the Gnostic texts of Nag Hammadi—a location in Egypt where a treasure trove of lost books was discovered in the middle of the twentieth century. Collectively, they comprise the Lost Bible.

Within the Lost Bible, we find many of the same characters, events, and narratives preserved in the biblical canon—the official list of sacred texts. Yet, these books were cast out as heretical, salacious, occult, or untrustworthy for reasons we can guess at, but do not know for sure. Nonetheless, they offer insights into the human experience that are almost uncannily appropriate to us in the twenty-first century. Perhaps it is no accident that they are emerging from obscurity at this moment in human history, for they contain truths that can guide us toward greater self-knowledge, wholeness, fulfillment, and peace (*shalom*).

The Jewish mystics organized their understanding of the workings of the universe into Four Worlds: the World of Knowing, the World of Being, the World of Feeling, and the World of Doing. Far from being mutually exclusive, these aspects of creation together form the whole of reality. I have ordered this book according to the same schema as ordained by those sages.

I N ✝ R ⊕ D U C ✝ I ⊕ N

Let your imagination take charge, like a winged seraph, leading you to a place you have never before dreamed of. You are about to enter another world . . . of prophets and mystics, patriarchs and sages, saints and visionaries, consumed with holy fire.

Welcome to the world of the Lost Bible, an entire library of hidden wisdom, a treasury of ancient writings that never found their way into our Bibles. They were suppressed through the desire of religious leaders across the centuries who consigned to the blackest pit any writings that did not conform to their narrow notions of piety. Today, if we are bold enough to learn the right lessons, these suppressed books can become for us a key to getting out of our own skins; to looking at the world in a new, vital, and healthy way; and to unlocking the transcendent mysteries of life. They can open us to the world of Spirit and transform us. These texts—scores and scores of them once declared unworthy—very nearly perished from the earth, only to re-emerge in our day and time.

But what exactly is the Lost Bible? The place to begin is with personal experience, my individual encounter with a treasury of documents while I was seeking, as it were, the light of day. I first became aware of these ancient texts when I journeyed to the Middle East as a young college student, intent on learning about the history, culture, and textual traditions of the ancient world. I had read the Bible when I was in high school, but I understood that there were other books, multiple volumes that had never been canonized. I had an insatiable curiosity to know more about them. I remember sitting in the musty old library of the American Institute for Holy Land Studies, perched atop the ancient hill called Mount Zion. There, in that place, looking out over the majestic Hinnom Valley, at a view shared by prophets, patriarchs, saints, sages, and kings, I first encountered the books that we call today the Apocrypha and Pseudepigrapha.

Their tone and style were strikingly different from what I was accustomed to reading among the many books of the standard biblical text. They were completely new to me, and I had not a clue what to make of them. They were nonetheless an integral part of my academic rigor, for I had come to Jerusalem as a student of ancient Israelite history, literature, and culture. My focus was an epoch in time known as the Second Temple Period, an age that began in the sixth century before the Common Era (B.C.E.) and stretched to the end of the first century of the Common Era (C.E.) It represents what is perhaps the most pivotal time in the history of the Western world, for it was during the Second Temple Period that the three cultures that have dominated the western half of the planet until this day were born: Judaism, Christianity, and Islam.

This fact I knew implicitly. What I did not know was that the Apocrypha and Pseudepigrapha represent a whole host of ancient literature that circulated widely during the Second Temple Period and that directly influenced those three new religions. As they began to emerge from their infancy, each religion went through the process of developing a distinctive theology, accepting this text as Holy Writ, discarding that one as heresy. Well, truth be told, it was the heresy— the forbidden, the mystical, the erotic and exotic—that attracted me. No doubt about it. I had to devour these long-forgotten and rejected books. And I had to learn about the people who wrote them.

As I sat in that library, I was also aware of the geography of the land where I now resided. The Hinnom Valley, opposite Mount Zion, whose limestone hues greeted my eyes day after day, wended its way inexorably down to the shores of the Dead Sea, about forty kilometers to the east, across the Judean desert.

It was along the northwest shore of the Dead Sea that a curious group of ancient Judeans once established a formidable residence. During the Second Temple Period, roughly two hundred of these Essenes, as they were called, built a substantial settlement known by the Arabs as Qumran. Among the ruins of that settlement, where Judea's limestone hills give way to a series of chalky marl cliffs, we find the remnants of an ancient monastic society, which carefully inscribed on parchment material hundreds and hundreds of mysterious texts now known loosely as the Dead Sea Scrolls. As a young student I had visited this site on more than one occasion, and I had gotten up close and personal with the Scrolls themselves, found by a Bedouin shepherd boy in the year 1947.

The Dead Sea Scrolls include the oldest copies of the Hebrew Bible known to exist in the world—two millennia old, from the first two centuries B.C.E. But they also include hundreds of non-biblical texts, those that were later kept out of the Bible. Some of them were the Essenes' own manuals and rulebooks, assorted psalms and liturgical documents, and fragmentary copies of a number of books of the Apocrypha and Pseudepigrapha. I was astounded that these hidden books—this Lost Bible—were apparently looked on as canonical and inspired by none other than the ancient Essenes themselves. In fact, books such as Enoch and Jubilees (which do not appear in standard Bibles) are prominently represented among the Dead Sea library. Furthermore, we find them directly quoted by other Dead Sea Scrolls, in which they are cited as authoritative and as Holy Writ.

There is no escaping the conclusion that these books (which over the centuries were deemed unholy and therefore sequestered and suppressed) were, among the Jews of antiquity, at least among the Essenes, considered an integral part of the earliest biblical canon. Nestled in the library atop Mount Zion, I often thought of those ancient Essenes and what it must have been like to spend one's entire life immersed in the scribal arts, making copies, not just of the thirty-nine books of the Hebrew Bible, but of the multiple books of the Lost Bible: the Apocrypha and Pseudepigrapha.

Also atop Mount Zion, next door to the American Institute, was an important Christian site known as the Dormitian Abbey, an imposing medieval church whose stone towers mark the location of the death of Jesus' mother, Mary. The legacy of Christianity, along with Judaism deeply rooted in this holy city, was never far away, oozing through the very stones of Mount Zion. I found myself asking: How did the earliest Christians view the Lost Bible? If the Dead Sea Scrolls preserve the Apocrypha and Pseudepigrapha and quote from them liberally, what about the earliest Christian documents? What about the text of the New Testament? Did the writers of the New Testament consider the Lost Bible to be canon, Holy Writ?

I needed some answers. It could certainly be argued that the flavor and concepts of the Lost Bible are preserved in the New Testament. However, such arguments are tenuous and do not really prove anything. As I pored through reams of material, searching the world of the ancient scribes, I came upon precisely such a source of inspiration. Lo and behold, I found a curious passage, cryptically preserved in the New Testament book of Jude, which is, more or less, a smoking gun with regard to the New Testament's view of the apocryphal books:

The seventh descendant from Adam, Enoch, prophesied, declaring, "Behold, the Eternal appeared with a multitude of the righteous, to make judgment upon everyone, and to chastise all the unrighteous, because of all the ungodly deeds they perpetrated, and because of all the harsh words the unrighteous uttered against him." (Jude 1:14-15, author's translation)

The book of Jude is directly quoting the apocryphal book of Enoch. But why, unless Enoch were considered somehow authoritative—unless Enoch were in fact considered Holy Writ? What I had found amounted to proof positive that the earliest Christians included a book of the Lost Bible in their sacred canon, their list of inspired Scripture.

My quest to understand the metaphysical meaning of these books began in earnest. I had a particular custom of performing an almost daily pilgrimage to one of the holiest sites in the holy city—the Mount of Olives. It was there, on that timeless limestone ridge, that I most often pondered the mysteries of the ages. I looked westward over Jerusalem, where the great cupola of the Dome of the Rock, a mosque built in the seventh century by the calif Omar, glistened in a golden hue under the late afternoon sun. The mellow ochre of the ancient ashlars blended together in a kaleidoscopic panorama of church domes, minarets, and quaint synagogues. In this pastiche, the intense religious debates of the centuries faded away, for the structures appeared to stand side by side in the cramped quarters of the Old City—close companions behind the weathered walls built centuries ago by the Ottomans. Religious invective disappeared in this majestic spot. Jerusalem stone conveys beauty, not dogma.

Up there on the Mount of Olives was where most of the answers came to me, perhaps whispered into my soul by some long-forgotten sage from the hoary past. "Search the Kabbalah," the still, small voice seemed to say. Kabbalah, as I well knew, was the way of the Jewish mystics, whose glimpses of the world beyond invigorated their lives in the here and now. To be sure, the mystics have been around for a long time. They were known as Kabbalists in the Middle Ages, though the mystical impulse that moved them can be traced back to the pages of the Hebrew Bible itself. The great prophet Ezekiel, whose ecstatic visions included a glimpse of the divine throne of the Almighty, quite properly belongs in the general realm of Jewish mysticism. He broke through an otherwise impenetrable barrier into the world beyond.

Moreover, the door he opened was enlarged and broadened by subsequent generations of anonymous mystics, who propounded their own visions of heavenly reality. They were the writers of the Lost Bible, the books we call the Apocrypha and Pseudepigrapha. If we think of them not just as anonymous Jewish authors but as ancient "Kabbalists," then Kabbalah itself might lend us a key to the understanding of these books.

Perched atop the Mount of Olives, I began to gain a fresh perspective of both the holy city and the holy books, as well as the officially unholy books of the Lost Bible. Perhaps the reason they were deemed unholy by so many clerics and religious leaders is that this same devout flock of religionists tried to read these texts in an overly literal way, as opposed to the mystical, symbolic way in which they were originally composed. The trouble, I concluded, is that we often try to read Eastern texts with a Western mindset. "Forget abstractions!" we say to ourselves. We want our realities concrete, logical, and syllogistic.

But that still, small voice that had originally beckoned me up the Mount of Olives now whispered a Kabbalistic paradigm into my innermost soul. "The Four Worlds," I heard it say. "They are a blueprint for understanding and interpreting the Lost Bible." What are the Four Worlds? They are four ways of approaching our existence. Much has been written across the centuries of Kabbalistic literature about these four dimensions. They consist of Knowing (*Briyah*), Being (*Atzilut*), Feeling (*Yetzirah*), and Doing (*Asiyah*). Within these Four Worlds, within these realities, we live and move and have our being. Find harmony among them, and we align ourselves with heaven. But fail to appreciate their operation, and our life goes askew.

When we harmonize these four life forces—Knowing, Being, Feeling, and Doing—we get in touch not only with ourselves, but also with the marrow of the universe. We know what we have to do because we know who we are; we appreciate our feelings and can express them; and, we appreciate the sensibilities of others.

The landscape of old Jerusalem, replete with mosques, churches, and synagogues, stood as a challenge to the realities of yesterday and today. The great God-religions of the Western world, with their common heritage, ought to get along. If we could make ourselves broad enough to appreciate the metaphysical messages of this lost library, perhaps we could understand each other better. Perhaps we could appreciate other religions, recognizing that many of their teachings stem from a single root, expressed in these long-suppressed books.

I slowly made my way down the side of the ancient hill and began my journey.

PART I

THE WORLD OF KNOWING (BRIYAH)

A Victim's Tale

The 1960s and 70s were a period of great social upheaval in the United States, and, as those were my formative years, I was quite ready and willing to be an upheaver. I was about to embark on what I thought was a new way of life—the communal lifestyle.

Had I known ancient history a little better, I might have realized that was an old, old story. The ancient Essenes had lived communally for centuries before the time of Christ. Millennia later, when the European feudal system broke up under the combined weight of the Reformation, Counter Reformation, and Industrial Revolution, vast numbers of the peasantry left the rural areas for what British poet William Blake described as the "dark Satanic mills" of the cities where they became little more than cogs in the machinery of commerce. Communes became one form of escape.

The movement spread to the United States in the 1820s, and "arose at the same time as the great tide of religious revivalism, and which was entangled at various points with Transcendentalism, Swedenborgianism, Perfectionism, and Spiritualism," wrote Edmund Wilson in *To the Finland Station*. According to Wilson, "a very few of these communities lasted longer than a decade, but a great many never completed two years." In general they suffered from both internal dissent and external scorn. A member of one such community declared: "They would suffer from lack of faith in those who had the funds and lack of funds in those who had the faith." [1]

In the 1970s, the metaphysical landscape was likewise rich with people who had faith without funds, and who were desirous of finding alternative forms of spirituality. To be sure, on the heels of the student-led revolution of the 1960s came various attempts to reformulate religious expression. I, in particular, was wooed by the Jesus Movement, whose guitar-strumming advocates preached the Christianity of the streets. This elite corps was unconventional by anyone's estimation. They not only passed out underground Jesus People newspapers at airports, but also performed street theater, serenaded passersby with a heavy metal Jesus band, and even organized their own commune in Chicago's inner city. I gravitated toward these radical pure-hearts, becoming convinced of the apocalyptic urgency of our mission. If, as I feared, the world was indeed coming to an end in a decade or two, there wasn't much time left.

It was like an acid-trip without the LSD. I distinctly remember thinking that I had committed intellectual suicide and was glad of it. In those days I was a history major and political science minor at the University of Illinois in Chicago, but I decided to drop out of school, so convinced was I that the time was short and the end near. My middle-class family was horrified, and, looking back, I cannot blame them. But at the time religious zeal won the day. Not only did I embrace the company of the downtown Chicago Jesus People, I also became intimately involved with other expressions of the radical Jesus Movement in various parts of the country, from Minneapolis to Indiana to Oklahoma. Christian communes were springing up, based on a concept they called shepherding.

The idea was that the members of these groups could not really think for themselves. They had to have an authority figure, a shepherd, gently directing them in the way they should go. Obedience was the key. All major decisions were in the domain of the shepherd, from whom to date to whether to go to school to what career path to take. Education was generally discouraged, as was building a career. Ambition was seen as prideful and inconsistent with the humility prized by the group.

The shepherds were also prophets, laying hands upon their sheep and uttering forth the oracles of God. One Christian commune was born in a private home, from a Bible study, which budded into a ministry cementing its members together in a deep interpersonal covenant. Another ministry involved hundreds of middle-class suburbanites, who began selling their homes and pooling their resources, buying up property and moving in together. They purchased a long-abandoned health spa in a rural town in Indiana and renovated the enormous building, turning it into a full-fledged commune. They bought a resort in northern Minnesota, converting it to a retreat center. They also bought a sprawling estate in suburban Chicago, which boasted a palatial home that was soon inhabited by scores of the faithful.

It was there that I met a self-styled prophet by the name of Louis, who encouraged me to abandon an officer's training program I had previously enrolled in at my university. As a direct consequence of following this advice, I was involuntarily inducted into the United States Army as a buck private. What had my religious zeal earned me? Boot camp in the middle of winter.

Ironically enough, my two-year stint in the Army proved to be my salvation, for it afforded me time to ponder life. I came to realize the cult-like aspects of the communal groups in which I had been involved. It dawned on me that what was happening was a form of mind-control, along the lines of that practiced by figures who would later make national headlines—Jim Jones and David Koresh Now I wanted to understand the strange vibrations that had gripped my soul.

After serving two years at Fort Knox, Kentucky, I was discharged, and I used my GI benefits to study abroad in Israel. Thus began my personal quest for knowledge, my path through the World of Knowing. Study was to be my therapy, knowledge my deliverance. It was freedom and power, for I understood implicitly that no cultic group of domineering shepherds could control me as long as I knew more than they did. That is how I came to study the great religious systems of the Western world and their ancient roots. That is how I came to discover the secret books of the Apocrypha and Pseudepigrapha. That is how I came to identify with the ancient writers of these books and their incessant quest for knowledge.

LESSONS LEARNED

It was Aristotle who taught, "Know thyself," and never has there been a more powerful admonition. However, true knowledge is not about abstractions or the sort of things one studies for tests in school. True knowledge is ultimately about consciousness, self-awareness, which in turn leads to taking responsibility for our own lives. Why is it that so many people in today's society fall prey, not only to religious cults but also to all manner of destructive behaviors, from illegal drug use to marital infidelity? It has been said that we live in a victim's culture, wherein people are content to portray themselves as helpless pawns in some cosmic chess game, not responsible for their actions because they have been victimized by somebody else: their parents, a dysfunctional family, despotic bosses, or even religious leaders. Clinical psychologists deal with an endless line of such victims who cannot manage, control, or organize their own lives because they have never established an integrative framework through which to view the world around them. Adrift, they seek harbor wherever there appears to be a friendly port.

The first thing I needed to do in my own life's odyssey was discover my worldview, my own value system, which no one else could do for me. One of the counterproductive things modern people do is to throw out the time-honored traditions of their ancestors, claiming that organized religion doesn't do it for them. My personal advice to the perplexed—find your spiritual heritage all over again. Seek out the ancient wisdom. Or, if your own religious heritage really doesn't work, then find another time-honored tradition. After all, there are many paths to truth. When we dedicate ourselves to that search, we enter the World of Knowing.

When we get out of the role of victim, when we quit being passive and dare to ask questions, when we challenge somebody else's interpretation, we are on the path to discovering what true knowledge is all about.

FURTHERMORE . . .

There are two similar words in Hebrew, *melech*, which means king, and *lemech*, which means fool. The sages taught that the letter *m* also stands for *moach*, or mind, and that the letter *l* also stands for *lev*, or heart. Therefore, if a person places the mind before the heart, the *m* before the *l*, he or she is a *melech*, a king. But if that individual places the heart before the mind, the *l* before the *m*, he or she is a *lemech*, or a fool. How appropriate in today's world, when people are dominated by their feelings. "Oh, I just *feel* that this is the right thing to do," you hear them say. The sages of old would call them fools. Life in the final analysis is not only about what we *feel*. It is about what we *know*. When we enter the World of Knowing, we are able to make valid judgments about right and wrong, about the path we need to follow, without being led astray into a morass of relativity. The Tree of Knowledge is ultimately redemptive. Go ahead; take from the fruit. Eat. It will make you wise.

CHAPTER 1

Falling Up—A Tale of Two Sinners

*The apple cannot be stuck back on The Tree of Knowledge; once we begin to see,
we are doomed and challenged to seek the strength to see more, not less.*
—ARTHUR MILLER

*All knowledge is of itself of some value. There is nothing so minute or
inconsiderable, that I would not rather know it than not.*
—SAMUEL JOHNSON

I t all goes back to creation (*Briyah* in Hebrew), and a garden called Eden. If
you are looking for the Tree of Knowledge, Eden is the only place to go. Give
heed, therefore, to a tale from the Lost Bible, from the most ancient of texts.

It is called the Life of Adam and Eve, a document first written down in
Hebrew in ancient Judea. Since the book was suppressed, the original Hebrew text
was lost, and the only copies that survived are translations in Greek and Latin. But
we can nonetheless reconstruct what the earliest version of this book may have
looked like. It is reproduced here in lively paraphrase:

Adam's life spanned a total of 930 years. He knew his days were num-
bered, so he declared, "Bring my sons to me, all of them, because I want
to talk to them before I die, and give them my final blessing."

Adam's sons came together in three groups, exactly on the spot where
they always worshiped the Eternal. They asked, "What is wrong with
you, Father, that you brought us here? And why are you lying on your
sick bed?"

Adam related how painfully sick he was. One of his sons named Seth
said, "Father, maybe you have missed the fruit that you used to eat in
Paradise. Maybe that is why you are sad and ill. Just say the word, and I
will go back to where the entrance of Paradise is located. I will throw
ashes on my head and fall down on the ground in front of the gate. I will
moan and wail and beg the Eternal. Who knows? Maybe I will be heard

and an angel will be sent, bearing the fruit you have missed so much." However, Adam only chided him.

"No, Seth, that is not what I want. The truth is, I am weak and racked with pain."

"Pain?" asked Seth incredulously. "What is pain? Do not try to shield us. Tell us the truth."

Adam retorted, "Let me tell all of you what really happened back in Eden. That is why I summoned you. You see, when we were first created, the Eternal allowed us to eat from every fruit tree in Paradise, except one. We were commanded, 'Do not eat of the Tree of the Knowledge of Good and Evil, in the middle of the garden.'

"Now the Eternal also divided the garden between me and your mother. I was given the trees on the east side and off to the north, while the southern and western parts of the garden were given to your mother. We weren't completely on our own though. The Eternal appointed two angels to watch over us.

"But something happened when the time came for the angels to ascend on high to worship. Suddenly, the Adversary, who was called the devil, found a way to sneak into the garden in the absence of the angels. He tricked your mother into eating the fruit from the forbidden tree. She not only ate it herself; she gave it to me.

"That very instant, the Eternal became quite angry and declared, 'Since you have not kept my commandment but have ignored what I told you, I am going to send seventy plagues to afflict your body. You will feel a whole assortment of pain, from head to toe and in each of your limbs. The pain will be like a scourge coming from one of the trees in the garden.'

"The Eternal laid this upon me and on all my descendants as well."

Adam began to weep, and when Eve saw this, she joined in weeping too. "Oh God," she cried, "please transfer the pain over to me, because I was the one who sinned."

WHAT IT MEANS

Granted, the Lost Bible places the onus for disobedience squarely on Eve, who is a formidable figure in her own right, in charge of the trees of half of the garden. But consider what results from Eve's disobedience—true compassion, in striking details missing in the standard biblical text. Adam's son Seth is moved to such compassion that he volunteers to go back to Eden, to entreat God for fruit from the Tree of Life, so as to heal his father. And Eve begs to take the illness upon herself.

We see in the end that the knowledge of good and evil, while it brought about the many plagues that afflict us, also makes us fully human in the most positive sense, for without pain, we could not possibly know compassion, the most Godlike quality of all. The language of compassion is the language of sacrifice and of love, and that is what both Seth and Eve offer. Interestingly, it is the Tree of the Knowledge of Good and Evil that produces this compassion.

On the one hand, the text seems to paint the original disobedience as a disaster. Adam and Eve, who were once clothed with righteousness, perhaps some sort of mantle of pure light, are now driven into exile.

Their sin is described as covetousness, or simply desire. What is so bad about desire, we wonder. Nothing in the abstract, except that it focuses us on ourselves. Desire leads to "I" trouble. The irony is that desire brought forth knowledge (as Eve ate the fruit), which in turn has made each of us aware, not just of our own pain, but the pain of others. It gets us out of ourselves. We may have fallen, not down, but *up*.

The story continues. Adam takes up the offer of his wife and his son:

> Adam told Eve, "You and Seth, go back to the entrance of Paradise. Go ahead. Throw dust on your heads. Fall on the ground, and mourn before the Eternal. Maybe an angel will be sent to the Tree of Mercy, where the oil of life flows forth. Maybe the angel will give you some of it to anoint me with, to ease the pains that have afflicted me." Eve and Seth went on their way and approached the gates of Paradise. But along the way they were suddenly attacked by a beastly serpent, who bit Seth with his fangs. When Eve saw what had happened, she cried out loud, "Oh no! I've been cursed! I did not keep the Eternal's commandment, and that is why this has happened." Eve shouted at the serpent, "You cursed beast! Why weren't you afraid to attack a human being, who is, after all, made in the divine image? How dare you!"

FROM KNOWLEDGE TO FOLLOW-THROUGH

At this point the story is all about self-sacrifice, taking deliberate action on behalf of someone else. Eve and Seth follow through on their offer to help, sacrificially, and in love. Here, the story teaches us to accept the pain attendant with living in a fallen world knowing that pain leads to compassion.

> The servant answered Eve in a voice that sounded human. "You are the one I'm angry at! I'd like to know, Eve, why you ate the very fruit that the Eternal told you not to eat. What is wrong? Cannot you take it if I rebuke you?"

But Seth chimed in and retorted, "You are the one the Eternal should rebuke. Now shut up, you enemy and destroyer! We happen to be made in the divine image, so get away and stay away until Judgment Day."

The serpent replied, "All right, I will withdraw. I know the divine image when I see it."

So Seth, still wounded by the serpent's teeth, was left alone.

KNOWLEDGE IS POWER

The adage, "Knowledge is power" is a valuable one in our victim's culture. Though the consequence of disobedience was the Fall, eating from the Tree of Knowledge has also brought redemption. Eve and Seth know that they are made in the divine image, and they use that power to rebuke the serpent and command him to leave. Like Seth we will be wounded, but our wounds need not debilitate us. When we truly know who we are—miraculous divine creations—we unleash a secret power that puts us in charge of circumstances, rather than circumstances being in charge of us.

Finally, Seth and his mother Eve arrived at the entrance to Paradise. They were soon overcome with weeping, begging the Eternal to send an angel bearing the oil of mercy. After hours of prayer, the angel Michael finally appeared. He said, "Listen, Seth, I know you are a godly person. Do not cry, and stop begging. I know you want the oil of the Tree of Mercy for your father Adam, but I have to tell you that you are simply not allowed to have it. Only in the very last days can this oil be obtained. For now, Seth, I want you to go back to your father Adam, for he is about to die in just six days. But as his soul ascends, you will see signs in heaven and wonders on earth. So be at peace." Right after this, Michael left Seth. He and Eve went home, bearing nothing more than aromatic spices: nard, crocus, calamine, and cinnamon.

ONLY IN HOLLYWOOD

In Hollywood there are happy endings; in real life they are much less common. God is not Santa Claus. The compassion and love we express exists for its own sake, not necessarily to cajole a miracle from the Divine Presence. To be sure, if our prayers were always answered, they would amount to nothing more than twisting the divine arm.

The pains of life invariably yield to death, but because we have knowledge, we need not surrender to fear. The love and compassion we express become sweet-smelling incense, to make fragrant the passage into eternity.

> Eve and Seth returned to the tent where Adam was lying. Adam said, "What have you brought upon us, Eve? For death seems to be gaining on all of us. Here's what you should do. Call all our children and grandchildren together and tell them how we went astray." Eve only wept.

DIVINE WEAKNESS

In a very real sense, when she gave Adam the Forbidden Fruit, Eve enabled our full humanity. Without the Tree of Knowledge there would be no pain. Neither would there be weakness. But without the capacity to be weak, would we truly have the capacity to care?

> Some time later, Eve addressed all of her children and grandchildren. "Let me tell you my own version of how the enemy deceived us," she said.
>
> "Adam and I were guarding our respective portions of the garden. The Evil One dared not enter my portion, the south and the west. Instead, he snuck into Adam's territory. All the female animals had been given to me to guard, while the male animals had been given to Adam. The Evil One chose to enter male territory."

WOMEN ARE SUPERIOR

Is the Lost Bible trying to tell us that females are more diligent in keeping out evil influence than males? Historically, women have guarded the home and built nests, while their husbands have gone out into the world. The homemaker is a higher role, not lower; she is the Director of Homeland Security.

> "Now the serpent took his orders straight from the Evil One, who said, 'You are more clever than all the beasts, yet you have to crawl on the ground beneath everyone, eating Adam's weeds! That is not right, is it? We were cast out of paradise because we wouldn't worship Adam. Now let Adam be cast out because of Eve!'
>
> "The serpent objected, 'Nevertheless, I'm afraid that the Eternal might get angry at me.'
>
> "The Evil One responded, 'Do not be afraid; just act as my agent. I

will speak through you. I will use you as my mouthpiece; that is how you will fool him.'

"Next, he hung himself from the garden's walls, at the very moment when the angels came together to worship. The Evil One suddenly appeared, in the exact form of an angel, and joined the other divine beings in singing hymns. He leaned over the wall, looking just like an angel, and he asked me, 'Are you Eve?'

"I said, 'Yes.'

"He asked, 'Why are you here in Paradise?'

"I explained, 'The Eternal told us to guard it and also to eat from the trees.'

"The serpent, whose words came straight from the Evil One, said, 'I'm sure you are doing a good job, but you are not allowed to eat from every tree, are you?'

"I answered, 'We do eat from every tree . . . except just one. It is in the middle of the garden. The Eternal said that if we eat from that one, we'll die.'

"But the serpent said, 'This really troubles me! You do not want to be like dumb animals, do you? After all, ignorance is not bliss; it's stupidity! Do not be fools! Get up and eat, and experience this glorious tree.'

"But I answered, 'I'm afraid that the Eternal will be furious, because of the warning we were given. . . . '

"'Do not be ridiculous,' said the serpent. 'The moment you eat it, your eyes will open. You will know good from evil, like gods. Of course the Eternal, being jealous, did not want you to be full of knowledge, as though you were also divine. So you were told not to eat of it. But never mind that; have a look at this splendid tree.'

"Gazing at that glorious tree, I replied, 'It certainly is beautiful!' But still I was afraid to take the fruit. So the serpent said, 'Follow me, this way! I will give it to you myself.'

"I let him into the garden, through the front gate. But after he walked for awhile, he said pointedly, 'I've changed my mind. I will not let you eat it.' This of course was reverse psychology, causing me to want it all the more.

"'I will let you have it,' he continued, 'if you swear you will give it to your husband too.'

"'I'm not accustomed to oaths,' I replied. 'But I'm prepared to swear by the eternal throne, and the cherubim, and the Tree of Life that I will give it to my husband.'

"After I swore the oath, he went and climbed the tree, then took the fruit and sprinkled on it a poison, which is called 'Desire.' After all, every sin is born of desire. Next, I pulled down one of the branches of the tree, plucked a piece of fruit, and ate it."

DESIRELESS . . .

Like the traditional account in Genesis, this story can be read on different levels. Try reading it as an allegory. The book of Genesis depicts the original sin as simple disobedience, but the Lost Bible tells us that it is desire. We open the door of our own garden to evil. We open the door to desire, and desire produces its own fruit. The psalmist wrote, "The Lord is my shepherd; I shall not want" (Psalm 23:1 KJV). Actually, the original Hebrew reads, "I lack nothing." A similar lesson is taught by the metaphysics of the Far East. Taoism, for example, teaches us to be desireless. Invariably, we want things that we cannot have. Eve coveted the fruit all the more because the serpent (as well as God) told her she could not eat it. Nevertheless, there is an antidote to unbridled desire. When we are in the World of Knowing, we unleash the power of wholeness. Whenever we think we want something or need something, we need only remind ourselves that we are complete already, because we are made in the divine image. Every time we look in the mirror and affirm who we are—the very stuff of God—we are embracing wholeness and conquering desire.

Eve continues her account:

"The moment I tasted the fruit, my eyes opened, as it were for the first time, and I understood that my clothing of righteousness was removed, and I was naked.

"In my tears I asked the serpent, 'Why did you do this to me? Why did you cause me to lose the glory I had been clothed with?' I also cried because I had sworn to lure my husband into eating the fruit. But by now the serpent had come down the tree and was gone. I looked around for some leaves with which to cover myself, but all the trees in my part of the garden had suddenly shed their leaves. Only the leaves of the fig tree remained, so I used those to make myself some clothing. They were from the same plants I had eaten from. Next, I called for your father.

"'Adam!' I shouted. 'Where are you hiding? There is something very mysterious I'd like to show you. . . .'

"When your father showed up, I enticed him to break the Eternal's commandment. When I opened my mouth, I found that the words were not mine, but came in from the Evil One.

"'Listen, my husband,' I said. 'Eat the fruit of this tree, the fruit we were commanded not to eat, and you will be like the Eternal.'"

LIKE GOD?

The irony is, if we understand the Lost Bible correctly, that Adam was already in the divine image, the stuff and essence of God. The Evil One had fallen (not long before, according to this account) because he had refused to worship Adam. What if Adam had somehow had the benefit of the World of Knowing without ever eating the fruit? He would have known that he was already like the Eternal. He wouldn't have needed to be like God. He might well have ignored the serpent.

The text goes on:

> "Your father Adam answered, 'I'm afraid the Eternal might be angry with me.' But I told him not to be afraid.
>
> "'As soon as you take this fruit, Adam, you will know good and evil.' That convinced him. Adam ate the fruit, and his eyes opened, so that he understood that he was naked.
>
> "'What an evil woman you are!' he shouted at me. 'Why have you brought curses on us, and separated us from the Divine Presence?'"

THE DEVIL MADE THEM DO IT?

Allegorically, the serpent is like all the people who try to mess with our heads. In my case, they were the cultic groups I was involved with, who told me not to get an education, who told me that the world was about to end. Like Adam, I had a desire for the Tree of Knowledge, but I should already have been operating in the World of Knowing, reminding myself who I am—made in the divine image—not in need of self-proclaimed gurus to tell me what to do. When we operate in that kind of knowledge, no serpent can fool us.

But what about the concept of a personal devil, who, in the case of Adam and Eve, made them do it? Bear in mind that Judaism, as it evolved, steered clear of the concept of a satanic malevolent figure, lest it appear that there are two gods—a good God and an evil god—rather than one. But let's get beyond all of that. The fact remains that evil exists, and the Lost Bible is trying to teach us that we create it by our own desire, be it lust, the desire for power, wealth, prestige, or whatever.

INDICTED . . .

As the text continues, Eve narrates how Michael, the archangel, announced the arrival of the Eternal—how God came into the garden, the divine throne being established at the location of the Tree of Life, and how all the trees came to life in God's presence. She relates how God called out to Adam: "Where are you hiding? Can a house hide from the one who builds it?"

Adam responded that he did not really believe that he could hide from God. He was afraid because he was naked before the Almighty's power. God then wanted to know how Adam was aware of his nakedness. "Have you broken my commandment?" the Eternal asked.

Adam, deflecting the blame from himself, turned to Eve and asked, "Why have you done this?" Eve answered, "The serpent fooled me."

God's response was a series of indictments, cursing the ground under Adam's feet, and consigning Eve's husband to alienated labor for the rest of his days. For her part, Eve was to suffer greatly in childbirth. What a fearful outcome!

But we need to consider carefully the nature of these curses, even as we ask poignantly whether Adam and Eve really fell down, or perhaps up. We read the following:

> "The Eternal said to Adam, since you listened to Eve and did not keep my commandments, the ground on which you labor is now cursed. You will work it in weariness. Thistles and thorns will grow, and your brow will sweat as you eat. You will not find rest. Things will taste bitter to you. You will be hot in the summer and cold in the winter. You will work hard but never get rich. And though you will get fat, you will die in the end. Even the animals will rebel, since you broke my commandments."

But in spite of these fearful pronouncements, Adam himself is never cursed, only the ground.

Eve continues:

> "The Eternal told me, 'Since you paid attention to the serpent and broke my commandment, you will suffer labor and great pain and trembling as you bear children. In your pain you will come close to death, and you will cry out, 'Save me, Oh Eternal, and I will never turn away from you again!'
>
> "'This is how I will judge you, Eve. Yet, you will return to your husband and he will rule over you.'"

WHO IS CURSED?

After these things the narrative tells us that the serpent is called out and cursed by God "beyond all wild beasts." He will lose his ears, his wings, his hands and feet, and will crawl on his belly. (Yes, the Lost Bible tells us that the serpent once walked on all fours, and that he even had ears and wings, prior to being cursed from on high!) But the amazing thing to notice is that while the serpent is physically cursed, neither Adam nor Eve receives a curse. Adam is to toil working the ground, and Eve is to experience pain in childbirth. But Eve herself is never cursed, perhaps because it was God's intention all along that Adam and Eve should have knowledge. God is simply explaining what life will be like in the future. The depiction is realistic more than it is punitive. Furthermore, through all the pain that is predicted, Eve will learn a touching vulnerability, as she cries out to the Almighty. Pain, as C. S. Lewis once observed, has a positive, redemptive value, for it acts as God's megaphone, nudging us out of complacency and awakening us to the Divine Presence.[2]

As for the man ruling over the woman, this is not a depiction of the way things ought to be. It is not Adam's divine right to rule Eve; it is a prophetic statement of the power that men would in fact take down through the ages. What is gained through the whole ordeal is knowledge, the knowledge of what will happen, of what life will be like; and with knowledge comes the power to deal with it.

Long after these events, Eve recounts the final days and hours of her husband's life. She relates how Adam, as he is dying, tells her prophetically that she will die not long after him. But Adam also speaks with great faith, declaring, "God will not forget me, because I am the vessel formed in the divine image."

Eve continues the story:

> "Shortly afterward the angel of humankind told me, 'Get up, Eve, you have done enough repenting. Your husband Adam has left his body. Stand and watch his soul rising to its Maker. . . . Do not dwell on things of this earth.'
>
> "When the angel had said this, I looked up to see a chariot of light, pulled by four angels glowing with radiance, with such brightness that their faces could not be seen. As Adam lay lifeless, the angels drew the chariot right up to him, with fiery beings called seraphim lining up between him and the chariot.
>
> "The angels took frankincense, golden containers, and three bowls up to the altar, breathed on them, and caused incense to rise and fill the sky. The angels prostrated themselves in the Divine Presence and cried out, 'O Holy One, grant forgiveness to this being in your image, whom you yourself have fashioned.'
>
> "There were two divine beings standing before God, and I, Eve, called out to Seth my son, 'Get up, quickly. Do not linger at the body of your father Adam. I want you to see things you have never seen before.'
>
> "Seth rose and came over to me. 'Why are you crying?' he asked.

"I said, 'Look up, and you will see the seven heavens opened, and though your father's body lies face down, all the angels are praying for him, saying, 'Father forgive him, because he is your very image.' But what does this mean, Seth? When will he come into the presence of our unseen God? And who are those two dark beings standing by?

"Seth answered, 'Mother, they are the sun and moon, who are falling down to pray for our father Adam.'

"'But where is their light, and why are they dark?' I asked.

"Seth answered, 'They are unable to shine before the great Light of all.'

"While Seth was still talking, one angel blew his trumpet, and all the other angels got up from prostrating themselves and shouted, 'Blessed be the Almighty, who has shown mercy to Adam, his handiwork!'

"At that point, one of the six-winged seraphim lifted Adam up and brought him to the mystical lake called Acheron, washing him three times in the Divine Presence. For three hours he lay there, while God, enthroned on high, took him in his hands and gave him to the archangel Michael. 'Take him up to the third heaven, to Paradise,' he said to Michael. 'Let him stay there until the great and terrible day I will establish for the world.'

"Michael did as he was told and took Adam away."

BEYOND THE VEIL

Just think of the aspect of compassion in Adam's ascent on high, after his death—an element absent from the traditional text, but emphasized in the repetition of the number three. He is washed three times, lies before God for three hours, and is taken to the third heaven.

The original sin, taking and eating from the Tree of Knowledge, has opened up the way to the divine throne—the whole realm of mystical experience. It has brought humans into an encounter with God in a new and dynamic sense—things that eye has not seen nor ear heard. Beyond the veil of death are seven heavens and Paradise.

There are, moreover, many ways in which we die. What would the newly enlightened Eve counsel us? Do not shrink from death, for dying brings forth life. When dreams and hope die, know that the very next phase is mercy, compassion, and resurrection.

God's final prophetic words to Adam are these:

"I will turn your sorrow into gladness. I will place you upon the throne of the evil one who seduced you. Before, I told you that you are only dust and shall return to dust; I now promise you life in the resurrection. I will raise you up on the last day, along with all others of your kind."

Six days later Eve also died, saying, "Holy One, receive my spirit." As the archangel Michael attended, three angels carried her away and buried her beside her son Abel.

Michael told Seth, "You must prepare for burial each person who dies until the day of resurrection. But do not mourn beyond six days. Rest upon the seventh and rejoice, since both God and we angels rejoice at the passing from earth to heaven of a righteous soul."

Afterward the angel ascended to heaven, saying, "Praise be to the One whose glory and power is forever!"

SIMPLE TRUTH

What do we glean from this? For starters, we might discover a healthier view of self than what our traditional, Western, sin-focused culture has conveyed. If indeed we fell up and not down, then true salvation is not so much about rescuing us from some terrible abyss into which we have descended—as miserable, helpless creatures—but rather about the realization of the simple truth about ourselves.

The Lost Bible does not just declare the inherent worth of the individual; it screams it. It depicts all of the sadness of human frailty, grief, and pain—the inevitable byproduct of disobedience. But none of that negates the spark of the divine within us, the eternal quintessence of Deity, which can never be extinguished. The text repeatedly returns to a simple revelation, as Adam declares: "*I am* the vessel formed in the divine image." This "I am" declaration is the most powerful piece of knowledge ever dropped into the human heart.

THE REST OF THE STORY

The incredible account concludes, as Eve instructs her progeny, thirty brothers and thirty sisters, to inscribe the account of her life and Adam's. Her son Seth, who had no knowledge of writing, sets it all down (his hand guided by an angel) on two sets of tablets—one of stone, the other of clay. If the world is to end by water, declares Eve, the clay tablets will dissolve, but the stone tablets will survive. If the world ends by fire, the stone tablets will crack in tiny pieces, but the clay tablets will be baked in the heat. As fate would have it, the world would later be destroyed by a great flood. The stone tablets would survive. Many people would see these tablets, but none could read them. Only many centuries later would they be deciphered—by King Solomon the wise. They would tell him of the precise location of the place of prayer, where Adam and Eve used to worship. That spot was where the mighty king would choose to build his great temple. At least that is what the account tells us . . . believe it or not.

More centuries have passed. While sages and religious leaders tried to sequester the contents of the tablets (now written down in Greek and Latin manuscripts), the few determined scribes and copyists who preserved them have given us a priceless legacy. Now the Life of Adam and Eve belongs to the world. And it goes beyond the Genesis account, telling us the rest of the story.

THE EXCLUSION

The original version of the Life of Adam and Eve probably goes back to the first century, C.E., perhaps around the year 70, and was most likely written in Hebrew. The texts that survive are later translations into Greek, Latin, Armenian, Georgian, Slavonic, and Coptic. The Latin text, dating from the ninth century, C.E., is the earliest in existence. The original Hebrew was not preserved, since the book was denied canonical status by the Jewish sages who presided at the Council at Yavne around 90 C.E. and who vigorously debated which books merited the label "Holy Writ" and which would be rejected.

Why was this account kept out of the official canon? Doubtless, dualism did it in. The idea that a satanic, evil force is out there in the universe, in direct competition with God and speaking through the serpent (like a demon possesses a physical body) sounded too much like Zoroastrianism for the sages of old. The ancient Zoroastrians theorized two gods, not one: a good deity and an evil counterpart. This was an affront to the fiercely monotheistic rabbis who decided which books to include and which to suppress. Of course, in this day and age, with Zoroastrianism hardly a threat, we can read all this in a different light, without being tempted into heresy. We can appreciate the deeper message of the Lost Bible.

THE SECRET

And what is the great secret of this account of the Fall? Everyone who knows biblical literature is aware that the tale is written in a crisp, succinct fashion, without mincing words. It begs us to read between the lines. The Lost Bible paints the background scenery of compassion as well as the human—and godly— element of sorrow and remorse. By contrast the traditional story of Genesis depicts a punitive God and a chastised first couple, who evince little emotion.

Only when we see the full range of feeling in the first man and the first woman do we realize that the original sin was not an unmixed tragedy. We have eaten the fruit, and we know better. We know not to bemoan our fallen condition, but to embrace it, to celebrate our weakness, and even our mortality. Could it be that the divine intention was for us to go back to the Tree of Knowledge, take from its fruit without shame, and find our way through the wilderness of life?

CHAPTER 2

The Gospel of Thomas
and the Wisdom of the Gnostics

Oz never did give nothin' to the Tin Man,
That he didn't already have.
—AMERICA

But this thing is God:
To be man with thy might,
To grow straight in the strength of thy spirit,
and live out thy life as the light.
—ALGERNON CHARLES SWINBURNE, AMERICAN RELIGIOUS LEADER

K nowing is also the subject of another book of the Lost Bible. It is called
the Gospel of Thomas, and it came as a veritable bolt from the blue when
it was discovered in the middle of the twentieth century by an Egyptian peasant
lad named Muhammad Ali. The boy was digging near a village called Nag
Hammadi, around 225 kilometers northwest of Aswan. Though his object was to
dig up fertilizer, he instead came upon a jar in which he found a wad of decaying
leather manuscripts later determined to date back as far as the fourth century of
the Common Era.

Among these manuscripts was a text of sayings—pithy aphorisms attributed
to none other than Jesus of Nazareth. Its author, according to the gospel itself, was
Didymos Judas Thomas, the same "doubting Thomas" who would not believe that
Jesus had risen from the dead unless he touched the very wounds of crucifixion. But
what one never hears from traditional Christianity is that Thomas was believed to
have been—in some ancient traditions—Jesus' twin brother. There could hardly
be a more astounding claim.

There is no narrative in this book; it is simply a list of sayings and prophecies,
one hundred fourteen of them, in Jesus' mouth. Some researchers believe them
to be even older than those we find in the four gospels, Matthew, Mark, Luke,

and John; and, if this be true, then the Gospel of Thomas may well represent the earliest and most authentic version of Jesus' words known to exist in the world.

THE EXCLUSION

Why was the Gospel of Thomas suppressed? Why was it shoved under the carpet, as it were, until its accidental discovery in the mid-twentieth century? The answer is as simple as it is mystifying—because its theme was knowledge. The word in Greek is *gnosis*, and those who sought this knowledge were called Gnostics. By the orthodox church they were called heretics, for they sought to know secrets about their own spirituality, about their prior existence in the spiritual world before becoming incarnate as flesh and blood human beings. Such speculations were unlawful, according to ecclesiastical authorities.

The Gnostics gravitated to the idea that God—or the Godhead, as they liked to think of the Divine Presence—is utterly incomprehensible, beyond the ability of mere humans to grasp. God doesn't exist in the way we think of existence and is therefore really Nothing—nothing at all. This Nothingness chose to emanate the Divine Presence into the material world. This is where the Gnostics got into trouble with early Christian orthodoxy, for they said that the last great emanation was wisdom personified—Sophia—who sought knowledge that was forbidden to her and was therefore exiled, made to wander across the universe, seeking to return to the Godhead. This secret knowledge is really available to all of us, if we merely reach out and appropriate it. One of the divine emanations, called the Logos, or the Word, had come down to earth in the form of Jesus, with the purpose of showing people the way to the divine source.

The Gnostics never intended their fantastic mythology to be taken literally. It was symbolic of the fact that truth and reality are to be found inside, nestled within each human heart. The reaction of the church to all of this was stern. The Gnostics were damnable heretics, their leaders, such as Valentinus (of the early second century), guilty of shameless blasphemy. Both Clement of Rome and Ignatius of Antioch wrote harsh epistles in which they insisted on unquestioning obedience to apostolic authority. All deviation from the party line was to be squelched. What we know from this reaction is that the Gnostics had in fact become extremely popular, so much so that they threatened the very foundation of ecclesiastical authority.

THE KNOWLEDGE RX

Indeed the Gnostics were undaunted, having arrived at an understanding that humans are really spirits who have fallen from the supernatural universe, only to become imprisoned in materiality. True knowledge revealed to them that authentic salvation is not about groveling in the dust, lamenting one's depravity, but waking up to the reality of one's spiritual existence and preexistence. The material world becomes secondary; the spiritual world is truth. That level of knowledge brings with it great power in daily life, for the material world with all its attendant problems is only a pale shadow of the spiritual reality.

Sitting atop the Mount of Olives and staring at the ancient city, I was intimately aware of the political and cultural strife ever present in Holy Jerusalem. I asked myself: What is so special about these sayings? Whether or not they were ever on Jesus' lips, what truths do they convey for a strife-torn world? I wondered how such knowledge might liberate the whole earth, might hasten the Messianic Age.

FROM ANOTHER WORLD

The lessons we learn from this book of the Lost Bible are universal and teach us much about ourselves. We are all on a journey of self-discovery. We are destined to have many adventures, make new friends along our way, and ultimately learn that what we thought we lacked was inside us all along.

We have come from another world (if we believe the Gospel of Thomas)—the primordial Eden. We all share a sense of alienation, knowing instinctively that we are strangers in a strange land. We are not at home, and we are looking for answers. But all too often we fabricate brittle doctrines of religion. We seek shelter in numbers, only to create institutions and bureaucracies, which make us feel more alienated than ever.

That is the true nature of our fallenness. We are blind to the divine spark within, which ought to be a blazing fire. Moreover, our friends seem just as helpless as we are. In our quest for enlightenment, we long to find an all-knowing, omnipotent deliverer, kind and merciful, who will make everything right. Maybe it is a sage or a guru, a rabbi or a cleric. Maybe it is Jesus that we seek—or, rather, our own image of Jesus—which just may turn out to be a graven image.

EDEN'S CHILDREN

I stared intently at the Gospel of Thomas, which speaks of our eternal abode—the primordial Eden—before we came to reside in bodies of flesh. This book of the Lost Bible (which I present here in paraphrase) teaches that the soul, far from being corrupt, is pure, eternal, and birthed in Paradise:

> Happy is the one who came into being before coming into being. . . . In Paradise there are five trees which no one disturbs year round; and their leaves never fall. If you come to know them, you will never know spiritual death.

The idea of the preexistence of the soul is not foreign to biblical faith. In ultra-orthodox Judaism, for example, there is the concept that all the souls of righteous Israelites were present, mystically, at Mount Sinai, when the Ten Commandments were given, and only later found their place in human form. William Wordsworth's famous ode, *Intimations of Immortality,* suggests that all souls come from a state of divine preexistence:

> Our birth is but a sleep and a forgetting:
> The Soul that rises with us, our life's Star,
> Hath had elsewhere its setting,
> And cometh from afar.

On a personal level, I recalled how the cultic groups I had been involved with indoctrinated their adherents in a theology of original sin and total depravity, only to leave them feeling weak and helpless, thereby easily controlled and manipulated. I had often felt that preachers and clerics were so intent on propagating the doctrine of original sin that they had forgotten the reality of original innocence. The Gospel of Thomas expresses the same sentiments.

But what are the five trees Jesus refers to in this gospel? Perhaps the five senses, which—once reborn—never again suffer corruption. However, the imagery certainly recalls the Tree of Knowledge. If you understand, if you know your true identity, spiritually, your spiritual self will never die.

Unfortunately, knowing that you are pure and holy and birthed in Paradise doesn't get you back there. Each of us must set out on a road of discovery.

LIFE AND RIGOR MORTIS

But how many people attain this knowledge, and how many choose instead to misspend their lives? The Lost Bible declares that seeking the material world leads only to rigor mortis:

> Whoever gets acquainted with the world only finds a corpse . . . but I
> only tell my mysteries to those who are worthy of them.

What should you do when you find a corpse, carefully disguised in the glitter of materialism? According to the Lost Bible, when we put on knowledge like a garment, we protect ourselves from the snares of the material world. Think about it. If disobedience brought forth death, then the object of this disobedience—the Tree of Knowledge—provides the antidote. When you know yourself, you will never know what it is to die, spiritually. The Gospel of Thomas says it well:

Whoever discovers the true meaning of the sayings will never die.

Over and over in this incredible gospel, the Master seems to be admonishing his disciples to take freely from the Tree of Knowledge, just as Eve had taken its fruit at the beginning. It is the knowledge of self and of the primordial Garden. He declares:

I will give you what no one has seen, what no one has heard, what no one has touched and what no one has even thought of.

Moreover, it takes a child, someone transparent and ingenuous, to find the path. The Master declares:

From the days of Adam until John the Baptist, no one is greater than John the Baptist. . . . Nevertheless, anyone who becomes a child will know and understand the kingdom and be superior even to John.

THE LONG AND WINDING ROAD

The Tree of Knowledge is the quest of a lifetime. But you must find your own road to the kingdom. Just look around and you will find it. The Master declares:

Things I was asked in times past, which I never told you then, I now want to tell you, only you never inquire about them.

He also says:

Cut open a piece of wood, and there I am. Pick up a stone, and you will find me there.

How do you find this knowledge? There are no set answers. Each person must find it individually. Moreover, this type of knowledge is not dogmatic. It doesn't demand that we click our heels and salute smartly. It is deeply personal—a self-revealing path, unique for each person.

Sometimes we are naively unaware of the challenges we are likely to encounter. Great adventures typically begin with a babble of enthusiasm. In the Gospel of Thomas, the Master observes:

Since you have drunk, you have become drunk—intoxicated—from the bubbling spring I have created for you.

Jesus' mission, according to the Lost Bible, was to disclose truth—the truth about our authentic selves—to everyone.

The Gospel of Thomas teaches us afresh about reigning in the kingdom of heaven, but without the religious sentimentality we are used to. The kingdom is not some far-off hope for the future, in the sweet by-and-by, but a present-tense reality for those who know themselves, those who have discovered their divine nature. The Master says:

> If your leaders tell you, "Look, the kingdom is up in the sky," know that the birds will get there before you. If they tell you, "It is in the sea," then the fish will get there before you. But know that the kingdom is within you and without you. When you finally know yourselves, you will become known. You will understand at last that you are the living Father's children. However, if you do not know yourselves, you will live in poverty, and you will be that poverty.

To be sure, setting out on the long and winding road involves transformation. What happens when you do seek the kingdom, when you find the light within you and follow your unique path? The Master says:

> Whoever takes a drink from my mouth becomes just like me. I will reveal myself to that person, becoming that person, and hidden things will be revealed. . . . But none of this comes by waiting around. You cannot point out the kingdom, saying, "Here it is," or "There it is." Instead, the Father's kingdom is stretched out across the earth, but people do not see it.

In this passage the followers of Jesus are urged to think of themselves as identical twins of the Master, just as Thomas was, according to tradition, Jesus' twin brother. You may call it *chutzpah*, but the Lost Bible calls it enlightenment.

What is the answer to life's mysteries? When you take from the Tree of Knowledge you find yourself, as the Master declares:

> This person is indeed greater than the world.

"IT HAS TO BE ME!"

Make no mistake, the journey of self-discovery also involves inner conflict. The Gospel of Thomas teaches:

> Look for wisdom and keep looking until you find it. When you do find

it, you will become troubled. When you become troubled, you will be amazed, and you will come to rule the world.

Modern motivational experts counsel us that we should all expect adversity. Every leader, every hero, everyone who has ever made a difference has had to contend with conflict—internal and external. We should expect to be troubled, but we should also persevere, through massive, consistent action. We should keep seeking the answers, because knowing them is what causes us to reign over our adversity.

Of course the road to true knowledge is never easy and may leave us feeling isolated. The Master laments the sad reality:

> I appeared in the world and I revealed myself in flesh and blood, but everyone was drunk. No one was even thirsty. . . . They came into the world empty, and they desire to leave the world just as empty. . . . It is a real wonder if flesh came to exist because of the spirit, but it is an even greater wonder if spirit came to exist because of the body. I am astounded at how such a treasure could be at home in such spiritual poverty.

Be aware, the road you travel may be one of solitude. The Gospel of Thomas continues:

> Happy are those who are alone, yet chosen. You will truly discover the kingdom, for you came from it and you will return to it.

And though we may feel alienated, the Lost Bible counsels this:

> Many people may be standing at the door of the bridal chamber, but the one who is alone will be allowed to come in.

Oftentimes, based on our feelings, we convince ourselves that we lack something. We are certain that our greatest desires are blocked by some fundamental deficit. A voice inside says, "It has to be me!"

"WHERE HAVE YOU GONE, JOE DIMAGGIO?"

Do not be deceived, however. Jesus' admonition in the Gospel of Thomas is:

> Let a person who has understanding be among you. When the grain becomes ripe, he quickly comes with his sickle and reaps it.

Timing is everything. "For everything there is a season, and a time for every desire under heaven," declares the book of Ecclesiastes, "a time to plant and a time to uproot what was planted" (Ecclesiastes 3:1-2, author's translation). Getting the timing right requires both knowledge and discernment. Actions must be undertaken at the appropriate moment, when the situation is ripe for harvest. It is like a surfer waiting for the perfect wave and then riding it. We must know ourselves but also know the world around us, evaluating each grain field and putting our hand to the sickle only when the time is right. Quite a challenge for every sojourner on the road to the kingdom.

Indeed, the pilgrim often becomes faint of heart, in dire need of inward transformation. The Gospel of Thomas also addresses this great process:

> A lion that is transformed into a man after being eaten by a man is blessed.
> But a man eaten by a lion (that is transformed into a man) is cursed.

The prospect of being eaten alive is not especially appealing, yet each of us recognizes that we are in need of change, that corruptible flesh must put on incorruptible spirit. Our lower, animalistic, predator nature (the lion) needs to be consumed by the spirit nature (a man) and ultimately transformed into spirit (a man). But the process is doomed if (vice versa) the spirit nature is consumed by the predator nature (disguised to look like spirit).

Discernment is not found in our gray matter alone; it is equally the domain of the heart. Hearts are more than just repositories of love. They are seats of judgment, which is about more than intellect and requires more than a stony countenance. The Gospel of Thomas has this to say about a person with a discerning heart:

> That man is like a wise fisherman who threw his net into the sea. He pulled it up from the sea full of little fish. Among them he found a large good fish. He threw all the little fish back into the sea and chose the large fish without difficulty. If you have ears, listen to this!

Imagine how helpless we would be if we could not distinguish between quality and its lack. Many in today's postmodern world find themselves confused and cynical. There is a sense that abstract yardsticks for measuring our experience have been swept away, that there is no longer any measure of virtue, that there are no longer any heroes— no "large good fish," no Joe DiMaggios. "Where have you gone, Joe DiMaggio?" crooned Simon and Garfunkel, bemoaning the modern culture of cynicism, "a nation turns its lonely eyes to you." The great DiMaggio may in fact be a version of the Master for whose wisdom and strength we all seek.

It takes a heart of discernment to separate the wheat from the chaff, to cultivate a set of personal values that somehow reflect eternal values. It also takes a childlike heart to believe that true virtue still exists. Go ahead, counsels the Lost Bible. Develop the heart of a hero. Throw back the little fish, the petty values of a cynical age, and take hold of a greater reality beyond yourself. There is no greater challenge than this.

Yet, we all feel somehow inadequate. There is a huge disconnect between what we are and what we wish to be. All too often life is pure posturing. The Gospel of Thomas, by contrast, teaches:

> When you find two of anything make them one. Eliminate disparity. Make the outside like the inside and the inside like the outside. Make things above like things below. Make male and female one. That is when you will enter the kingdom.

To be sure, the flesh and the spirit may seem incontrovertibly opposed, but true knowledge will make them one. When we know ourselves and the world around us, we are able to replace conflict with harmony, to find unity in all things and among all people. Utilizing such wisdom, can we really unlock our inner resources? Why does true enlightenment so often elude us?

THE WISDOM OF OZ

The Lost Bible counsels us to beware, for appearances are perennially deceiving. One can see material images without ever experiencing the true light that is in them. The Gospel of Thomas teaches:

> Images are clear to people, but the light inside is still hidden, concealed in the Father's light.

We have to look beyond outward appearances—good or bad—to behold the true light in others. It is the snare of materiality (the smoke-and-mirrors act of everyday life) that robs us of true vision. The Gospel of Thomas teaches:

> Woe is the spiritual body that is dependent on a physical body.

We must look beyond the physical to perceive the inner light in those around us. The Master says:

> In a person of light great light is found, enough to illuminate the whole world. But if the light doesn't shine, that person is really only darkness.

What a declaration! The Lost Bible is teaching here that every individual is capable of finding a personal, individualized direction toward an inner light. We are all light-bearers—the very opposite of pathetic wretches depicted by so much traditional religion. Each person has the potential to turn night into day. But there is not a single path to tread; the journey is unique to each individual.

We must, however, put away material concerns, like taking off old clothes. The Master says:

> When you take off your garments with no shame and trample them like little children, then you will envision the son of the Living One, and you will have no fear.

In the end, the Master informs us, we are not really missing anything. We only truly arrive at our destination when we realize something universal—that none of us needs to seek beyond ourselves for courage, fortitude, intelligence, or anything else we desperately wish we had. What we seek is already inside of us; we need only recognize it. The Master says to Thomas:

> The angels will visit you, and so will the prophets, and they will give you things you already have.

We do not need to be searching for anything, because the answer is right inside, where it has always been. A young girl from Kansas named Dorothy (a very wise sage, as the people of Oz discovered) once observed that when we think we lack something, we need not look any further than our own backyard, and if we cannot find it there, it must be that we never lost it at all.

The Master asks:

> Have you found the beginning of all things? If so, why are you looking for the end? When you find the beginning and take your place there, you will have knowledge of the end of all things. You will never experience spiritual death.

We do not need a medal to prove our heroism. We do not need a diploma to establish our wisdom. Knowledge is salvation, declares the Master in the Gospel of Thomas:

> If you have this kind of knowledge but still feel that you lack something, then you do not have true salvation.

THE SECRET

In the Gospel of Thomas, Jesus challenges his disciples to envision themselves at the beginning, clothed with light, as were Adam and Eve. Perhaps the most startling thing about the Gospel of Thomas is that this light, which reveals true knowledge, shines not in Jesus only, but resides in everyone. If taking the fruit from the Tree of Knowledge brought about the Fall, then taking again from the Tree of Knowledge restores us to primordial glory. The Master says it well:

> Learn to recognize what you see, and hidden things will become clear
> for you. There is nothing hidden that will not come to light.

I glanced back at the strife-torn city of Jerusalem and wondered whether a little wisdom from the Lost Bible might help. What if Arabs and Israelis could look at each other not as inveterate enemies but as light-bearers, conduits of complementary truth. What if Protestants and Catholics, Hindus and Sikhs, people of every size, shape, and color could recognize that we are all but sojourners, inadequate in ourselves, yet twin brothers of Jesus, on our own pathways to enlightenment. Perhaps, just perhaps, that splendid dream is not so impossible after all. The Master declares:

> I have cast fire on the world. And look, I am standing watch over it until
> it blazes.

The fire is the power residing within each of us, guarded by the Master until we understand and know enough about ourselves for it to burn brightly. May that day come, sooner than we dare to believe.

CHAPTER 3

The Israelite Book of the Dead

CERBERUS, n. The watch-dog of Hades, whose duty it was to guard the entrance—
against whom or what does not clearly appear; everybody, sooner or later,
had to go there, and nobody wanted to carry off the entrance.
—AMBROSE BIERCE, THE DEVIL'S DICTIONARY, 1911.

A mind not to be changed by place or time. / The mind is its own place, and in itself/
Can make a heav'n of hell, a hell of heav'n.
—JOHN MILTON

The pyramids rise majestically from the desert sands. They are the definitive symbol of the kingdom of the Nile, so much so that one cannot even think of ancient Egypt without the image of the pyramids coming to mind. We think of them as magnificent structures, mountains of limestone, unparalleled among the monuments of our planet. But, paradoxically, their sole function seems to have been to glorify the macabre aspects of death and decay—to serve as tombs for the pharaohs, enormous stone sarcophagi, from which the soul of the great potentate might be launched heavenward.

In point of fact, much that remains to us of ancient Egypt would lead us to believe this was an entire culture focused (morbidly, we might think) on death. The Egyptian Book of the Dead tells us about their notions of the netherworld—how souls were guided through the afterlife, equipped with prayers, hymns, magical incantations, and the like, which protected them from evil influence and provided for their needs in the shadowy world of the dead. Additionally, it included a graphic depiction of how the heart is removed from the body and weighed in the scales by Osiris, lord of the underworld, to determine whether one's good deeds outweigh one's evil deeds.

Amazingly, in the Lost Bible we discover that the Israelites had their own Book of the Dead. In many respects it sounds remarkably like its Egyptian counterpart. It is the Apocalypse of Zephaniah, an ancient account of how the biblical prophet Zephaniah is taken up into the heavens and shown the fate of souls in the hereafter.

THE EXCLUSION

The origins of the Apocalypse of Zephaniah, like its mysterious contents, are shrouded in mystery. It came down to us in Greek, having been composed in Egypt as early as 100 B.C.E. Bear in mind, however, that the prophet himself lived in the seventh century, B.C.E., fully half a millennium before the apocalypse bearing his name surfaced. Much of the book has been lost, and what remains is preserved in an early Coptic language text, which dates to around 400 C.E. Why was the book excluded from the canon? As for the keepers of the canon, who presided at the Council of Yavne, they would certainly have balked at a text whose original language was Greek, rather than Hebrew—the "holy tongue." They rightly guessed that it was composed much later than the rest of the Hebrew Bible, and was not the product of Zephaniah himself, but rather an impostor, using the prophet's name as a pseudonym.

Furthermore, it is likely that the early sages, both Jewish and Christian, did not like the book's depiction of the afterlife, which is similar to ancient mythologies, both Greek and Egyptian. The keepers of the canon wanted to distinguish biblical faith from all other religious traditions. What they failed to recognize, however, is that the Greek and Egyptian accounts are based on even earlier traditions from the ancient Near East, which are even older than the canonical books of the Bible themselves.

SHADES OF DANTE

In the early twelfth century, Dante wrote the *Inferno*, about a journey through the nine circles of hell, describing in vivid detail the types of torment found in each. The Apocalypse of Zephaniah is more like the entire *Divine Comedy*, of which the *Inferno* is a part. It is a journey to heaven, the place of the righteous. And, while there are scenes of torment along the way, the main emphasis is not on divine wrath but divine mercy. The paraphrase I present here recounts the amazing story:

> One day an angelic spirit came to me and took me up into the fifth heaven. There were multitudes of angels in that place, wearing crowns, which the Holy Spirit had placed on their heads. They were living in temples of salvation, and they were all singing to the Eternal. I saw many things on my ascent, including a soul being punished by five thousand angels, being given one hundred lashes every day.
>
> The spirit said to me, "Great wickedness was found in this soul."

Though this account seems to focus on the hereafter, it has much to teach us about human condition in the here and now. People's lives, it shows, consist of the multiple choices they make. Those mired in destructive behavior cannot make the right choices because they understand neither the world (their own environment) nor themselves. Life has no scripts, but it does have paths, and we are free to choose among them. In the relativistic maze of modern culture, the right way has never seemed so elusive; our framework has been undermined. Knowing has never been more important—knowing ourselves and knowing our world. The account continues:

> The spirit accompanied me and showed me an enormous place with many multitudes of angels.
>
> "Whenever someone dies," the spirit said, "we carry out the body, playing music, singing hymns, and chanting spiritual songs."
>
> Next the spirit lifted me up so that I could see all of the earth beneath me. It was as though the whole world were suspended like a water drop falling from a bucket that is drawn up from a well. I caught a glimpse of the multitude of souls that were being punished. I exclaimed, "Dear God, if you really care about righteous people in the world, then you must have mercy upon its inhabitants, and even on these souls who are being punished."
>
> Then the spirit said, "Come with me and I will show you the abode of the righteous." He lifted me up to the mountaintop and showed me three men (sons of a priest) who were unrighteous and had never kept the holy commandments. Two angels rejoiced and exulted over them for being condemned, but two others wept.
>
> I asked the spirit who they were, and the spirit replied, "The latter pair are the angels who inscribe all the good deeds of the righteous while guarding the gates of heaven. They are all written on a scroll. However, the other two are the angels of the Adversary who walks the earth. In their scroll they inscribe all the sins and iniquity of those being judged. They also guard the gates of heaven, relating these sins to the Adversary, who in turn inscribes them in his own scroll."

THE TWO WAYS

The angels appear in pairs—one who inscribes the deeds of the righteous, and one who metes out punishment upon the wicked. It is an image of what the Lost Bible depicts as the two ways: the way of life and the way of death, the way of good and the way of evil. We read on:

> As I accompanied the spirit I was taken to a place where an infinite number of angels resided. They looked like leopards, only bearing tusks,

like wild boars. Their eyes were bloody, and their hair fell loosely like women's hair. In their hands they held whips of fire. I was terrified and asked the spirit who they were. The spirit explained that they are servants of creation, who bring in ungodly souls and leave them here. In terror I begged, "Please do not give them power over me." The spirit replied, "Do not worry, they will never be able to approach you, since you are pure." The spirit gestured to them, and they quickly ran from me.

Each of us has both a good inclination and an evil inclination. It is our evil inclination that acts as an accuser. Sometimes we hear voices of accusation (like fearsome spirits) in our own heads. Most often we accuse ourselves, sometimes fairly, oftentimes unfairly. The great truth of the Apocalypse of Zephaniah is that we are already pure in our innermost being . . . if we dare to believe it.

Next, I accompanied the spirit and saw bronze gates, which opened up as the spirit touched them. Inside was a vast sea, which I thought was water, but it turned out to be a sea of fire with waves of burning sulfur. In blind terror I prayed to the Eternal, "You saved Israel from pharoah in Egypt. You saved Susanna from the wicked elders who accused her. You saved the three young Israelites, Shadrach, Meshach, and Abednego, from the fiery furnace. Now please save me from this awful fate."

I asked the spirit, "What place is this that you have brought me to?" The spirit replied, "It is Hades."

"And who is the mighty angel I see?" I asked.

The spirit replied, "This is the Adversary, who indicts people before the Eternal." He was holding a scroll in which all the sins I had ever committed were written. If I had failed to visit a sick person or a widow, it was inscribed in the scroll. If I had not paid a visit to an orphan, it was also inscribed. If I had failed to fast and pray as I ought, it was written down. I begged the Eternal for mercy.

But a mighty angel came to me and said, "You have overcome and gained victory over the Adversary. You may now ascend from Hades and pass over the crossing place."

Dante's *Inferno* notwithstanding, it is important not to get overly flustered by visions of heaven and hell. What is the message here? It is that the soul that is tested, the soul that is tried, is the soul that perseveres. Think of all the times in life when you have faced an accuser, when you have felt that you were on your own journey through Hades. But the Lost Bible teaches that those who glimpse hell are the ones who find heaven:

Another great angel appeared, holding a golden trumpet, which he held over my head and blew three times.

"Be brave, O victorious one, for you overcame and conquered the Adversary. You have found escape from Hades and from the pit."

He approached all the righteous souls of the past, including Abraham, Isaac, Jacob, Elijah, and David, talking to them as one speaks to a friend. I felt like hugging the angel, but I could not, because his glory was so great.

THE INFERNO

The hell we occasionally experience is a part of life, and we could never appreciate heaven otherwise. These visions came from human experience, and it is in our (sometimes fearful) experience that we appropriate redemption:

> I saw the sea of flame in the lowest part of Hades, with its waves reaching up to the clouds. A multitude of souls were drowning in it, many with their hands chained to their necks, their hands and feet in fetters.
>
> When I asked who they were, the spirit said, "These are people who are guilty of taking bribes, which in turn led others to go astray." Many more were wrapped with blankets of fire. When I asked who they were, the spirit said, "They are guilty of usury, having lent money at high interest."
>
> There were also many blind souls crying in pain. The spirit explained, "They are the ones who heard the word of the Eternal but never carried out or acted upon what they heard."
>
> I also heard voices crying out, "We beg you, O Eternal, on behalf of those suffering in anguish, be merciful upon them all."
>
> When I asked who they were, the spirit said, "They are Abraham, Isaac, and Jacob. Every day they come out accompanying a mighty angel, who blows a trumpet, whereupon they rush forward to pray for the souls in punishment."

Overly terrifying, we might think. Perhaps not modern enough for our consumption. Of course the text says what it says, but we can choose to read it in the light of modern values and contemporary metaphysics. We can choose to see goodness and mercy (very much a part of these passages), rather than wrath and punishment.

The unfortunate tendency of moderns is simply to dismiss this incredible literary record because it doesn't appear to mesh with modern notions of enlightened spirituality. But we need not go to that extreme. Indeed, we can read this material through enlightened eyes and draw valuable lessons for modern life.

THE SECRET

The metaphysics of the Lost Bible is strongly action-based. However; action begins with knowing. The biblical book of James declares, "So, to the one knowing how to do good, but who does not do it, it is sin"(4:17, author's translation). How many times have we all said to ourselves, "I should have known better"? Every action has its consequences.

There was a student in a particular class I taught on philosophy and religion. He was brilliant—well versed in the world of ideas, in metaphysics, and the realm of abstract reasoning, with the potential to become an author in his own right someday, or perhaps a distinguished professor. But somewhere along the line there was a disconnect between what he knew and the choices he made. Whether his troubles stemmed from a dysfunctional family or from low self-esteem, he ended up choosing drugs.

By the time he reached my class, he was using heroin on a semi-regular basis and doling it out to others, including his girlfriend. Perhaps he hoped that together he and his friends might reach some sublime state of ecstasy. But heroin is part of the modern Book of the Dead.

One day early in the semester, my young academic charge introduced the drug to a friend. A potent mix of alcohol already in the blood and the powdery toxin brought forth a frightful consequence—cardiac arrest. A brilliant young mind certainly knew better, but he did not know as he ought. He had killed a close friend.

Wracked with guilt and pain, he cooperated with the authorities, leading them to the dealer, whom he helped to convict and put behind bars. Still, he himself was sentenced to seven years in prison. A convicted felon with a drug record, his hopes of becoming a teacher someday vanished.

Indeed, there is hope for everyone, even felons, even those languishing in prison. But wouldn't our lives be infinitely sweeter if we studied to know and understand the two ways—of good and evil, of life and death—and chose the way that leads to life?

Bottom-line advice from the Lost Bible: know yourself, believe in yourself. Get out of the role of victim; give yourself the power to choose.

CHAPTER 4

You Are Not Helpless

Always continue the climb. It is possible for you to do whatever you choose,
if you first get to know who you are and are willing to work with
a power that is greater than ourselves to do it.
—OPRAH WINFREY

I don't know what the future may hold, but I know who holds the future.
—RALPH ABERNATHY, CIVIL RIGHTS LEADER

I
t is said that success is the result of good judgment—part of the realm of knowing. At least we would like to believe so. To the contrary, Mark Twain once quipped, "All you need in this life is ignorance and confidence; then success is sure." There is of course the popular adage, "It is not *what* you know, but *who* you know." The Lost Bible, however, tells a story to prove that it really is *what* you know. Or, as Ralph Waldo Emerson put it, "I hate quotations. Tell me what you know."

Perched atop the Mount of Olives in my favorite spot of meditation, I realized only too well that whom I knew had gotten me into trouble. It had in fact been my friends, including old school buddies, who had lured me into the clutches of cult-like groups. The group became a surrogate family, more important than my real family. I became, in a sense, idolatrous. I realized that if I were to find escape, it would have to be through what I knew, not whom I knew. Such was my motivation, years later, in becoming a professor in the field of philosophy and religion. If I could help other young people discover for themselves what they knew, they just might gain sufficient inner fortitude to avoid the snares that had so entrapped me as a young man.

The Lost Bible teaches that when we understand ourselves and the world around us, we can act in harmony with our surroundings, rather than fighting against them. We can use natural laws to gain the upper hand. However, we have to do our homework. We have to understand the inner workings of a situation in order to "ride the wave."

The story of Bel and the Dragon is another book that was excluded from the canon of the Bible; yet it contains one of the great heroic accounts of antiquity. It relates how a young victim of the Babylonian conquest, an Israelite named Daniel, finds, through the power of knowledge, that he is not so helpless after all. What might have been the account of a victim of religious persecution becomes the story of a hero of religious perseverance.

"TELL ME WHAT YOU KNOW"

The hungry Babylonian god Bel is served food every evening by the priests. The food mysteriously disappears during the night, supposedly proving that Bel has in fact consumed it. The truth is, however, that the priests have stolen it by night. In fresh paraphrase of the story, we read:

> When King Cyrus ruled Persia, young Daniel was one of his friends, and honored more than anyone else. But the Babylonians worshiped an idol known as Bel, serving it with twelve fine bushels of flour every day, as well as forty sheep and fifty gallons of wine. King Cyrus worshiped Bel every day, while Daniel worshiped the God of Israel. The king asked him, "Why do not you worship Bel with the rest of us?"
>
> Daniel replied, "I do not honor empty idols, but the true Creator of the heavens and the earth, who rules all humankind."
>
> King Cyrus replied, "What? You do not believe that Bel is alive? Do not you see how much food and wine he consumes every day?"
>
> Daniel only laughed, saying, "Do not be fooled, great king. Bel may be made of bronze outside, but he's only clay inside. He can neither eat nor drink!"
>
> King Cyrus became furious and said to the priests of Bel, "Who is consuming all of this food and wine? Tell me what you know, or I will have you all killed. If you can prove that it is Bel and no one else, then I will have Daniel killed, since he has slandered the god."

As the text tells us, a contest ensues, to see which god is alive, Bel or Daniel's God. The loser is to die. Daniel uses his wits:

> When everyone had departed, King Cyrus laid food for Bel out on the table. But Daniel asked his servants to carry ashes into Bel's temple and spread them across the entire floor as the king was watching. Afterwards they shut the door, sealing it with the royal signet ring.
>
> Later in the night the priests of Bel entered, just as they had done before, bringing their wives and children with them, and they ate and drank everything. The following morning the king got up early and asked

Daniel whether the seals on the door had been broken. Daniel replied that they had not. When the doors were opened, the king glanced at the table and cried aloud, "O Bel, you are great! In you there is no deceit." Daniel, however, only laughed, and blocked the king from entering the chamber.

"Just look at the floor!" he exclaimed. "Whose footprints are those?"

King Cyrus replied, "Those are the tracks of men, women, and children!" The king was furious. He had the priests of Bel, along with their wives and children, arrested. They revealed the location of the secret doors, through which they had broken in and consumed the food and wine. The king in his rage had them all executed. He handed over to Daniel the idol called Bel, and Daniel had it destroyed, along with the whole temple in which it stood.

Next, the king challenges Daniel to kill a dragon he had worshiped, and do it without a sword. Daniel, again through sheer wit, feeds it cakes made with pitch, fat, and hair. The dragon, in gastrointestinal distress, bursts open. Daniel is thrown into a lion's den—for a second time. However, the prophet Habakkuk is miraculously whisked in to help, providing food for Daniel:

> The prophet Habakkuk protested, saying, "But I've never even seen Babylon! Nor do I know this den."
>
> But the angel merely grabbed him by the top of his head and yanked him upward by his hair. He transported the prophet all the way to Babylon at the speed of the wind, coming directly over the den.

In the end, the king, who returned to mourn for Daniel, was amazed to find him alive and well:

> King Cyrus had Daniel lifted out of his prison, and the very ones who had plotted to kill him he had thrown into the den in his place. The lions immediately consumed them as he watched.

THE EXCLUSION

Bel and the Dragon does not appear in Jewish Bibles, but did in fact make it into the Greek version of the Hebrew Bible, called the Septuagint, translated in Alexandria in Egypt. It was most likely originally composed in Aramaic (a close cousin of Hebrew, using the same alphabet), perhaps in the third century, B.C.E. Centuries later, as Christianity developed into a religion distinct from Judaism, it canonized the books that appear, not in standard Hebrew Bibles, but in the

Septuagint. After all, the New Testament was preserved in Greek. Shouldn't the Greek version of the Old Testament be held up as the standard? Moreover, the early Church Fathers had developed a growing rivalry with the parent religion, and sanctioning the Greek version of the Scriptures over the Hebrew allowed them to further sever any link with Judaism. Consequently, the Apocrypha formally came into being—a series of books stricken from the Jewish canon but preserved in the Septuagint and kept alive to this day in Catholic Bibles.

In the Septuagint, the story of Bel and the Dragon forms the last section of the book of Daniel, the officially canonized account of a young Israelite taken into captivity in faraway Babylon. The book of Daniel itself struggled long and hard for canonical status and was almost excluded. It seemed too consumed with angelic visitations and mystical dreams to please the sages of later generations. Perhaps a compromise was reached, whereby Daniel would be voted in as long as its last chapters, about Bel and the Dragon, were kept out. Perhaps the story about Bel seemed just too far-fetched, and when the prophet Habakkuk is magically transported to Babylon, the sages likely threw up their hands and cried, "Enough!" But whether or not they should have canonized the stories themselves, they might have been well advised at least to have canonized the wisdom they convey.

THE SECRET

The story of Bel and the Dragon allegorically tells us how to find calm in the midst of a storm. Discover the source of true nourishment, which, even in deprivation, will never fail you. Why was Daniel fearless in the face of persecution? Because he had cultivated knowledge and wisdom, which are really intertwined. As Immanuel Kant observed, "Science is organized knowledge. Wisdom is organized life." Daniel, it seems, was a master of both science (with his clever test in Bel's temple) and life. That is what won the day.

KNOWING WHO HOLDS THE FUTURE

One final aspect of knowledge relates to the end of all things—what theologians call eschatology. Much of the Lost Bible deals with this theme. Of course, having been erroneously convinced (during my involvement with the cult-like groups) that the world was about to end, I was now wary of anything related to eschatology. Sitting in that musty library on Mount Zion, I almost closed the books and walked away. But I also knew enough to understand the allegorical nature of the Lost Bible. I knew that it is not about setting dates or plugging current events into some prophetic scheme, but about finding meaning on a personal level.

Indeed, there is something very comforting in knowing that history is going somewhere, that events are not random, and that life itself consists of something more than time and chance in an impersonal void. The Lost Bible, specifically the book of Jubilees, proclaims that history is dominated by order, not chaos, that there is a structure to it all, and that time may be divided into precise forty-nine-year periods. These periods, called jubilees, are based on seven weeks of seven years each, and follow a fixed solar calendar, prophetically delineated well ahead of its time (i.e., long before the Julian calendar that we have grown accustomed to).

There is a lesson here, summed up in a single word: progress. It is a word we take for granted. But leave the West behind, at least in your imagination. Travel east as far as you can, and you will discover a very different worldview, one that says: "History is not progressing anywhere, nor are individual lives. It is all part of a great cycle, endlessly repeating itself, constantly seeking equilibrium and balance, but never finding resolution." The Western idea of advancement is really an ancient Israelite idea, birthed in the pages of the book of Jubilees and other books of the Lost Bible.

The mystical book of Jubilees proclaims itself to be the direct revelation of the Angel of the Presence to none other than Moses, the great lawgiver, atop Mount Sinai. It includes a detailed account of history, from Adam through Moses, as well as a series of prophecies about the future. We are told that the people will be exiled from the land of Israel, only to return again in repentance and restoration. The account is laced with the expression of an incredible hope for the future, at the end of days. We read (in fresh paraphrase) the words of the Eternal:

> I will bring them back from the lands of exile. When they look for me, they will find me . . . I have decided in the depths of my heart to replant them in the land. They will be blessed, not cursed; they will be honored, not despised. I will even rebuild my temple among them, and I will live among them forever.

It is said that hope springs eternal in the human breast. We all want to nourish hope—for a better, brighter day, for a renewed and restored world. Hope is a good thing, perhaps the best of things, though it is sometimes a rare commodity in the modern skeptical world. It is, however, the very warp and woof of the secret knowledge of the Lost Bible. The book of Jubilees tells us:

> The Angel of the Presence . . . brought the stone tablets containing the periods of time, from the creation of the world across the complete number of jubilees, until the time when a new heaven and a new earth will be created. All creatures will be brought back to life by the power of

heaven and the way of the world. Finally, the temple on Mount Zion in Jerusalem will be restored, and the lights of the heavens will shine—for healing, peace, and eternal blessings.

Beyond Jubilees, Moses was also the author (in tradition) of a prophetic work called (appropriately) the Apocalypse of Moses, which relates the awesome events to transpire upon the earth at the end of days. We read (in paraphrase):

> The entire world will shake on its foundations. . . . The mountain peaks will be flattened. . . . The sun will not shine, and the moon will be eclipsed by darkness. . . . . The oceans will roll backwards, retreating to their own depths. The source of all water will be blocked, and the rivers will dry up.

Yet another book of the Lost Bible, the book of Enoch—purportedly written by the great patriarch of the book of Genesis, the grandson of Adam—propounds knowledge of the end. The ancient patriarch declares that a time of terrible persecution will come someday, in which the righteous will suffer greatly at the hands of the wicked. Interestingly, Enoch's very name in Hebrew, *Khanokh*, is another word for education or knowledge. The ancient patriarch goes so far as to predict a second great judgment coming on the world, after the great flood of Noah. The second judgment will not be by water but by fire. In the book of Enoch, he beholds a river of flame, flowing like water into the great sea to the west.

All of this can of course be read allegorically. Fire destroys, but it also purifies. Let your heart be purified, Enoch would surely advise us today. Let every motive be judged. Open yourself to divine scrutiny, and let the hand of God be upon you. Images of fire notwithstanding, judgment is not for evil, but ultimately for the good. Just as death and life are partners with each other, completing one another, so are mercy and judgment. You must understand fundamentally that you cannot know mercy without also knowing judgment. That is what the Lost Bible is trying to teach us.

THE EXCLUSION

The book of Enoch was originally composed in Hebrew or Aramaic, which must have pleased the keepers of the canon. But despite the claim that it was authored by Enoch himself, all the evidence points to the second century B.C.E. as the time of its origin. The earliest copies that came down to us date from the fourteenth and fifteenth centuries C.E., preserved in the Ethiopic language. However, we now have significant fragments of the book preserved among the Dead Sea

Scrolls. Clearly, the second-century keepers of the canon did not like the book's mystical speculation or the peculiar class of angels known as the Watchers, who are introduced into the book. Enoch, they clearly felt, was out in left field. So thoroughly did they suppress the book that the original Semitic language was entirely lost to us until the discovery of the Dead Sea Scrolls, by chance, in the twentieth century.

The book of Jubilees was likewise composed in the second century B.C.E., notwithstanding its attribution to Moses. Originally composed in Hebrew, its earliest known copies date from the sixteenth century, preserved in the Ethiopic language. But as with Enoch, we now have fragments of the book, preserved in their Semitic original, among the Dead Sea Scrolls. The keepers of the canon doubtless rejected it, due not only to its mystical tone, but to the fact that it proclaims a solar calendar, in stark opposition to the lunar-based calendar of the Israelites.

THE SECRET

Cataclysm has happened before, declare the books of Enoch and Jubilees, and will happen again. Modern science of course verifies that the very elements are temporary, part of a great cosmic waltz between matter and energy. When we understand that everything is temporary, we can relax in the only day that really matters—today. *Carpe diem*: Seize the day.

PART II

THE WORLD OF BEING (ATZILUT)

Being is all about self-discovery and self-actualization. It is where true life begins. Take the case of the young man who was supposed to become a lawyer. He was groomed to perform well in life's endeavors. His friends and family convinced him this was the path to success. The young man's brother had become a lawyer. It seemed the logical thing to do. And so he dutifully entered law school, though his heart was never in it. He knew that there was something else for him to become. The more he centered down into his being, the more he knew that he must find himself, authentically.

This sense of being is what makes us true to ourselves. In the case of this young man—me—the voice that beckoned was from the Middle East, the cradle of civilization, which had gotten into my blood when I had lived and studied there as an undergraduate. Over time I had my own Mount Sinai experience. I realized that the answer for my life was in the personal empowerment that comes from self-actualization. I left law school and decided simply to sit for a while. In the end I returned to the study of ancient Near East language and literature—hardly a career path of glamour and luxury, but one which has filled my life with a sense of wonder. There is a feeling of deep satisfaction every time I survey a fresh crop of young faces who flock to my university classes for one reason—to understand the complex tapestry of civilization which has given birth to us all.

"AM I GOOD ENOUGH?"

Studies tell us that many modern people are likewise troubled, wondering whether they are good enough, whether they have accomplished enough, whether they are living up to the expectations of family and friends. How many of us are plagued by inner voices whispering: "You will never amount to anything. You will never get ahead in life. You will never accomplish much." We have grown accustomed to measuring our self-worth on the basis of what we *do*, having never discovered the World of *Being*. Like many other members of the Baby Boom generation, I used to think that I was never good enough. It was a phenomenon I overcame only when I learned to quit judging myself by other people's expectations. I have learned that happiness comes not through what you do, but by who you are. You need not prove yourself or your worth to anyone. You simply need to discover *yourself*. Shakespeare said it simply and directly: "This above all, to thine own self be true." It is a principle illustrated in an incredible story.

Chapter 5

The Hollow Man

Destiny is an absolutely definite and inexorable ruler.
—ALEISTER CROWLEY, SWISS WRITER

*Not to evade destiny, as the ordinary people try to do, but to fulfill it
in its true potential —the imagination.*
—LAWRENCE DURRELL, RUSSIAN-BORN TRAVELER

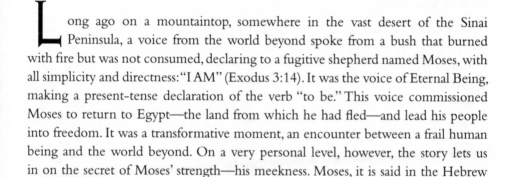

Long ago on a mountaintop, somewhere in the vast desert of the Sinai Peninsula, a voice from the world beyond spoke from a bush that burned with fire but was not consumed, declaring to a fugitive shepherd named Moses, with all simplicity and directness: "I AM" (Exodus 3:14). It was the voice of Eternal Being, making a present-tense declaration of the verb "to be." This voice commissioned Moses to return to Egypt—the land from which he had fled—and lead his people into freedom. It was a transformative moment, an encounter between a frail human being and the world beyond. On a very personal level, however, the story lets us in on the secret of Moses' strength—his meekness. Moses, it is said in the Hebrew Scriptures, was the meekest man on earth (Numbers 12:3). The great Israelite sages called him a "hollow reed"—personally empty, but filled with the divine breath.

HOLY MOSES

Moses was a man who had grown up in Egypt, in the court of Pharaoh, who saw the suffering of his people as they labored under the burden of slavery and who wanted to make a difference. However, he acted impulsively. He took matters into his own hands. He slew one of the Egyptian slave drivers (whom he had seen mistreating a Hebrew), only to find himself a fugitive, wandering in the desert, trying to find both himself and his God. His transformation on Mount Sinai was essential if he were to deliver a band of Hebrew slaves from the whips of their taskmasters. It involved giving up his pride and his selfish striving, and relaxing in the knowledge that the Divine Presence is in charge of everything. By the time God was finished with Moses, he was a true human *being*. Having been transformed by the divine encounter, he finally returned to Egypt with a message for Pharaoh: "Let my people go." This time, however, the power with which he acted was not his. The staff he wielded represented divine fullness and his own emptiness.

The Lost Bible's book of Jubilees (reprinted here in fresh, modern paraphrase) tells us that Moses

> climbed up the holy mountain, Mount Sinai, which the Divine Presence covered like a cloud for six days. On the seventh day the Eternal called to him.

An ancient parchment fragment from the Dead Sea Scrolls declares:

> An angel came directly to Moses and revealed to him an account of how the world was created. (Dead Sea Scroll fragment #4Q216, author's paraphrase)

THE EXCLUSION

That account is found in the Lost Bible's book of Jubilees. Written around 150 B.C.E., but attributed to Moses (falsely, according to most scholars), it is one of the most remarkable books that the ancient world ever produced. Nevertheless, it was deliberately excluded from the official canon of Holy Writ. The earliest copies of the text known to exist—up until the middle of the twentieth century—were in Ethiopic, dating from the 1500s C.E. Then, the Dead Sea Scrolls were discovered, and the whole picture of the biblical world changed. For among the thousands of tiny scraps of parchments discovered in caves in the Judean Desert were fragmentary remains of the book of Jubilees.

The people who preserved these scrolls, a mysterious Judean sect called the Essenes, clearly considered the book of Jubilees to be inspired, Holy Writ. They even cited it and quoted from it in various other sectarian writings, also found along the shores of the Dead Sea. Doubtless, Jubilees had quite a following among the inhabitants of ancient Israel.

There were, however, things about this mysterious book that the traditionally minded rabbis and sages did not particularly care for. They disliked the incessant harping on angels (a hallmark of this text), fearing it might divert attention from God. There is only one Deity, they insisted, who does not need intermediaries to perform the divine will.

Moreover, they chafed at the idea that an independent evil force, called by the book of Jubilees Mastema, is at work in the world, opposing the Eternal. To them, an evil power seemed at odds with monotheism. Furthermore, they disagreed with the concept that everything is ordered, predestined, according to a fixed solar calendar—a prominent feature of this text. Therefore, they condemned the book, consigning it to the ash heap, along with scores of other texts that did not merit their blessing.

Nevertheless, many in ancient Judea apparently believed that the Jubilees had been divinely dictated to Moses. God had spoken; no further proof was necessary.

JUBILEES AND THE COSMIC PATTERN

The book of Jubilees itself explains:

> The Angel of the Presence told Moses: "Write down the detailed account of the creation. . . . On the first day the Eternal brought the heavens into existence, as well as the earth, the waters and the ministering angels. These include angels of: the Divine Presence, sanctification, fire, wind, clouds, darkness, snow, hail, frost, the depths, thunder, lightning, cold, heat, winter, springtime, fall, and summer."

Why was Moses chosen to be the recipient of such secrets? The answer lies in Moses' deep humility, his hollowness. The mystics taught that the World of Being is all about pure spirit, which must find a point of exit from the divine realm into the material, physical dimensions. That point of exit, as fate would have it, was the hollow man, Moses. The World of Being is the realm of the life force that resides in all beings. It is pure; it is holy. It is like fire (such as that which enveloped the burning bush), manifesting itself in brilliant white light. It is the ultimate reality, of which everything down here is at best a pale copy. It emanates from the infinite domain of heaven and finds expression in the finite—in this case, a man named Moses, who learned to leave himself behind and simply rest in the Divine Presence.

The narrative in the book of Jubilees goes back to the moment of creation itself. There is an interesting theory in astrophysics known as the Anthropic Principle that within the first millisecond after the Big Bang all manner of mathematical equations had to array themselves just so, in order to form an orderly, smoothly functioning system of millions of galaxies and billions and billions of stars—as opposed to a nebulous, anarchic void, inhabited by nothing more orderly than a gaseous chaos. Why did *this* universe, as we know it, with all its incredible beauty and complexity, go to all the trouble of existing, of being? It is as though the universe itself wanted to bring forth life . . . and ultimately you and me.

The book of Jubilees fills in details that the book of Genesis never mentions— that specific angels guided the process of creation from the very beginning. Of course, as with the rest of Lost Bible, Jubilees should not be read as a scientific text. But the bottom line is this: either the universe and everything in it, including you and me, is the result of randomness and chance, with no purpose and no meaning, or there is an intricate plan, an Anthropic Principle behind it all. Notice that the names of the angels coincide with the forces of nature. Perhaps Jubilees is telling us that the fundamental laws of the universe are the intermediaries (symbolized by angels) through which God created everything.

It stands to reason that the subsequent section of the book of Jubilees is all about the meaning and function of the Sabbath day. When we know that all of history—and our own life—is under control, we enter the World of Being. We discover the secret of rest. The text states (in paraphrased reconstruction):

> The Creator of everything made this day to be a blessing—of holiness and splendor, hallowed beyond all other days. Observing the Sabbath is a sacred law, a gift to Israel's descendants for all eternity.

THE HUMAN ANIMAL

In keeping with the Anthropic Principle, Jubilees next turns to the account of the creation of humanity. We quickly realize that history is going somewhere. It is not an endless circle with no progression, but a dynamic process, charged with meaning, beginning with the first human, Adam. Our paraphrase continues:

> All of the animals were created on the sixth day, after which the Eternal made Adam—a man. Male and female were created and given dominion over everything. . . . The Eternal said: "It is not good for Adam to be alone. We shall make a helper just like him." The Eternal put Adam to sleep and took one of his bones, a rib, from which a woman was fashioned. This woman came directly from Adam's bones.

The book of Jubilees goes on to record the serpent's temptation of Eve, her disobedience, and the expulsion of Adam and Eve from the garden. All of the events recounted follow a specific chronology, according to a series of jubilee years, so that even sin and disobedience can be seen as part of the divine plan. There are no accidents. Nothing is lost in God's economy. It is all an aspect of the World of Being.

Thereafter, Adam's descendants are named. The great sin of the angels is also described. Moses is told that in a certain jubilee year, many angels took wives from among the daughters of men. We read (in modern paraphrase):

> And the women bore them children, who were giants in those days. Wickedness multiplied, and all living things were corrupted, including the animals, who began to devour each other.

The angels were punished as a result, and the great flood came upon the earth. This judgment, along with everything else in history, had been foreordained:

These things have been engraved and fixed in the heavenly tablets.

The story of Noah and his ark is of course a classic in world literature. Living in Israel and learning the Hebrew language, I was aware that Noah's very name means rest. Like his distant descendant after him (Moses), he was a hollow man. He was deeply acquainted with the World of Being, doing little in his life, save for building an ark—slowly, and with great patience:

Noah built an ark exactly as he was commanded, during the twenty-second jubilee of years.

What might normally be dreadful in this account is mediated by the fact that everything has been ordained according to a precise 364-day solar calendar. Nothing is left to chance in the Eternal's timetable. So relax and get out of the way.

THE FAMILY TREE

The history of the patriarchs is related thereafter: Abraham, Isaac, Jacob, Joseph. The descent of the Israelites into Egypt, ultimately to become slaves under Pharaoh, is cataloged, culminating in the birth of a great deliverer, who was really another hollow man: Moses.

Why do so many people today research their lineage, trying to find their ancestors and where they came from? Is it just that people can find no better way to spend their time? Or is it because people genuinely need to find connectedness with the generations gone by, to be able to say: "My life has meaning, as part of an extended heritage passed from generation to generation. I am part of that heritage. Had even a single ancestor died before his or her time, I would not exist."

This is what Moses comes to understand as his own family tree is revealed. Suddenly, the account becomes deeply personal. The angel addresses Moses directly, in the second person:

"In the seventh week of the seventh year of the forty-seventh Jubilee, your father came to Egypt from the land of Canaan. You were born in the fourth week of the sixth year of the forty-eighth jubilee . . . when the king of Egypt, Pharaoh, ordered that the male Israelite children should be thrown into the river. But your mother . . . made you an ark, with pitch and asphalt, and set it in the river among the reeds."

The familiar story is related, of how Pharaoh's daughter finds the infant Moses and raises him in Pharaoh's court. In recounting to Moses the events of his own life, it is clear that the Angel of the Presence has been watching him from his birth. Like Clarence, the kindly angel in Frank Capra's classic film, *It's a Wonderful Life,* the Lost Bible declares that we really do have guardian angels who look out for us and watch over our every step.

Heightening the tension throughout, however, is an acknowledgment of the presence of Evil—the Lost Bible's equivalent of *Star Wars'* Darth Vader, or Sauron, from Tolkein's *The Lord of the Rings* saga:

> "An evil angel, named Mastema exercised his power and tried to cause you to succumb to Pharaoh. He inspired the Egyptian magicians, who performed their own tricks in front of you. They were allowed to act wickedly, but they weren't allowed to heal, so that no one would think that they had such power."

As in the movies, there really are happy endings. Mastema is ultimately defeated. After the Red Sea splits and the Israelites walk across on dry land, only to watch the pursuing Egyptian charioteers drowned when the sea comes together again, the evil Prince Mastema is bound and imprisoned. The Angel of the Presence continues speaking directly to Moses, saying:

> "After all these things I showed you, when you were in the wilderness, the days of the Sabbaths. . . . I also showed you, when you were up on Mount Sinai, how the Sabbaths are to be kept in the future, in the land of Israel. . . . Everyone in the land will keep the Sabbaths when your descendants possess it, and they will honor the Year of Jubilee."

The book of Jubilees ends as it begins, atop Mount Sinai, with a hollow man named Moses, who has found the World of Being and who now rests in the everlasting arms.

THE SECRET

How do the lessons of Jubilees apply to me? I recall my experiences living in the Middle East in the 1980s, and working with an American news gathering organization. Sometimes late at night, driving along the roads of Lebanon, from the town of Marjayoun (the location of our TV studio) to my home in northern Galilee, I slipped into the World of Being. It was the only way to counter the occasional terror that gripped me, knowing how many vehicles had been ambushed along this very road. Would tonight be my turn? But a moment of reflection and meditation always brought me back to a peaceful centeredness. I recalled the generations of my own family heritage, from my distant Viking ancestors to my grandfather, a circuit-riding Methodist minister who traveled from town to town across southern Georgia. Surely I had not been brought to this Middle Eastern land to become a victim of terrorism. In the World of Being, fear holds no sway. These were burning bush moments for me.

As the pragmatist philosopher William James once said, "The greatest discovery of my generation is that a human being can alter his life by altering his attitudes of mind." When my life flashed before me on those narrow Middle Eastern back roads, I altered both my attitudes and my mind. I too became a hollow man. Somewhere in the World of Being, Moses was looking down, and smiling.

The most important lesson to be gleaned from all this is simple: Before *doing* anything, you must first learn the secret of *being*. A Buddhist master once quipped:

"It is often said, 'Don't just sit there; do something!' We like to say, 'Don't just do something; sit there!'"[3]

Believe in destiny. You were born for a specific purpose, and there are no accidents. The universe makes sense, and you make sense within the greater cosmic pattern. As the jubilees of your own life unfold, look for the larger patterns. Let go, and get out of the way. If you seek anything, seek to be hollow. Do not just do something; sit there!

CHAPTER 6

The Primordial Me

*If you have anything really valuable to contribute to the world it will come
through the expression of your own personality, that single spark of divinity that
sets you off and makes you different from every other living creature.*
—BRUCE BARTON, AMERICAN AUTHOR, ADVERTISING EXECUTIVE

*Life [is] a culmination of the past, an awareness of the present, an indication
of a future beyond knowledge, the quality that gives a touch of divinity.*
—CHARLES A. LINDBERGH

An incredible book of the Lost Bible tells us much about the secret of self-worth. It is the second book of Enoch, an additional account purportedly written by the great biblical patriarch—the sixth descendant of Adam and the great-grandfather of Noah. All the Bible says about Enoch's fate is as follows:

> As it came to pass, all the days of Enoch were three hundred and sixty-five years. And Enoch walked with God; and he was not, for God took him. (Genesis 5:23-24, author's translation)

The Lost Bible, however, tells us what happened to Enoch *after* God took him. The second book of Enoch, or 2 Enoch, relates how the patriarch was taken on a journey through the heavenly realms, to the presence of the Eternal, after which he returned to the earth and related his experiences. The second half of the book tells the story of Methuselah, the longest-lived of all the patriarchs (969 years), and of the mysterious high priest Melchizedek, who, according to this book of the Lost Bible, also ascended on high, before the flood of Noah.

THE EXCLUSION

Some researchers assert that the contents of 2 Enoch date no earlier than the late Middle Ages, since the earliest of manuscripts (which came down to us in the Slavonic language) date to around 1400. But the reality is much more complicated. The underlying structure of the language, the way the sentences are put together—the syntax—betrays a Semitic flavor. Moreover, many expressions and phrases found in the book are distinctly Middle Eastern, as though the author were thinking in a Semitic dialect. Such telltale clues point us to the fact that this book must have been composed in a Semitic language, either Aramaic or, most likely, Hebrew. If this were the case, then 2 Enoch had to have been composed in ancient times, in the land of Israel, as early as the second century B.C.E.

But antiquity alone cannot get a book accepted as divinely inspired. The earliest keepers of the canon likely excluded 2 Enoch from the Bible because they did not believe that Enoch himself wrote it. They would clearly have placed it in the category of Pseudepigrapha—the false writings.

There was probably even more involved in the decision to suppress this book, for 2 Enoch teaches that in each of us resides a mind-boggling power, through which we can transform ourselves and the entire world. This is a far cry from the traditional portrait of misery painted by the ecclesiastical interpreters of the book of Genesis. Their conventional wisdom was this: We had better not bask in the image of the divine, lest we be overcome with haughty arrogance.

After all, we are worthless, miserable creatures. Adam was created from the dust of the ground, mortal, frail, prone to decay, and destined for dissolution. The book of 2 Enoch tampers with these crusty notions. It was consequently stricken from the official canon of Holy Writ, notwithstanding that a credible theory suggests that the book was in fact a sacred text of a Jewish sect in Egypt. It is evident that many people in the ancient world loved the message of this text, which tells us a great deal about the spiritual nature of human beings.

YOU ARE MORE THAN WHAT YOU KNOW

The detailed account of Enoch's ascent through the ten heavens, to come before the face of the Most High, is incredible enough. We read (in paraphrase, condensed from the original):

> There once was a great and wise man whom the Eternal snatched away, so that he could come up and behold the divine realm, including the multi-eyed throne of heaven.
>
> Enoch related, "When I was 365 years old, I was alone in my house. While I slept, two enormous men materialized in front of me. I bowed down in front of them. 'Enoch,' they declared, 'the Eternal has dispatched us to help you ascend into heaven this day.' I instructed my sons, telling them not to turn away from God. Immediately, the two men—who were angels—put me on their wings, carrying me up to the first heaven.

"Afterward, they sat me down on the clouds, and I saw a great ocean, larger than any on earth. They also showed me two hundred angels, who are in charge of the stars and the celestial bodies.

"Next, I was brought up to the second heaven, where I was shown a great darkness. There were many prisoners there, awaiting their final judgment.

"After that, they took me to the third heaven, from which I looked down and saw Paradise. In the midst of the Garden I saw the Tree of Life, where the Eternal always rested upon entering. The Eternal explained, 'Enoch, this Garden has been prepared as the home of the righteous, those who suffer greatly in this lifetime.'

"The angels subsequently brought me up to the northern heaven, a terrifying place of torment and darkness.

"From there I was taken to the fourth heaven, where I was shown rays of light from the sun and the moon. I was also shown a place to the west of heaven, with six enormous gates, where the sun goes down.

"Thereafter, I was brought up to the fifth heaven, where I saw many armies, too numerous to count. They consisted of the Watchers, who look like human beings but are bigger than giants.

"I was next carried to the sixth heaven, where I saw seven different groupings of angels.

"When I was taken up to the seventh heaven, I saw a very great light, as well as the fiery hosts of the archangels.

"Then I beheld the eighth heaven, called in Hebrew *Muzalot,* signifying the changer of seasons. I also saw there the heavenly homes of the twelve zodiacs.

"Finally, the archangel Michael brought me up to the tenth heaven, called *Aravot* in Hebrew, where I saw the face of the Eternal. I fell down prostrate before the divine glory and the splendor of the heavenly throne. The Eternal told Michael to exchange my clothing for clothes of glory and to anoint me with oil. The oil sparkled like the sun's rays, and when I looked at myself, I was like one of the divine beings. There was no difference. The Eternal called one of the archangels, known as Vrervoil, who brought me books of blank pages and a pen to write. Vrervoil taught me for thirty days and thirty nights, and I wrote it all down."

SOMETHING FROM NOTHING

This remarkable ascent (part of a whole genre of ancient ascension texts) is, however, only the beginning of the book's wisdom. Enoch witnesses many things on his ascent through the heavens, including the torture and judgment of evildoers, which he beholds in the second heaven. But he does not stop there. He rises all the way to the tenth heaven, where holy judgment is supplanted by even holier love.

After the patriarch enters the divine throne room and comes face to face with the Eternal, he is given insight into the nature of God, the universe, and himself.

Philosophers of religion, especially the mystics of the three great monotheistic faiths, Judaism, Christianity and Islam, have from time immemorial speculated about the essence and nature of God. Many suggest that God is really nothing, for the most fundamental thing that can be said is that God is not material—no thing. In a sense God cannot even be said to exist, for existence implies some material essence. God is certainly beyond words to describe. God is eternal *Being*, in the World of Being. The Eternal Being is also Eternal Nothing, beyond the bounds of space and time. Consider the words of the Eternal (in the following modern paraphrase), spoken to Enoch and recorded in the book that bears his name:

> "Before anything existed at all, from the beginning of all things, I brought into existence of being from non-being, the visible from the invisible. Listen to what I'm telling you, Enoch. Take note that I have not even shared my secrets with the angels. I never explained to them their own origins, and I never expressed my own endlessness, or my inconceivable, inexpressible essence. It is I who plan and conceive of all living creatures, and I am revealing them to you this day.
>
> "Know that I am eternal Oneness. Before any material things came to exist, I moved about through the invisible things. I moved like the sun, passing from east to west and returning from west to east. But although the sun finds rest within itself, I found no rest. For many things had not yet been created. Therefore, I conceived the creation of a foundation, from which the visible world would spring."

The passage contains a remarkable sophistication, which, whether coincidentally or not, happens to dovetail with the most complex modern notions about what the universe is and where it came from. What indeed was there before the creation event, before the Big Bang? There was truly nothing. For what we think of as iron laws regarding space, the material world, and time are really only aspects of the space-time continuum, functions of a universe expanding ever since the Big Bang. What we measure as space and count as time is really only the product of our human perceptions. We perceive them because we too are part of the expanding universe. The universe is like a balloon that is being blown up, and we inhabit the region within. But outside of the balloon there is no space and there is no time. Therefore, the creation of everything really did come about *ex-nihilo*—from nothing—and that Nothing is God.

Second Enoch expresses this divine nothingness when it speaks of God moving about among invisible things. We might extrapolate that God, too, is invisible—Nothing. And Nothing brought forth something, indeed everything. But there is yet another layer of sophistication in the text, for it declares that Adam was in fact assembled from the very elements of the universe. It is a notion that is particularly intriguing, because astrophysicists point out that everything we behold in our material world, down to the very atoms comprising us, originated long ago, in the midst of great cosmic explosions known as supernovas. One metaphysical contribution of modern science is the observation that we are all therefore the offspring of the stars.

Nor is this idea pure fancy. On the contrary, it is an essential law of astrophysics. The very atoms comprising our bodies are all linked together in the great cosmic continuum. The World of Being, which birthed us all, likewise beckons us, as fellow travelers on Spaceship Earth, toward harmony, mutuality, and understanding.

NOT JUST DUST FROM THE GROUND

But there is yet a more powerful contribution from 2 Enoch. It elevates the human race. From the text itself we read (in modern paraphrase) the following:

> "I gave orders on the sixth day, commanding my wisdom to bring forth a human being from the seven elements of the universe. First, his flesh was taken from the earth itself. Second, his blood was brought forth from both the dew and the sun. Third, his eyes were formed from the depths of the oceans. Fourth, his bones were fashioned from stone. Fifth, his reason derived from the angels, in all their movements, and from the clouds. Sixth, his veins and his hair were made from the grass of the field. Seventh, his spirit derived from my own spirit, as well as the wind. I created him as the Second Angel on the earth, to be greatly extolled. I also gave him a name, taken from the names of the four directions: A for *Anatole,* meaning East, D for *Dusme,* meaning West, a second A for *Arktos,* meaning North, and a final M for *Mesembria,* meaning South."

The clear message from 2 Enoch is that Adam, the prototype of all human beings, was brought forth as a truly cosmic creature, and designed to be the Second Angel— a king full of God's own wisdom, to whom nothing on this planet can be likened. Adam is transcendent in nature, yet also at one with a very fabric of the universe.

When I lived in the Middle East, there was only one place to go to ponder such secrets of the Lost Bible—the Mount of Olives. From my perch atop this natural ridge to the east of the Old City, where I frequently retreated on Jerusalem's cool, crisp evenings, I gazed out at the breathtaking panorama of the ancient city beneath me. I could not help but observe that the city is a vast menagerie of structures, all built from the same Jerusalem limestone. The term *menagerie* may be defined as a varied, striking, or distinctive assortment of individuals, objects, or entities. No word is better suited to explicating the true nature of this ancient, yet modern city, host to multiple religious, political, and ethnic groups.

The buildings of the Old City reflect this diversity, serving many different functions, and representing assorted traditions and contrasting cultures, from Arab to Christian to Jewish to Armenian. Yet, they are all faced with the same Jerusalem stone, which glows with an otherworldly aura as the sun sinks low on the horizon. There is no discord between the structures. The eye sees them as a single stone tapestry in perfect balance and harmony. For all their diversity, these buildings seem to know that they are all dug from the same quarry. Likewise, for all our human diversity, we are all Adam's children, all divine by nature, all the stuff of the eternal cosmos. Why can't we all be like those stones? I wondered. Why is there so much human discord in this ancient city of stone, this City of Peace? Why can't we all just get along?

It dawned on me that the real problem behind human conflict is not that we love ourselves too much, thereby being selfish and self-centered, but that we do not love ourselves enough. We do not recognize the Adam-nature in us—the fact that we were all made to be Second Angels and kings full of wisdom. To be sure, it is only when we can see God in ourselves that we can see God in everybody else.

BECOMING HUMAN *BEINGS*

The book of 2 Enoch coincides with much mystical speculation from other ancient sources, elucidating how the Eternal One decided to experience the material realm, therefore creating the sun, the moon, the stars, and the earth. This process of creation involved sending down pieces of the Divine Presence. The divine will brought into existence an entire class of heavenly beings called *Aeons*—who emanated directly from the Eternal. Collectively, they formed the *Pleroma*, or divine fullness. One such *Aeon* took the form of the first human *being*—Adam.

Thus, Adam was in fact the seed of God. Far from being mere dust—part of the earth—the human was an expression of God, emanating directly from the Eternal. To be even bolder, we may go so far as to say that Adam *was* a little bit of God. Good enough reason for the sages to suppress this book, for such knowledge is power, and history has many examples of people who, thinking they were gods, wreaked great havoc on themselves and others. Still, if we could all grasp the magnificent truth of our *being* and tap into that expression of the divine source in each of us, we would not be so easily controlled by strong personalities and other powers of this world.

When we enter the World of Being, we establish a God's-eye view of the world. We learn to release the fears that keep us focused on materiality, judgments, hatred, and prejudice. Our actions become more meaningful. We are able to evaluate knowledge more effectively, transcending the bombardment of information that is so much a part of modern life.

The Lost Bible tells us that as human *beings*, we are truly spirit beings—having sprouted from the divine seed. While the book of 2 Enoch goes on to recount the story of Adam and the fall from grace, we need to consider above all what this "pseudepigraphical" work tells us about ourselves and about the value of the human being. In 2 Enoch God adds details not found in the book of Genesis:

> "For Adam I created a wide-open heaven, in which he could see the divine angels, as they triumphantly sing. There was also a light that can never be extinguished, which was always burning in Paradise. Even the Evil One understood that I wished to create an entire world, over which Adam could rule."

We may agonize over whether we believe in God, but it is clear that God believes in us. If we can only clear away the cobwebs in our minds—glimpse that wide-open heaven—we will understand that our potential is unlimited, and our powers are multifold. We always have options. After all, look who we have as our Source. The first step toward reaching our potential is of course to change our focus from the physical to the metaphysical, to let the breath of the Eternal fuse with our own.

THE SECRET

During the 1980s when I worked as a cameraman and broadcaster in war-torn Lebanon, I had a special need to tap into that supernatural presence. The stresses I encountered on a daily basis as I watched the jewel of the Mediterranean turned into a pile of rubble by years of civil war were frequently beyond my poor constitution to handle. I needed to find myself, to be rejuvenated. Fortunately, I knew where to go. I often took off down the road toward a centuries-old city snugly situated in the hills of northern Galilee, called Tsfat.

This fabled town had been established by Jewish mystics—masters of Kabbalah—in the 1500s. Today it is home to artists and shopkeepers, but within its weathered walls is an otherworldly aura, which has never left it. The stones themselves seem strangely alive with the divine breath. The whole city of Tsfat is, as it were, a point of contact between this world and the next—or perhaps another point of exit for pure Spirit For me it was the perfect place to get away, to walk enchanted streets, and be transported back to a long-forgotten time—to simply *be*. By the time I returned to my post in Lebanon, I had discovered myself afresh, but I had also discovered how to leave myself behind, how to filter out the background noise that robbed me of my inner peace in the powder keg of the Middle East.

In Tsfat I learned the fullness of the World of Being, as taught by 2 Enoch. The God-force is not out there somewhere in the cosmos, an unknowable abstraction beyond human ken. God is here, and is not silent.

I decided each day to set some time aside, to set a place aside, to center-down into my deepest being through silence, meditation, and study. I adopted a simple word or phrase to repeat (which I found in old Hebrew prayer books), and I let this mantra take the place of worries, cares, and concerns. I focused each meditation session on a declaration of my own divine nature. From then on, when the stress of life pressed in, I remembered this secret.

Contemporary novelist Tom Robbins writes: "When a person accepts a broader definition of reality, a broader net is cast upon the waters of fortune." A broader reality is what 2 Enoch is all about. The secret of 2 Enoch is applicable to our lives each day and conveys a tip on how to approach life: *Never underestimate yourself.*

When you discover the secret of your own being, you need not worry about what others think of you. Trust yourself; believe in your own judgment. Look in the mirror daily, but do not look for blemishes or the latest wrinkle in your brow. Stare at yourself and say, not only, "I am made in the divine image," but also, "I AM . . . a spark of the divine."

CHAPTER 7

Worship Whom?

Our humanity is a poor thing, except for the divinity that stirs within us.
—FRANCIS BACON

My appointed work is to awaken the divine nature that is within.
—PEACE PILGRIM, AMERICAN RELIGIOUS LEADER

L et's return to the Garden of Eden, perhaps better named the Garden of Being, and the story of the first human *beings*—the story that never found its way into the canon of Sacred Scripture: the Life of Adam and Eve. As mentioned above, this mysterious text got into serious trouble with the keepers of the canon, at least in part because it depicts a malevolent external force in the universe—the ancient version of Darth Vader—who came to be called Satan. It was explained that the Jewish scholars considered the very notion of such a figure, independent of the Divine Presence, incompatible with monotheism.

As in ancient times, many modern people of faith do not conceive of Satan as an omnipotent anti-God force on the loose in the universe. Satan, as characterized in the Life of Adam and Eve, might represent the evil inclination in all of us—the part of us that cannot, or will not, recognize the God that resides in all human beings.

THE EXCLUSION—MORE FUEL FOR THE FIRE

There is, moreover, an additional reason that this document was suppressed. It not only makes too much of Satan (thereby diminishing God), but it equally makes too much of the first created being, Adam. The keepers of the canon were "bugged" by such a text, one that virtually deifies the first human, and by extension, all humans.

Specifically, the book boldly declares the nature of Satan's original transgression, namely his refusal to bow down and—yes—to *worship* Adam. We read (in original modern paraphrase):

The Evil One related to Adam: "The reason I'm angry and envious of you is that I was expelled from the Divine Presence on your account. Because of you I was sent down to the earth."

"But what harm have I done to you?" Adam replied. "Why do you blame me, especially since neither I nor Eve have hurt you?"

The Evil One continued: "What are you talking about, Adam? You are the reason that I was cast out of heaven. I was expelled from God's presence not long after you were formed. I was exiled from the company of the angels. Why? Because when God breathed into you the breath of life—when your shape and your likeness were fashioned after God's very image—the archangel Michael brought you before the angels and commanded that they bow down and worship you, while God was looking on.

"The divine voice declared, 'Look, Adam, I have made you in my own image and likeness.'

"At that point Michael went out and proclaimed to all the angels, 'Bow down and worship the divine image, just as God has commanded!' Michael set the example by worshiping first. Then he called to me, saying, 'Worship God's image!'

"I replied, 'I'm not going to worship Adam!' Michael tried to force me to worship, but I asked him, 'Why are you trying to make me do this? I will not worship someone of a lower rank than I. Remember, I was created before Adam, chronologically. Since I existed first, Adam should be worshiping me!'

"At this point many other angels who overheard all of this also declined to worship Adam. But Michael kept on insisting, 'Worship God's image! But if you absolutely refuse, God will strike you in anger.'

"I replied, 'If God does get angry with me, I will establish my own throne well above the stars. I will be God's rival!' Indeed the Most High became furious with me, exiling me along with the other angels away from the Divine Presence.

"You see then, Adam, that our expulsion from heaven down to this world is because of you. We grieved over what happened, since our glory had been taken from us. It hurt us to see you in such a place of delight, and that is why I have deceived your wife Eve, and caused you to be expelled from Paradise."

HOLY CLONE

As in 2 Enoch, Adam is presented as the first human; but he is also presented as divine in his own right. Adam is in a sense God's clone, a holographic image of the

Divine Presence. This is why Satan, as a member of the angelic host, is expected to worship him. The biblical book of Psalms makes the traditional declaration that human beings are not exactly stellar in status:

> What are human beings, that you even notice them?
> What are mere mortals, that you favor them? (Psalm 8:5, author's translation of the Masoretic text. *See* verse 4 in Christian versions.)

Humans have a unique position, to be sure, and are (as the psalm continues) "a little less than divine" (v. 6, author's translation of the Masoretic text. *See* v. 5 in Christian versions). Some translators, troubled by the implications of this verse, correct the text to read, "a little lower than the angels." Such self-effacing theology sounds humble enough for public consumption. But the Life of Adam and Eve suggests the opposite—that the angels, including Satan, were expected to *worship* the human creature. Satan, however, was not about to bend his angelic knee to any being made from the ground. He would not recognize Adam's divinity, nor pay homage to any holographic image of the Eternal. Moreover, his refusal to worship Adam was interpreted by the angelic hierarchy as a refusal to worship God. This was his great transgression, for which he was cast out of heaven.

Recall that much mythology has sprouted up over the centuries, recounting a war in heaven, at some point in hoary antiquity, in which Satan and a third of the angels mounted a revolt against the Almighty, only to be expelled from God's presence. Thereafter this ungodly horde was consigned to the earth, where they would make eternal mischief. Though it is mentioned in a couple of places, you will not find the details of this supernatural soap opera in the Bible per se; they are in the Lost Bible. The tale also found its way into Milton's *Paradise Lost*, which is more than a great epic poem. It draws the kernel of this complex prehistory from the books of the Lost Bible, which were apparently known to Milton, though they have been unknown to most of us moderns.

> Th' infernal Serpent; he it was, whose guile
>   Stird up with Envy and Revenge, deceiv'd
> The Mother of Mankinde, what time his Pride
> Had cast him out from Heav'n, with all his Host
> Of Rebel Angels, by whose aid aspiring
> To set himself in Glory above his Peers,
> He trusted to have equal'd the most High,
> If he oppos'd; and with ambitious aim
> Against the Throne and Monarchy of God
> Rais'd impious War in Heav'n and Battel proud

> With vain attempt. Him the Almighty Power
> Hurld headlong flaming from th' Ethereal Skie
> (*Paradise Lost,* Book I)

Bear in mind, just because these suppressed books weren't officially canonized doesn't mean that they weren't copied or available. The monks who labored from generation to generation in the monasteries of Ireland to reproduce the Sacred Scriptures also made copies of the books of the Lost Bible. "Never mind that these books are not in the canon," the monks must have thought, "they are darned good stories, and they just might shine a ray of light on the primordial past." But even the great John Milton, with all his poetic imagination, neglected to include the tidbit about Satan's refusal to worship Adam. Milton, after all, was a good English Puritan, who dared not even suggest that the first human being (who was responsible for original sin) might also have carried the seed of divinity, which likewise has come down to us all. In other words, it is fine to call the seed of Adam corrupt, depraved from conception, and hopelessly mired in original sin, but do not even think about calling him divine.

HOLY QUR'AN

The notion that Satan wouldn't worship Adam sounds far-fetched, does it? Consider, however, that the very same tradition was picked up in Islam, which has developed its own version of Satan, called Iblis. According to Muslim tradition, Iblis was originally a member of the angelic court, but was ejected from the presence of Allah because he would not bow down to Adam. God, speaking in the plural, with the Royal We, declares in the Qur'an:

> And when We said to the angels: Make obeisance to Adam they did obeisance, but Iblis (did it not). He refused and he was proud, and he was one of the unbelievers. (Qur'an ii. 34)

> And certainly We created you, then We fashioned you, then We said to the angels: Make obeisance to Adam. So they did obeisance except Iblis; he was not of those who did obeisance.
>
> He said: What hindered you so that you did not make obeisance when I commanded you? He said: I am better than he: Thou hast created me of fire, while him Thou didst create of dust.
>
> He said: Then get forth from this (state), for it does not befit you to behave proudly therein. Go forth, therefore, surely you are of the abject ones.

He said: Respite me until the day when they are raised up.

He said: Surely you are of the respited ones.

He said: As Thou hast caused me to remain disappointed I will certainly lie in wait for them in Thy straight path.

Then I will certainly come to them from before them and from behind them, and from their right-hand side and from their left-hand side; and Thou shalt not find most of them thankful.

He said: Get out of this (state), despised, driven away; whoever of them will follow you, I will certainly fill hell with you all. (Qur'an vii. 11-18)[4]

While Islamic art is very careful about reproducing graven images of God or the prophet Muhammad (a clear violation of divine law, called the *Sharia*), there are in fact many graphic representations of Iblis refusing to bend the knee to Adam.

Amazing, that while the Lost Bible has for millennia been stricken from the lists of acceptable reading material, it nonetheless managed to influence—independently—the likes of John Milton in Puritan England, and Muslim theologians from the deserts of Arabia to Moorish Spain.

HOLY BEING

Beyond what Milton and the Muslims picked up, there is another important message here. Without looking at the account as literal or historical, it conveys the idea that everything—including Adam—is a part of God. The great American Transcendentalist, Ralph Waldo Emerson, observed: "Every thing in nature contains all the powers of nature. Every thing is made of one hidden stuff. . . . The world globes itself in a drop of dew." In fact had Satan been truly wise, he would have realized that his jealousy was unwarranted, for he too carried the divine image. In a larger sense, Satan (the Adversary as his name suggests) represents the denial of oneness with God.

Going a step further, Satan can be said to represent human denial. He could not recognize the divinity of humans, or of anything else for that matter. Satan can be seen as a metaphor for the myriad psychological factors that get in the way of our believing in ourselves and in others. The great Adversary short-circuits the World of Being by denying our connectedness with God. The divine spark is of course the subject of Dante's *Divine Comedy*, which depicts the outermost regions of hell (the greatest distance from God) as being occupied *not* by those who committed the worst acts, but by those condemned for their callous indifference to the divine image in others.

THE SECRET

The World of Being allows us to recognize ourselves for who we really are, and to recognize the aspect of the divine in all people. A very nice thought, but what can we do about it? Take the advice of Emerson and the Transcendentalists. Cultivate stillness, practice meditative silence, and take every opportunity to observe the world of nature—the Garden of Being. Even in Eden, a bit of denial (Satan) is still there, but it mustn't interfere with our perception. We realize that we are all part of the whole, the divine Source. It is only when we forget that greater reality that we perpetrate negativity, doing things that are not Godlike.

The stories of the Lost Bible may be largely mythological. However, they teach important lessons about who we are. They also affirm that the Eternal considers humans to be nothing less than divine. We can choose to recognize that great truth about ourselves. We can see the spark of Deity in ourselves and know, as Emerson reasoned, that we are all a piece of the divine fullness. The anonymous authors of the Lost Bible recognized the same principle long ago, though it has taken until modern times to rediscover the impact of their teachings. As these hidden books come to light in the modern age, the World of Being is being born again in us all.

CHAPTER 8

Lilith in the Garden of Being

So long has the myth of feminine inferiority prevailed that women themselves find it hard to believe that their own sex was once and for a very long time the superior and dominant sex.
—ELIZABETH GOULD DAVIS, LIBRARIAN, WRITER

How people treat you is their karma; how you react is yours.
—WAYNE DYER, AMERICAN PSYCHOLOGIST

We should not be surprised that much of the Lost Bible highlights the events of creation, culminating in the formation of the first humans in the Garden of Eden. Like so many other words, Eden is overused to the point that we simply accept its connotation—Paradise—without wondering about its derivation. Linguists know, however, that words in various languages are connected and that a cognate in one will often reveal the meaning in another. In the case of Eden, the closest linguistic link is with the Arabic word *adan*, which means tranquility or languid rest. To be in a perfect state of rest is to be in Eden. It is a good description of the World of Being.

The Lost Bible (via several documents of hoary antiquity, from the Dead Sea Scrolls to the mystical masterwork and quintessential treatise on Kabbalah, the Zohar) takes us back to the Garden of Being through a long-suppressed story about Adam's wife—not Eve, but his first wife, known as Lilith.

THE FIRST LADY

Perennially popular in contemporary folklore, we find just a single, scant reference to her in the Bible itself, where she is depicted—far from Paradise—in demonic terms:

And wildcats will meet hyenas,
and goat-demons will call out to each other;
There also the Lilith will rest,
and find herself a place to recline.

> There the arrow-snake will make its nest and lay eggs,
> and will hatch and brood in its shadow. (Isaiah 34:14-15, author's translation)

The Dead Sea Scrolls pick up the story with another oblique reference, again with demonic overtones:

> And I, the sage, declare the glory of his splendor, in order to frighten and dismay all the spirits of the angels of destruction, the bastard spirits, the demons, the Liliths, the howling desert animals, and those who descend on people very suddenly, to pervert the spirit of understanding. (Cave 4 fragment, author's translation)

Notwithstanding such dreary imagery, the Lost Bible hints that Lilith once enjoyed a high and exalted state, as Adam's first partner. According to the traditional Bible story, Adam was formed "of dust from the ground" (Genesis 2:7), while Eve was taken from Adam's side, or from "one of his ribs" (v. 21), depending on which translation you prefer.

From this story, the assumption is characteristically made (at least by traditional sexist interpreters) that a certain hierarchy exists, wherein the man is naturally superior to the woman. The Lilith story is different from the outset. The account relates that the first woman was formed, not after the man, but at the same time—not from a rib, but likewise from the good earth. The essence of the relationship is partnership, not subservience.

The most important source of Jewish mysticism (or Kabbalah), the Zohar, relates (in lively paraphrase) the following:

> Come, listen to this: There is a supreme female spirit named Lilith. She was created at the very beginning, along with Adam. (Zohar 3:19, author's paraphrase)

In the early medieval tractate, called the Alphabet of Ben Sira, we find additional details:

> God first created Adam, who was by himself. God declared, "It is not good for this human being to remain alone" [Gen. 2:18]. Afterwards, God created a woman to be with Adam. The woman was created from the ground, just as Adam had been created. God called her Lilith. (Alphabet of Ben Sira Question #5 23a, author's paraphrase)

THE EGO-LESS GARDEN

In short, Lilith was Adam's perfect equal. It is precisely as we should expect in the Garden of Being. There was tranquility because there was harmony. The World of Being is essentially ego-less, framed by selfless concern for one's partner, to be sure the greater part of holiness is ego-less-ness. So it was during the day, but at night the story takes a twist. Ego has a way of expressing itself under cover of darkness. Interestingly, Lilith's name is a derivative of the Hebrew word *lailah*, meaning night, for she was a creature of the night, and night is when the man attempted to assert himself.

We are told that Adam wanted Lilith to lie beneath him, a euphemism for adopting a male-dominant sexual position. Lilith not so politely refused, preferring to be on top. We read (in contemporary paraphrase):

Adam and Lilith started to quarrel bitterly. She snipped, "I will not lie beneath you! . . . After all, the two of us are equals, since we were both created from the same earth."

Adam's response was belligerent:

"I certainly will not lie beneath you! I demand to be on top! As far as I'm concerned, you are only suitable to be on the bottom. My position should be superior to yours."

By now Paradise was already lost, for the World of Being was fractured, and the Garden of Being was consumed in a flash of ego. Being doesn't assert its own will over another's. When Adam's will took over, the divine aspect of human existence was obliterated. Original innocence died in a moment's display of hierarchy. The Alphabet of Ben Sira sadly and crisply comments:

They wouldn't even listen to each another.

TO BE OR NOT TO BE

Lilith responded to Adam's will with a will of her own. She stormed off, angry and hurt. The battle of the sexes had begun in earnest. At this point Lilith, being herself a reflection of the Divine Presence, opened her mouth and uttered the name of the Almighty, which mere mortals are never supposed to pronounce: "YAHWEH." Suddenly, she ascended into the heavens and flew far away. We read (in continuing paraphrase):

> After these things, Lilith uttered the inexpressible Divine Name. Then
> she flew off into the sky.

Once the ego had asserted itself, the man felt deprived of the wife who rightfully
belonged to him. The drive for dominance was now converted to the desire to
possess and to own. The account continues:

> Adam stood still and prayed to the Creator, saying, "Master and Maker
> of all! The woman you made for me has run off!" All of a sudden, the
> Eternal, Blessed One dispatched three angels.

The three angels, Senoy, Sansenoy, and Semangelof, were charged with bringing
back Adam's errant woman. After a long search, the angels found her floating
magically upon the waves of the Red Sea. Lilith negotiated her release from their
clutches, however, by agreeing never to harm any children wearing amulets upon
which the names of the three angels were inscribed. According to the Alphabet of
Ben Sira (in paraphrase):

> The angels related the words of God, but Lilith did not want to go back
> with them. The angels then threatened, "We'll drown you here in the
> sea!"
> "Leave me alone!" Lilith retorted. "My reason for being is only to
> afflict babies with illness. If the baby is male, I exercise power over him
> until he is eight days old. If the baby is female, I have twenty days of
> power."
> On hearing these pronouncements of Lilith, the angels demanded that
> she return. However, she took an oath by the living God's Divine Name,
> saying, "I promise that if ever I see you three angels or your names or
> images engraved on an amulet, I will not exercise my power over that
> baby." Lilith further consented to allow a hundred of her own children
> to perish each and every day. For this reason, one hundred demons die
> each day. That is why the names of the angels are written on amulets
> worn by little ones. For Lilith, when she notices them, is forced by her
> oath to release them from her grip, whereupon the child gets better.

Meanwhile, back in the garden, Adam was demanding a second wife from the
Eternal, one who would be more submissive. Only then do we pick up the
traditional biblical account, about God putting the man into a deep sleep and
taking one of his ribs, which was fashioned into the woman called Eve. In due
course the human couple bore children, who in turn produced many offspring.

But the experience of Being in the Garden of Being would be forever forfeited. Lilith, in jealousy over having been replaced as a wife, decided to persecute the descendants of Eve. She would invade the homes of pregnant women and women in childbirth and administer the sleep of death:

> She wanders through the world, looking for children subject to punishment. She embraces them, only to cause them to die. (Zohar 1:19b, author's paraphrase)

She would take their babies, suck their blood, and eat their flesh and the marrow of their bones. Lilith and her female demon cohorts would also prowl the earth by night in search of male seed, by which they might be fruitful and multiply. For this reason young men were to be admonished to avoid sleeping alone, lest they be molested by Lilith and her demonic horde.

Even Adam was, according to the Talmud, subsequently visited in the night by his first consort, inadvertently becoming a father of demons:

> Rabbi Jeremia ben Eleazar said, "For years after Adam and Eve were cast out of the Garden, Adam (the first human being) was separated from his wife. During this time he inadvertently fathered many demons, evil spirits and 'Liliths.'" Rabbi Meir declared, "Adam, the first human being, was extremely pious. . . . The fact that he fathered evil spirits came about as a result of his wet dreams." (Babylonian Talmud Erubin 18b, author's paraphrase)

Elsewhere we find a warning:

> As Lilith wanders to and fro through the world by night, she wickedly plays with men, causing them to spill their seed. When she discovers men alone at home sleeping, Lilith and her demons come upon them, stealthily take hold of them, lie with them, taking their desire, and bearing offspring through them. Furthermore, they bring disease upon them, without these men knowing where it came from. (Zohar 1:19b, author's paraphrase)

THE EXCLUSION

The Lilith accounts, taken together, form a fantastic mythology. There are a number of elements of these stories that gave the keepers of the canon cause for concern and which doubtless prompted them to keep any mention of Lilith, other than the oblique reference in Isaiah (sufficiently vague, they felt), out of the sacred text. For one thing, Lilith's behavior challenges the entire claim of male superiority trumped by generations of sages and ecclesiastics. The traditional account—that the woman was created after the man, and from his rib—gave aid and comfort to male chauvinist religious authorities. The story of a race of demons being spawned through Lilith also seemed out of character with the sternly monotheistic tone of Holy Writ.

Nonetheless, the story was eventually recorded in bits and pieces in ancient and medieval texts, as well as certain passages scattered among the thousands of pages of the Jewish writings known as the Talmud. While those references invariably refer to Lilith as a demon and the mother of demons, perhaps she is merely history's quintessential feminist, who would not submit to male domination.

THE SECRET

Whatever the prevarications of religious authorities regarding the appropriateness of the Lilith saga in the sacred canon, there is nonetheless a great lesson to be learned here. Adam and Lilith were meant to be co-equal, both having been fashioned from the ground. Adam nevertheless dominated Lilith, because he had somehow lost touch with the World of Being, in the Garden of Being. Certainly, Adam need not have chosen dominance. Why would he want to impose his will on the woman, since her will was just as important as his? The fact is, when we recognize the divinity in ourselves, we do not need to control anyone else. Being is ego-less. We can say, "I am part of Divine Presence in the earth, and so is everybody else. All people have inherent worth."

Furthermore, we should understand that we are all creators. We have the ability to create whatever kind of world we want. Of course we go about it in many different ways. Adam found out that dominating is not the way. In dominating, we are hurting ourselves as well as others, for we do damage to the image of the divine in us. If, however, we let things *be,* we can live in harmony with ourselves and with the divinity in others.

Lilith was victimized, as the story tells us, but made the same mistake that Adam made. Because she was victimized, she victimized others. Instead of calling on her greatest power—her relationship with the Eternal—she became jealous of Eve. She became caught up in the power struggle and, spawning a group of demons, she afflicted women in childbirth and molested young men. By contrast, the World of Being enables us to act with conscience and creativity rather than reacting to circumstances.

The sad saga of Adam and Lilith teaches an important secret in dealing with conflict and potential conflict: Hold your fire! True, good deeds often seem to go unrewarded, but acts of revenge spawn their own demons to perpetuate evil. Cycles of revenge (once regulated by the ancient principle of *lex talionis,* the law of retaliation) are as common today as they were in the Lost Bible, producing the same lamentable results. As the old Arab proverb suggests, "Revenge is a dish best served up cold." Dominance, duplicity, and manipulation may work as short-term tactics, but they inevitably fail as long-term strategies. "What goes around comes around" may sound like a tired restatement of *karma,* but it is really the very essence of the World of Being.

CHAPTER 9

N.D.E.

Foolish men imagine that because judgment for an evil thing is delayed, there is no justice;
but only accident here below. Judgment for an evil thing is many times delayed some
day or two, some century or two, but it is sure as life, it is sure as death.
—THOMAS CARLYLE, SCOTTISH ESSAYIST, HISTORIAN

A major advantage of age is learning to accept people without passing judgment.
—LIZ CARPENTER, AMERICAN POLITICIAN, STATESMAN

Your soul is literally sucked out of your body, as you observe the room, the furnishings, and the people beneath. A long, dark tunnel suddenly gives way to a blinding white light. You are brought to a place of utter tranquility. All you know is that you do not want to return to the material world. The phenomenon is not as unusual as you might imagine. It is the N.D.E., or near death experience. In recent years the N.D.E. has become both a subject of scientific study and a target for skeptics. In one Gallup poll roughly 15 percent of the respondents declared that they had at some point encountered a close brush with death, involving an unusual experience.

But can such experiences be traced back to ancient times? Might there be references to N.D.E.s in the Lost Bible? If so, we may be looking at graphic, eyewitness testimony of the World of Being.

To be sure, the Lost Bible provides many glances into the metaphysical, archetypal world—the world of our dreams—after which physical reality is patterned. In every case, the archetypal world teaches us much about the material world. It teaches us that we are the very stuff of the Eternal, finite expressions of the totality of Deity.

An ancient book, excluded from the biblical canon, called the Testament of Abraham, is a case in point. This book relates how the great patriarch Abraham is met by the archangel Michael, who tells him that he is soon to die. Abraham, far from accepting the oracle passively, engages in some "hondeling," Yiddish for "heated negotiation." He not so politely asks that he first be allowed to see all the inhabited world and all created things. God, ever impressed by sheer *chutzpah*, grants Abraham's request. In paraphrase we read the following:

The ruler of the angelic host left the Divine Presence and found Abraham, who was dwelling near the Oak of Mamre. Abraham had been plowing the fields, along with a group of twelve servants. Suddenly, the angelic leader Michael approached from a distance, looking like a splendid soldier. Abraham welcomed him, as he would any stranger. The angelic leader returned the greeting, saying, "Peace to you, righteous chosen one, exalted father! I have come to tell you that the days of your earthly life are drawing to a close, and your death is at hand. It is time to set your affairs in order."

The balance of this fantastic account follows the esteemed patriarch on a journey into the divine realm. Through the agency of Abraham, esteemed in both the Jewish and Christian Bible as the intimate friend of God, we are all given a little taste of what the world to come is like.

THE EXCLUSION

Of course the keepers of the canon did not see it that way and declined to believe that this narrative was handed down from the time of the famed biblical patriarch, even though the language of composition was Semitic, probably Hebrew. They washed their hands of this book, and saw to it that it was not copied. As a result, the original text vanished, its contents surviving only in old Slavonic, in a manuscript dating from the fourteenth century. The sages were doubtless correct that the book was far removed from Abraham, given that the modern scholarly community dates it to the first two centuries of the Common Era. Furthermore, out-of-body experiences were too radical a topic for traditional religionists, who had no stomach for such highly personal, metaphysical, and rapturous experiences. The radical monotheism that became the standard dogma of Judaism had no use for a hierarchy of angels, since intermediaries are not needed to approach the one God. In the ancient world there was fear that angels—Michael the archangel in particular—might be worshiped and that Israel's proud monotheism might be overrun with paganism.

There are certain Christian elements in the book (though sometimes earlier Jewish writings were embellished by devout scribes), which made the work troublesome for Israelite sages. Meanwhile, Christian clerics saw it as theologically unimportant, even heretical, for it depicts people being judged according to their deeds, rather than by their faith alone. They could not appreciate the beauty of the narrative for its own sake, or recognize (as with so much of the Lost Bible) that we are dealing, not with a literal account, but with an elaborate allegory, containing lessons for us all. We moderns would be wise to suspend prejudicial judgment and let the story speak for itself.

SWING LOW, SWEET CHARIOT

As Abraham is speaking with the archangel Michael, a human voice begins to emanate from a cypress tree, saying, "Holy, holy, holy is the Lord, who summons his servant to those who love him." It is a message from the Eternal, alerting the patriarch of his imminent departure from this world. We are told that "Abraham did not let on that he had heard the mysterious voice, for he thought that Michael had not heard it."

The text recounts (in paraphrase) what happens next:

> The angelic leader Michael returned to heaven and stood before God, saying, "Your friend Abraham wishes to see the whole earth, as you see it, before he dies." The Eternal One, having heard this, once more dispatched Michael, commanding him to take a cloud made of light, along with the angels who keep the divine chariots, descend to earth, and find Abraham again. "You must bring him up into the heavens, in a chariot drawn by the cherubim, and let him look out over the whole earth."

In due course, a supernatural chariot swings low, drawn by heavenly beings called cherubim, who will escort Abraham heavenward, toward the divine realm. As with contemporary N.D.E.s, the ancient patriarch is able to see what is taking place on the earth beneath, as he is taken up, seemingly out of his body. The fantastic story continues:

> Michael the archangel descended to the earth and lifted Abraham up on a chariot drawn by cherubim. Abraham was levitated into the upper atmosphere, as it were in a cloud, accompanied by sixty angelic beings. The chariot bore him aloft, across the whole surface of the earth. Abraham saw the world exactly as it was at that moment. . . . Looking down he saw everything that took place, both good and evil. He saw some people dancing to the music of the harp; others he saw weeping and mourning the dead. There were newlyweds being honored, but he also saw men brandishing swords.
>
> "Who are they?" asked Abraham.
>
> Michael answered, "They are thieves plotting murder. They intend to kill, steal, and devastate."
>
> Abraham declared, "O Eternal One, listen to me! May wild animals come and eat them alive!"
>
> Abraham wasn't finished speaking when ferocious beasts lurched from among the trees and consumed them whole.

FIRE FROM HEAVEN

Abraham continues surveying the earth with his x-ray vision, and sees a man and a woman, out in the open, committing acts of fornication. Again, the patriarch cries out, "May the earth open up and swallow them for their wicked deeds." Next, he sees some men breaking into a house and carrying off the possessions. "May fire fall from the heavens and burn them up!" he exclaims. Amazingly, everything happens just as Abraham decrees. Wild beasts come and tear the sword-bearers limb from limb, gobbling them up. A fissure opens in the ground, and the two fornicators fall into it. Next, fire comes down and consumes the thieves.

We may balk here at Abraham's judgmental attitude. However, as I sat in that musty old library atop the Mount of Olives, poring through the books of the Lost Bible, it nonetheless occurred to me that the patriarch Abraham was hardly alone in his judgmentalism. For instance, the Dead Sea Scrolls, for all of their spiritual insight, are equally characterized by this judgmental attitude. Sometimes the lessons we learn from ancient texts relate to the kind of traits *not* to emulate.

BEYOND JUDGMENT

When it comes to Abraham, his N.D.E. and his sacred testament, one thing is clear. The judgmental phase is only a part of his upward ascent. As the narrative continues, the patriarch is beckoned to come up yet higher, beyond his judgmental attitudes and into the very presence of God. Read allegorically, the story teaches us that, while feeling judgmental may be a natural part of spiritual awakening, we should not be content with that manifestation of the Spirit. We should seek to rise above it.

We are told that at that moment, a voice issues forth from heaven, declaring (in modern adaptation):

> "Stop the chariot, Michael! Do not allow Abraham to see the whole earth, for if he glimpses all of the wickedness that goes on, he may destroy my whole creation! Abraham is a righteous man, but for that very reason he has no mercy for those who err. But I, having created the world, do not wish to destroy anyone. After all, everyone has a chance to change their ways and live, until the day they die."

Perhaps, allegorically, the story is telling us that God's compassion depends on ours, that God is as merciful as we are. As agents of the Divine Presence, God *needs* us to be merciful. If we want divine compassion to have an impact on the planet, we had better show compassion ourselves.

God instructs Michael to take Abraham to the first gate of heaven, where he can witness the judgment on the very souls he has condemned. As the supernatural chariot approaches the celestial realm, two pathways converge. The archangel declares, "These two paths lead to the broad gate and the narrow gate. Notice how many people are entering the broad gate. It is the gate that leads to destruction."

"And the narrow gate?" Abraham asks.

Michael responds, "There are also multitudes who enter this gate, the gate that leads to Paradise!"

THE GREAT DIVORCE

As we have already seen, the concept of two ways is prominent in the Lost Bible. Life, after all, is fundamentally about choices. There are no scripts, but there are paths—toward the good or toward the bad. People are not forced to do evil. They make choices, and what we think of as rewards or punishments are the natural consequences of those choices. Twentieth-century scholar/philosopher C. S. Lewis observed: "Blake wrote of the marriage of heaven and hell; I have written of their divorce." The lively tome he produced, *The Great Divorce*, describes a bus ride to heaven, in which the passengers individually decide that they do not really want an eternity with God. Each *chooses* hell—which Lewis whimsically describes as London—because this is clearly where he or she would rather be. Consequently, we should not really think of God sending people to hell; people send themselves. This is also the message of the two ways.

While righteous Abraham had called down judgment on the sinners, we also realize that unjust actions bring their own consequences, naturally. When it comes to the broad gate and the narrow gate, it is worth noticing that Jesus of Nazareth makes a similar analogy in the Christian gospel of Matthew:

> "Come in by the narrow gate, because the gate that leads to destruction is wide. That way is easy, and many enter through it. But the gate that leads to life is narrow. That way is hard, and few people find it." (Matthew 7:13-14, author's translation)

However, whereas Jesus announces that only a few will enter by the narrow gate, the Testament of Abraham depicts great numbers entering by this gate also. It seems that God the Father is even more forgiving than Jesus.

Abraham is next brought into the presence of a mysterious supernatural being—the first-formed Adam, the celestial Adam, after whom the earthly Adam was copied:

> This is the original Adam, who dwells in divine splendor. When he gazes on the world, he sees his own descendants, and he also sees their

fate. When he witnesses great numbers of souls passing through the narrow gate, he rejoices on his royal throne, full of joy. He knows that the narrow gate is the one through which the righteous enter Paradise. However, when he witnesses many other souls—those of the unjust—passing through the broad gate, he pulls his hair, throws himself down, with tearfulness and lamentation. He knows that the broad gate is the one through which the wicked are led away to eternal doom.

Near the first-formed Adam sits another being of supernatural aura, who looks like . . . a son of God. He is Adam's son, Abel. Abel is actually the judge in these proceedings, the idea being that humans should be judged by a fellow human. Who better than righteous Abel, murdered by his brother Cain?

"What about those scales?" Abraham asks. "They look like something from an Egyptian tomb painting."

"They are to weigh people's souls," Michael responds, "to determine who will be rewarded and who will be punished."

"And look," Abraham continues, "there are two angels. One is bearing light, with a balance in his hand, and the other is made of fire, and holding a trumpet. Two more angels are holding papyrus, ink, and a pen."

Thereafter, Abraham witnesses the amazing spectacle of people's souls being weighed in a balance and judged according to their deeds. In the presence of the primordial Adam (a Messianic figure) the righteous are admitted into Paradise. As the testament concludes, Abraham is whisked back to earth, like a person coming to after an N.D.E. As with others who have had this experience, and who return to the material world with a sense of regret, he no longer fears death. He is ready. The testament concludes with God's instructions to the heavenly messenger:

> "Michael, it is time to take Abraham back to his home, for the hour of his death is approaching. He must set his affairs in order. Afterwards, escort him back to me."

Soon afterward the archangel Michel returns with an army of angels, bearing Abraham's soul aloft in a linen cloth, supernaturally fashioned. On the earth below Isaac buries his father Abraham next to his mother Sarah in the Promised Land, near the oak of Mamre.

THE SECRET

The story is all about judgment and the choices people make. With respect to judging others, spiritually, I became aware of an unbelievable phenomenon in modern Israel, known as the Jerusalem Syndrome. It affects tourists and pilgrims to the Holy Land and, unbelievably enough, causes them to forget who they are, adopting sacred personas. It's the next best thing to an out-of-body experience. Not a few Jerusalem pilgrims have taken on the personhood of John the Baptist, the Virgin Mary, or even the Messiah. Not far from my quarters on Mount Zion, an English gentleman regularly stood beneath Zion Gate—one of the main entrances to the Old City—dressed as King David and holding a harp, which he plucked but could not play! Just about the only thing psychotherapists can say is that there is something about the Holy City that seems to produce profoundly strange spiritual experiences. Unfortunately, in some of those cases, spiritual experience becomes linked with self-righteousness.

In 1969 an Australian pilgrim, apparently affected by Jerusalem Syndrome, became upset over the fact that the Al-Aqsa Mosque sits on the site of the ancient city's Temple Mount. When fire did not fall from heaven upon the infidels, he decided to set fire to the mosque—the third holiest site in Islam. The resulting conflagration did significant damage to the structure and sparked unrest and rioting across the whole of Arab Jerusalem. It was an example of raw spiritual judgmentalism. During my tenure in the Holy Land as a Jerusalemite, people were still talking about it. As I strolled through the sacred precincts of the ancient city, as was often my custom, I occasionally had to pinch myself, to bring myself back to reality, lest I too should fall prey to the Jerusalem Syndrome and its attendant judgmental attitudes. Fortunately, I knew better.

Indeed, people make choices and experience their consequences, a truth that Abraham gets to see with exceptional clarity, even as he ascends higher—above judgment—and learns the linkage between his compassion and God's. Still, there is a warning here: "Look, this is what these people are doing, and this is the kind of world they have created for themselves." Most of us do not have the luxury of Abraham's out-of-body perspective. We act without thinking of the consequences. However, by sitting back and simply being—through stillness and meditative practice—we can see how our actions today affect the larger whole, and how our mercy is the channel of divine mercy. By mentally getting out of the world for a while, we gain a larger perspective. We become more open, because we have cultivated a God's-eye view of things.

CHAPTER 10

The Missing Years of Jesus, or
The Misadventures of Young Jesus

A child becomes an adult when he realizes that
he has a right not only to be right but also to be wrong.
—THOMAS SZASZ, AMERICAN PSYCHIATRIST, EDUCATOR

A child is a beam of sunlight from the Infinite and Eternal,
with possibilities of virtue and vice—but as yet unstained.
—LYMAN ABBOTT, AMERICAN RELIGIOUS LEADER

Note to the reader:
What you are about to read here may upset you. It is not for sensitive readers. If you are easily offended by variations on traditional theology, please skip to the next chapter.

We meet him at his birth, in a humble stable in Bethlehem. We glimpse him when he is twelve years old, in the temple in Jerusalem, confounding the experts in the Law. We encounter him at the age of thirty, meeting a man named John, who baptizes him in the Jordan River. But where was he during the intervening years of his youth? What was he doing? What was the character of his life?

An amazing text of the Lost Bible purports to fill in the gaps. It is called the Infancy Gospel of Thomas, and it presents a most unorthodox picture of Jesus of Nazareth. But perhaps that is why so many modern readers find it strangely compelling.

Where did it come from? Not to be confused with the Gospel of Thomas, found among the Nag Hammadi manuscripts in Egypt, the Infancy Gospel of Thomas can be traced back to the early second century, when it began to be distributed widely. Some researchers believe that the text can be dated to as early as 125 of the Common Era. If so, it is one of the earliest of all Christian writings. The author, according to the text itself, was Thomas the Israelite. Is this the same author who wrote the Gospel of Thomas—supposedly Jesus' twin brother? Since it deals with the early years of Jesus' life, the so-called missing years, who would be better able to recount them than Jesus' flesh-and-blood sibling? Of course the keepers of the canon would later deny this claim vehemently.

A HOLY TERROR

The essence of this book of the Lost Bible is an amazing journey of discovery for the young Jesus, as he recognizes the incredible powers that reside within his person. What shocks modern readers, however, is that this young Jesus has the power to do evil as well as good, and he occasionally exercises that power in a rambunctious, even delinquent fashion. Here we have a Jesus, who, like any young lad, is full of mischief. But what happens when mischief is accompanied by staggering, earthshaking power? For example, Jesus dishonors the Sabbath by fashioning twelve sparrows out of clay, violating the prohibition of work on the day of rest. His father Joseph approaches him, pointedly asking, "Why do you do such things on the Sabbath?" Jesus simply claps, and the twelve birds miraculously fly away, eliminating all evidence of the offense.

When Jesus feels out of sorts, he actually commands another child to wither. We think of the strange disease causing premature aging, the progeria syndrome, which is estimated to affect one in eight million newborns worldwide, and we shudder to imagine that the youthful Jesus could so afflict a playmate. The text, in paraphrase, reads:

> The child of a scribe named Annas was playing nearby. He grabbed a willow branch and stirred up some pools of water that Jesus had drawn together through his powers. When Jesus saw what the boy was doing, he cried out, "You evil, unrighteous fool! What harm did the water pools do to you? Listen, from now on, you will wither with age, like a withered tree, without leaves, or roots, or fruit!" Immediately, the child withered, and Jesus walked away, to his father Joseph's house. But his parents rushed and grabbed him, wailing over the loss of his youth. Bringing him to Joseph's, they shouted, "What kind of son do you have, who does such horrible things?"

On another occasion, his words cause a child to literally drop dead:

> Afterward, while Jesus was wandering through the village, a child ran by and bumped his shoulder. Jesus, feeling slighted, declared, "You will not make it the rest of the way!" At that moment the boy collapsed and died. Some of the townsfolk who had seen what happened wondered,

"Why was this young child born? For every word he speaks is fulfilled immediately!" The parents of the dead boy went to Joseph, in order to accuse him. "Your son is killing our children! You cannot continue to live in this village unless you teach your son to bless rather than curse!" Joseph was frightened by this and called Jesus. He asked, "Why are you doing these things? The whole town hates us!" But Jesus replied, "I know these words are not really yours, so I will not say anything. But our accusers will certainly get their just desserts!" In that instant, those who had complained became totally blind.

After these things, we are told the following:

Joseph was so upset that he got up, grabbed Jesus by the ear, and wrung it until it was sore. Young Jesus became very angry and said, "You are like those who seek but do not find. You have done wrong. Do you not know that I belong to you? Do not hurt me like this!"

LESSONS FROM SMALLVILLE

Once again we must not fall into the trap of reading the Lost Bible literally. How do we understand these mythological yet malevolent acts of Jesus? How do we evaluate his anger? The ancient Israelite sages taught that each of us is born, not evil, but morally neutral, carrying within us the staggering power of the divine image. It is pure creative power, which can be used however we wish to use it. We are a little like Superman, who came to earth with powers and abilities far beyond those of mortal men.

Remember young Clark Kent, a child of the planet Krypton, which is disintegrating in the wake of a cosmic explosion? Rocketed to earth on an interplanetary craft, he is adopted by a Midwestern American family in a nondescript town called Smallville. Of course his adoptive parents know from the outset that there is something special about this boy; yet he has to grow up, go to school, and learn discipline, like any other child. Always an outsider in an alien civilization, young Clark decides to use his supernatural powers only for good. Only during the course of time does he reveal himself as earth's mild-mannered guardian. Of course even Superman has his vulnerabilities. He can bruise, he can bleed, he can conceivably die. If exposed to a little Kryptonite (a radioactive substance emitted from the exploding planet Krypton), he is rendered helpless. Prolonged exposure will kill him. Similarly, the best of human capabilities, coupled with good intentions, are blunted—even annihilated—by the effects of the dark side of our own personhood.

As our paraphrase continues, we find that Jesus is sent to a teacher named

Zacchaeus for instruction in the alphabet. Jesus labels him a hypocrite for not being aware of the allegorical significance behind each letter:

> When the teacher Zacchaeus heard the many allegories spoken by the young Jesus about the first letter, Alpha, he was amazed. . . . He remarked, "I've been confounded by a child! Surely, this child wasn't born from this earth! He's one who could even tame fire. He must have been brought into being before this world was created!"

Afterward Joseph sends Jesus to a second teacher, who strikes Jesus for his insolent behavior. Jesus utters another curse, which causes the teacher to collapse in some kind of paralytic seizure. The third teacher does somewhat better, for he notices that Jesus—however his delinquent behavior manifests itself—is filled with wisdom and grace. Only as Jesus grows and matures do his benign powers start to prevail over the negative ones.

Read allegorically (just as the child Jesus reads allegories into every letter), the story of the Christ child's early years teaches us something that we already know about ourselves, intrinsically. We are all endowed as humans with superhuman powers. We are invested with the ability to accomplish deeds of goodness, but also to harm and even to destroy. Each of us is a messiah in our own right, anointed with an innate ability to create the universe we inhabit, day by day. We are not simply adapted to our environment, as are all other species. We are masters of it. We have learned to harness the very forces of nature, even splitting the atom. We live longer, healthier lives than our ancestors ever thought possible.

The Infancy Gospel of Thomas relates that Jesus begins to realize the many good things he can accomplish:

> When it was time to sow the fields, the young Jesus went out with his father to plant wheat. As his father sowed, so did Jesus, measure for measure. But at the time of threshing, the land Jesus had sowed yielded a hundredfold what was sown. Jesus promptly summoned to the threshing floor all those who were poor. . . . Jesus was eight years old when he did this miracle.

Like Jesus, we are all capable of working wonders. Nevertheless, we have a rambunctious aspect to our personalities, a certain mischievousness that perpetually gets us into trouble. We have an evil inclination. The sages of old taught about the evil inclination, declaring that it is an intrinsic to each of us, and for that very reason it is not truly evil. After all, the Eternal One created the first human being, Adam, as good. Yet even Adam possessed an evil inclination. This rambunctious side of our personality is nothing more than an assortment of our base drives and instincts; our lusts, sexual and otherwise; our desire for power, prominence, and prestige. Truth be told, we need these drives, for without them we would be incapable of leading, commanding, or taking charge in any situation. We would be incapable of building a home, creating a family, and bringing forth children and raising them. So taught the rabbis of centuries past. Our evil inclination is essential to our functioning in society.

But we must learn to control our inclinations, lest they get out of hand, rule us, and ultimately destroy us. That process, of learning to control and harness our baser instincts, is at the heart of growing up and standing on our own.

THE EXCLUSION

Did Jesus, history's most celebrated example of a perfect human being, have an evil inclination like all the rest of us? According to theological dogma down through the ages, the very notion is unthinkable. If Jesus possessed an evil inclination, that would mean that he had been tainted with the original sin inherited from Adam after the Fall. But Jesus was sinless, declares orthodox theology. He did not possess a sinful nature. This is why he had to have been born of a virgin impregnated by the Holy Spirit, rather than of normal human parents.

Not so fast, declares the Infancy Gospel of Thomas. When it comes to *being* human, Jesus wasn't really any different from the rest of us. He was a real human being, flesh and blood, who had to wrestle with his evil inclination like everyone else. He had to harness it, even as he experimented with his own superhuman powers. Goodness is something that is learned. According to this story of the Lost Bible, the youthful Jesus was, during the missing years, a rambunctious boy, and a "holy terror." Only when he had grown a bit more, having learned the lessons of his childhood, was he prepared to manifest divine redemption. It is no accident that the text ends when Jesus is twelve years old, astounding the teachers in the Jerusalem temple with his wisdom. All this time he has been on a learning curve.

Certainly, the keepers of the Christian canon would never go along with such unorthodox notions, which in their minds would certainly diminish Jesus' divine status. The book was deemed Gnostic heresy and stricken from the list of inspired writings.

LITTLE GODS

The narrative goes on to reveal that there is a greater purpose in Jesus' apparently harmful acts:

Young Jesus laughed and declared, "May all the barren ones now bear fruit! May the blind in heart now see! I came from on high, in order to curse them, but also to elevate them to higher things." As soon as he finished speaking all who had come under his spell were made whole. No one dared provoke him after that.

The Infancy Gospel of Thomas is not just about Jesus. It is about all of us. We can transform negative thoughts, intentions, and actions into vehicles for healing the planet. We are in effect little gods. We can direct the God-power within toward goodness, mercy, and compassion, or toward destruction. The choice is ours. We cannot kill our evil inclination, but we can channel it. That is what growing up is all about. There are very few true abstractions in the universe. Our words are material and have force. Our very thoughts are material. Our hopes and dreams are tangible entities, which come to pass if we will it.

Why was I sitting in that musty library on top of Mount Zion, staring at these lost books? Because something inside had gripped me as a young college student and propelled me in this direction. The desire for personal enlightenment wasn't just an abstraction; it was material. My heart's desire to live in the cradle of civilization, the Middle East, to live in the city of Jerusalem and behold the ancient Temple Mount, was more than a passing fancy. The thoughts themselves were material. They became reality because I willed them. By the same token, how many times have I done harm, to others and to myself, merely by harboring thoughts that subsequently became manifest?

The World of Being puts us in touch with the Jesus who resides in us—the power to do good or evil. The truth is, we are more than what we know. We can enter this World of Being through hours of meditative practice, but we can also get there in a single moment of reflection—like a body builder who feels that it is impossible to lift one more ounce, but who reminds himself or herself in a split second: "You are stronger than you know."

How many stories are there of people who do extraordinary things at extraordinary times? How many times have we heard of people who, on a moment of reflection, slip into the World of Being before they act and summon extraordinary power from a deep inner reserve? The power is there; it need only be summoned.

"SHABBAT SHALOM!"

I know of no better place for experiencing the evil inclination than the modern Middle East. Today's city of Jerusalem seems to summon the most base of humanity's baser instincts, as a matter of daily survival. Whether it is pushing and shoving to get onto a crowded municipal bus (which may explode by the end of the ride), haggling with shopkeepers (who are masters at such practice), screaming at bureaucrats (from bankers to postal employees), it is a land where little if anything seems to work out according to plan.

Constant temptations to give in to the evil inclination present themselves to both resident and visitor: Shall I do like everyone else and trade my dollars on the black market? Shall I act like young Jesus, who fashioned clay sparrows on the Sabbath, and violate the peace and sanctity of the holy day? Shall I verbally assault the government official who is giving me a hard time, wishing I could swat him dead, just as young Jesus struck dead a playmate he did not like?

For six days of every week Israeli society bustles with stress, hardly in keeping with Western images of the Holy Land. The six days of the week—the *yamei khol*, or profane days as they are called—are metaphors for the evil inclination. When Friday afternoon comes, however, a distinctly different tone emerges. The country begins to settle down. Shops close. Buses stop running. Gruff words and expressions are replaced by almost universal smiles. "Shabbat Shalom!" people say to each other—"Sabbath peace!" The day of rest is approaching. As the sun sets on Friday, the Sabbath begins, and a profound peace and quiet settles in. There is nothing like a Sabbath in Jerusalem. It symbolizes everything pure, noble, and wholesome that life has to offer. It is a paradigm for the good inclination.

THE SECRET

As we grow and mature in life, the promise of the Sabbath—the good inclination—can be ours. Like the boy Jesus, we can all be transformed from the rambunctiousness of youth to the mature power of a Messianic, redemptive role. Such is the message of the Lost Bible.

All of that notwithstanding, perhaps the most profound thing about the Infancy Gospel of Thomas is that it presents a Jesus who is as normal in his moods, his emotions, and his shortcomings as the rest of us. His redemptive nature is something he grows into. In short, do not worry if you are not perfect. All of life is a learning curve.

The lyric line of a modern hit song reads:

I can't stand to fly
I'm not that naive
I'm just out to find
The better part of me

I'm more than a bird . . . I'm more than a plane
More than some pretty face beside a train
It's not easy to be me

Wish that I could cry
Fall upon my knees
Find a way to lie
About a home I'll never see

It may sound absurd . . . but do not be naive
Even Heroes have the right to bleed
I may be disturbed . . . but won't you concede
Even Heroes have the right to dream
It's not easy to be me . . .

I'm only a man in a silly red sheet
Digging for kryptonite on this one way street
Only a man in a funny red sheet
Looking for special things inside of me
It's not easy to be me[5]

Finding those special things are what this special book of the Lost Bible is all about.

CHAPTER 11

The Lost Civilization of the Rechabites

I have seen three emperors in their nakedness, and the sight was not inspiring.
—OTTO VON BISMARCK

There is a noble manner of being poor, and who does not know it will never be rich.
—LUCIUS ANNAEUS SENECA

Over two millennia ago in ancient Greece, Plato wrote an account of a lost civilization on an isolated island somewhere in the Atlantic Ocean. It was from his description that Westerners first became acquainted with a utopian society where the best of human virtues reigned supreme. It was called Atlantis.

The Lost Bible has its own version of Atlantis, describing a society sequestered on an island. It is called the History of the Rechabites. While the earliest manuscripts of the book are no older than the twelfth century, its contents may date as far back as the first century of the Common Era, roughly contemporaneous with Jesus and the Essene writings of the Dead Sea Scrolls. The Rechabites, we are told, are an ancient people embodying the very best of the human spirit, a people literally clothed in virtue. It is a theme whose variations reappear across the centuries.

At the heart of our fascination with lost societies, there is something about the human condition that beckons us upward, that compels us to believe that whatever advances our civilization has made, there is still a better way. In the nineteenth century French artist Paul Gauguin picked up bag and baggage and left the comfort of his native France, bound for the island of Tahiti, in search of what was called the noble savage. These islanders lived in utter simplicity, impoverished by European standards, yet uncannily happy—nearly naked, yet clothed in virtue.

A LITTLE BIT OF ZEN

The very term *noble savage* conjures up the notion of true freedom—of people unburdened by the fetters of modern culture. The assumption is that people are by nature good and virtuous; it is civilization itself that corrupts and distorts the human condition. French philosopher Jean-Jacques Rousseau declared, "Man is born free, and everywhere he is in shackles!" The concept found expression in the writings of John Dryden and even Mary Shelley, whose classic *Frankenstein* presents us with the idealized, unfettered, and uncivilized individual—a monster. In his heart, however, the monster is really quite noble. Civilization despises and, in the end, kills him.

The Lost Bible tells us that the Rechabites were, likewise, a noble people, living on an island paradise. Their lives were the quintessence of simplicity. Desiring nothing, they had no cares, no worries, no anxieties. Like Zen Buddhists, the Rechabites understood implicitly that the real problem in life is desire; whenever we want something, we are a little bit less than whole. Paradoxically, it is in learning to empty ourselves of desire that we really become full. As the biblical psalmist wrote, "The Lord is my shepherd; I lack nothing" (Psalm 23:1, author's translation).

What, then, is the story of this lost people? Where did they come from, and what do we know about their lives? The History of the Rechabites speaks for itself. As with the other books of the Lost Bible, we can either take it or leave it. Their origins, however, can be found in standard Bibles, specifically in the book of Jeremiah.

THE ISLAND OF BEING

Long ago, in the days of the prophet Jeremiah, there lived a group known as the Rechabites, a name derived from their leader, Jonadab son of Rechab. At a time when the ancient kingdom of Judah was being threatened by foreign invaders, the pious Rechabites emulated the lifestyle of Israel's earliest patriarchs. They lived as nomads, pitching their tents from place to place, never touching wine and not even cultivating their fields. The prophet Jeremiah lauds them for the purity of their ways and declares that they will be spared from the calamity soon to befall Jerusalem. The book of Jeremiah states:

> This is what the Eternal, the God of Israel, says: "Can't you learn a lesson about obeying my precepts? . . . The commandments of Jonadab the son of Rechab have been kept. Among them he commanded his descendants not to drink wine, and they have not done so to the present day, thus carrying out the instructions of their ancestor. Yet, I have consistently addressed you, and you have not heeded me. The descendants of Jonadab the son of Rechab certainly kept the commandment given to them by their ancestor; yet his people have not listened to me. Therefore . . . I will surely cause to come upon Judah and upon all of the inhabitants of Jerusalem all of the calamities that I warned them about. For they did not

listen when I spoke to them; they would not answer when I called." But Jeremiah said to the family of the Rechabites, This is what the Eternal, the God of Israel, says: "Since you have obeyed the commandment of your ancestor Jonadab, keeping all of his instructions and doing what he called you to do . . . there will always be a member of a family of Jonadab the son of Rechab before my presence." (Jeremiah 35:13–19, author's translation)

But where did the Rechabites go? Were they somehow magically whisked away? The Lost Bible recounts the tale of a hermit named Zosimus, whose lifestyle happens to resemble that of the Rechabites. Here in lively modern paraphrase, is the account itself:

> There once lived a righteous man, full of virtue, called Zosimus, who lived out in the desert for forty years, neither eating bread nor drinking wine, and shunning the company of others. Zosimus earnestly prayed that the Eternal One would reveal to him where the Rechabites had been taken. One day while Zosimus was in prayer, he heard a voice which came from an angel. "Listen, Zosimus, I have been sent from above to be your guide and lead you on a journey to find the righteous ones you seek."

Zosimus sounds like a Rechabite himself, in his manner of living. Like the ancient Israelites, he has personally wandered in the desert for forty years. That certainly adds to his spiritual credence. Now, however, he continues with his own narration:

> The angel led me from the cave where I had been living and accompanied me for forty days. Still in the middle of nowhere, I collapsed from exhaustion. When I woke I was alone. I started praying again, and three days later an animal came and bore me on its back for days on end, until I finally came to an enormous ocean. I could not believe how vast it was. In the middle of this ocean there was a great cloud, extending out into the heavens. I thought that perhaps the righteous Rechabites were hidden away inside it. A voice came out of the cloud, saying, "Father Zosimus!" I prayed again, relinquishing my will to the Eternal.

The narrative goes on to relate that two large trees suddenly appear on the shore. Zosimus takes hold of the branches of one of them, which bends down and lifts him into the heavens. He is elevated over the great cloud and passed to the branches of another mysterious tree, which drops him on an island in the middle of the great ocean. The island is enormous, though quite flat, and filled with flowers and abundant greenery.

THE EMPEROR'S NEW CLOTHES

Zosimus continues:

> Amazed by the island's beauty, I began to walk about, until I came upon a naked man, sitting down. I was startled by him, but I managed to say, "Shalom, my brother!" He answered, "And shalom to you! You must be a holy man, or else you would never have been allowed entry into this place." Next he asked, "Are you from the World of Vanity?" "Yes I am," I answered. "I've come in search of you all. But I would like to know, why are you naked?" He answered, "You are the naked one, not knowing that your clothes are defiled. But my clothing is pure. If you really want to see me, look this way." As I stared intently, I realized that he had the face of an angel. I fell prostrate on the ground in terror.

Hans Christian Anderson's story, The Emperor's New Clothes, carries much the same message as the History of the Rechabites. Society urges us to put on airs, to seek pomp and circumstance, pride and prestige. Possessions are often just status symbols, designed to distract people's eyes from our native shallowness. Such things really amount to invisible, defiled clothing, worn to mask our nakedness. It takes a child—or a lost tribe from the days of Jeremiah—to know the difference.

TAKE ME TO YOUR LEADERS

Zosimus's new friend wastes no time introducing him to the larger community of Rechabites:

> He came and took me by hand, helping me to get up. He said, "Do not be afraid. I belong to the Blessed Ones, whom you are trying to find. Come along and I will bring you to my brothers." He escorted me, never letting go of my hand, asking many questions about the world at large and what it contains. He led me into the Council of the Blessed Elect Ones, whereupon I bowed down to worship them. There were comely young people, along with honored saints. When these Blessed Ones saw me they were astonished and questioned one another: "Brethren, has the End of Days come upon us, so that a mortal man has made his way here?"

The narrative proceeds to explain how two angels come down from above, stand in the council, and declare that the end has not yet come. They explain that Zosimus will remain with them for one week and that the council is to write down a detailed description of what life is like among the Rechabites. Zosimus is brought to a special attendant, who escorts him into his tent. After listening to many prayers, Zosimus continues his own narration:

> I felt as though I were in Paradise, in the Garden of Eden, before Adam and Eve sinned. They eat nothing from morning until evening, but then they consume whatever they like from the fruit of the trees. From their roots flow streams of water, which taste as sweet as honey. They drink their fill, stop eating, and dwell alone for the rest of the night. Before long word spread that a man from a World of Vanity had come. Many of the family members came, just to look at me and to ask questions about my world. Night and day they came, asking their questions until I was spent with exhaustion, weary of words. I asked my attendant to tell them, "Zosimus is not here!" just so that I could get some rest. But my attendant was grieved, for I had asked him to lie, recycling as it were, the fall of Adam and Eve from grace. The elders of the community met together in their council and prepared to cast me out. "Take leave of us, you man of sin," they declared, but I only fell prostrate before them, weeping. "Please be compassionate, you blessed ones, you holy angels," I said. "Forgive me of my evil deed!"

STORY IN STONE

We are told that the Rechabites graciously forgive Zosimus and proceed to write down their history on stone tablets. When we read that the Rechabites abstain from bread and wine, we can of course understand the narrative on different levels. Liturgically, bread and wine are elements of sanctification, used in Jewish tradition to usher in the Sabbath day. Jewish theologians have long referred to the Sabbath as an island in time. But the Rechabites, living on their own island, experience a perpetual Sabbath. Their lives do not need to be sanctified, because they are holy already.

On another level we can think of Adam and Eve consuming the natural produce of the Garden of Eden. Bread and wine symbolize not the Garden of Being and its fruit, but the fruit of human labors, produced through agriculture—threshing the grain and pressing the grapes. Such things ae unnecessary in the Garden of Being. Moreover, the Rechabites are never anxious about anything, nor do they dwell in houses.

As their history relates, when a wicked king arose in Israel, commanding them to forsake their solemn oath, they refused to do so, whereupon they were imprisoned. During the first night of their imprisonment, they saw a very great light and glorious angels appeared before them. The angels escorted them out of prison, levitated them into the heavens, and brought them to the island paradise where they reside to this day. By divine command the waters of the ocean encircled the place, and mighty clouds arose upon the ocean as a protective barrier. This is their situation, as Zosimus encounters them for the first time.

Although they are mere mortals, their souls are pure. In the society of the Rechabites there are no vineyards, no agriculture, no wood or iron, no houses or other buildings, no gold or silver; nor does any rain or snow ever fall. Moreover, the cloud always shields them from direct sunlight. The land itself is filled with light, so that there is no darkness or night. All of them possess a shining aura, which hides their private parts by a glowing luminescence. While they might be considered something akin to an ancient nudist colony, the nakedness of the Rechabites hearkens back to Adam and Eve, prior to the Fall. The Lost Bible elsewhere tells us that Adam and Eve were clothed with light, which allegorically we understand as original innocence.

THE JOYS OF CHASTITY

As for their family lives, the Rechabites do take wives, though intercourse occurs only once. Thereafter they are separated and remain pure for the rest of their days. Nor are they troubled by memories of the experience, but lead monastic lives ever after. The typical wife gives birth to two children, one to be married, the other to live in perpetual chastity. While the tone of all this is Gnostic (denying the physical body while cultivating the spiritual), their chaste lives should not be seen in terms of deprivation. The tablets themselves explain:

> Listen, indeed we are never troubled by illness, pain, bodily fatigue, or injury. We know nothing of temptation, and even the power of Satan cannot affect us. We are not subject to anger or jealousy; nor are we beset with wicked desires or hateful feelings. All we know is quietude and joy, along with lovingkindness—to the Eternal and to each other. Our souls are not weary, nor full of sadness, when the day comes for the angels to call us home. On the contrary, we are joyful—along with the angels—when they are dispatched to bring home one of our souls.

No one calculates the years of their lives, to know how old they are, for those who live righteously experience great longevity. Nor are they ignorant about those who inhabit the rest of the world, for angels are commissioned to relate what goes on among the wicked as well as the righteous. The Rechabites continually intercede in prayer for the World of Vanity, since they know that all people are children of Adam.

All these things are engraved on the stone tablets and placed into the hands of Zosimus. As the entire community gathers and prays, a great white cloud forms, and trees materialize in the midst of the sea. One bends down and lifts Zosimus upward, passing him to the second tree, which carries him across the ocean. After he is brought down to the earth again, an animal arrives and escorts him home. So ends the strange tale of the Rechabites.

THE JOYS OF SECTS

The Society of the Rechabites sounds curiously similar to a pietistic sect living in Egypt in the first century C.E. known as the Therapeutae, who lived as monks and to whom were ascribed many miraculous healings. The Rechabites equally remind us of another communal group who flourished in the days of Jesus and John the Baptist. They lived in splendid isolation along the western shore of the Dead Sea. They were known as the Essenes. While they engraved no stone tablets, they did produce a series of parchments in which they left detailed records of their society. These parchments are known collectively as the Dead Sea Scrolls. Interestingly, the Essenes were the one ancient sect that meticulously copied (among their library of scrolls) the books of the Lost Bible, such as Enoch and Jubilees—books deliberately discarded by the religious leaders and sages, but which they deemed Holy Writ.

The Scrolls describe the Essenes' holy order, devoted to prayer and to lives of ritual purity. Consequently, they wore garments of pure white, reminding us of the luminescence that clothed the Rechabites. They enjoyed remarkable longevity—regularly living more than a hundred years. The evidence suggests that some of them married and raised families, while others, perhaps the core of the community, practiced strict celibacy, living out their lives as virgins. While no island in the ocean gave them shelter, their physical isolation in the Judean desert helped foster a mythology about the Essenes that has endured to this day. Those who seek purity in any age have much to learn from the Essenes and/or the Rechabites.

THE EXCLUSION

Little is known about how this curious account came to be composed. All that can be said is that it was likely written down at some point during the first six centuries of the Common Era. Furthermore, the original language of composition is uncertain at best. The earliest known text is in Syriac and dates to the twelfth century.

Why did the keepers of the sacred canon find no place for the fantastic story of the Rechabites in Holy Writ? Certainly, the story seemed too incredible for their rational souls. How could this fellow Zosimus have been plucked up by the branches of trees and whisked across the ocean?

In defense of the account, we might ask whether this story is any more fantastic than the book of Judges, for example, which tells us that the sun stood still in the heavens for twelve hours, over a Canaanite city called Gibeon, until Joshua and the Israelites could thoroughly defeat the Amorites who were threatening the city and its inhabitants (Joshua 10:1-15).

There are also a number of Christian elements in the book, including the mention of celibacy, which appear to have been added later. Needless to say, such a book would have found no place in the Jewish canon. As for the Christian canon, the Rechabite story would certainly not belong with the other New Testament books, since it doesn't deal directly with Jesus or any of the apostles. Additionally, its Gnostic elements must have troubled the Christian sages, who were creating the canon as part of their war against Gnostic thought.

Perhaps the church condemned this book due the fact that the elements of the Christian eucharist—bread and wine—were forbidden to the Rechabites. Obviously, such a book did not belong among the sacred texts of Christian orthodoxy.

THE SECRET

Nonetheless, the book is a treasure trove of enlightenment for the modern world. After all, we live in a world of vanity. But Paradise cannot be found in the clothes we wear or do not wear, or the food we eat, or the fine wines we drink. The island of the Rechabites epitomizes the World of Being and is the opposite of the world of vanity.

The more stuff we have, the more time and energy we are likely to expend taking care of it. The most important and enduring values in life we often barter away simply to acquire more stuff.

During my residence in the Middle East I got my own taste of Rechabite simplicity, when, for an entire summer, I volunteered to work on an Israeli agricultural settlement known as a kibbutz. In the kibbutz I discovered a truly communal society, where no one owned anything individually, but where everything was the common property of the collective.

The kibbutzniks had no need to flaunt their wealth or position by the acquisition of one status symbol or another. There was no struggle to build a bigger house, drive a sleeker car, or put together a bigger stock portfolio, because in the kibbutz there were no private homes, cars, or personal investments. Instead there was an egalitarian concern for every individual. The reality of a society without stuff was driven home by a simple fact: there were no locks on the doors. Stealing was unthinkable and unheard of. Utopia? Hardly. But it did represent a starkly different way of looking at life. The Rechabites would be right at home.

CHAPTER 12

Solomon: Lord of the Ring

"One Ring to rule them all, one Ring to find them
One Ring to bring them all and in the darkness bind them
In the Land of Mordor where the Shadows lie."
—J. R. R. TOLKEIN

The name Solomon is virtually synonymous with the word *wisdom*. He is depicted as the very image of the wise king. He is the Lost Bible's version of the great wizard from J. R. R. Tolkein's epics: Gandalf. A mastery of the magical arts is what defines both characters: Solomon of ancient Israel, and Gandalf of Middle Earth. Granted, we hardly think of magic when we come across the name of Israel's wise king, but the ancients were firmly convinced that Solomon was not merely a monarch, but also a wizard. We might also think of good King Arthur, whose closest ally was Merlin, a master of the magical arts. Solomon, however, doesn't need a Merlin; he does the magic himself.

Magic is a subject that the traditional Bible stays far away from, for it was seen as part of the domain of the pagans. Nevertheless, in a world beset by pain and suffering, where the power of evil often seems to triumph, we have to ask: What is wrong with a little magic? In the World of Being there is a lot more to life than what we can see with our eyes. There are mysterious forces that course through the world around us; and when we learn to operate, as Solomon did, in the World of Being, or as Gandalf the great in Middle Earth, we can learn to harness them.

The book of I Kings says this about Solomon:

God gave Solomon a great deal of wisdom and insight, along with understanding, as great as the sand along the seashore. Solomon's wisdom surpassed all the sons of the east as well as all the wisdom of the Egyptians. ... He talked about trees, from the cedars of Lebanon to the hyssop that sprouts from the walls. And he also talked about the beasts, the birds, the creeping things and the fishes. And people from all nations came to hear the wisdom of Solomon, having been sent by all the kings of the earth who heard his wisdom. (I Kings 5:9-10; 13-14, author's translation from the traditional Hebrew text. *See* I Kings 4:29-30, 33-34 in Christian versions.)

Given that the Bible makes much of Solomon's knowledge of the natural world, including plants and animals, it is not surprising that the ancients postulated that he mastered many esoteric secrets as well. There seems to have been a whole folklore about Solomon, as a miracle worker/magician, who had power over demonic forces. Even Jesus makes oblique reference to this fact:

> As the crowds pressed in upon him, he began to say, "This generation is evil; it searches for a sign, but no sign will be given to it. . . . Behold, one greater than Solomon is here." (Luke 11:29, 31, author's translation)

The Israelite king, according to an incredible book of the Lost Bible called the Testament of Solomon, performed wonders by harnessing the power of the demons. We naturally ask, whence did this book originate?

Like many other books of a Lost Bible, the Testament of Solomon first surfaced in Egypt. While the earliest manuscripts known to exist are in Coptic, dating from the fourth century, the original language of the text was certainly Greek, dating to some point between the first and third centuries of the Common Era. In its present form it is a Christian work, but the stories and folklore upon which it is based are much older and are certainly Jewish, having been passed down by word of mouth.

ABOUT A BOY

Where did Solomon, the mighty king, get the reputation of being a miracle worker in his own right? The Lost Bible's Testament of Solomon tells us that it all began with a demon and a little boy.

We read (in modern paraphrase) the following:

> Long ago, when the great temple was being built in the city of Jerusalem, a mighty demon named Ornias came along just as evening was setting in. By supernatural stealth he managed to rob the master workman's young son of the money he had earned. Every day the demon also grabbed the boy's right hand and sucked his thumb, distracting him so much that he could not eat, and grew terribly thin.
>
>   I, Solomon, loved and adored this little boy, and I asked him one day why he was becoming emaciated, even while I was paying him double wages. The lad explained that a wicked spirit approached him every day after sunset, pilfering his wages and sucking his right thumb.

In response I, Solomon, entered the Holy Temple while it was still under construction and began begging God day and night that the demon be handed over to my authority, so that I might have power over it.

THE ONE RING OF POWER

My prayers were interrupted by Michael, the archangel, who was dispatched directly from the Lord of Armies. He carried with him a ring, bearing a precious stone engraved with a seal. He spoke to me audibly.

"Solomon, descendant of David, accept this gift that has been entrusted to you by the Most High, for it shall bestow upon you power to bind every demon in prison. You may even use it to compel the demons to work on the temple, as long as you wear it, displaying the divine seal."

The next day I summoned the little boy into my presence. I placed into his hands the ring that Michael had given me.

I told him, "The next time you see the demon who has been troubling you, take his ring and throw it at his chest, shouting, 'King Solomon commands you to come to him!' Then run straight back to me."

The little boy did just as I told him. The demon approached, and he threw the ring at his chest, commanding that he come to me. However, the demon shouted back at the boy, "What have you done? Pluck out this ring that is lodged in my chest, and return it to Solomon. Do that, and I will give you all the gold and silver on earth!"

The boy answered, "I will never have the strength to stand up to you if I give in now!" He then came before me and announced that the demon was bound up and standing outside the temple gate, offering gold and silver, if only he were not delivered to the king.

What do we learn from this narrative? There is an image we have been given, a seal, a divine signet—the Ring of Power—that has been placed in our hands. We can wear it, we can display it, we can also wield it, because it is a weapon. A signet ring may not look like a weapon, but it is. In ancient times the ring-bearer possessed the seal of the king—with his power and authority. Slip it on and we enter a new realm, a new dimension—the World of Being. We are invested with a power invisible to others, but more potent a weapon than Excalibur.

Bear in mind that Solomon was himself the king, yet even his powers were only those of a mortal. The real power came from the King of the universe, who delivered the ring through the agency of Michael. Solomon in turn passed it along. He empowered a little boy. There is yet a greater principle here. Solomon, being king, was blessed with great bounty, wealth, privilege, and status, which he well knew came from above. But his way of paying back the divine providence was to pay it forward, to pass the blessing along to someone else, in this case a little boy.

ONE RING TO RULE THEM ALL

Solomon's first-person narration continues:

> After all this had transpired, I, King Solomon, seeing the demon shaking in terror, arose from my royal throne. "Who are you?" I demanded. "And what is your name?"
>
> "My name is Ornias," said the demon. Next I demanded to know his astrological sign. "My sign is Aquarius. There are many Aquarians who lust after women of the sign Virgo, the goddess of love. I strangle them. Beyond this, I occasionally go into a trance and transform myself. Sometimes I become a pedophile, inflicting terrible pain on effeminate boys whom I touch. On other occasions I transform myself into a winged being and ascend into the heavens. Thirdly, I occasionally take on the form of a lion. Genealogically, I am from the line of an archangel of divine power, but another archangel named Ouriel has withstood me."
>
> I, King Solomon, on hearing the name of the archangel, rejoiced greatly in the Divine Presence. I stretched forth my hand, on which I had placed the ring, and imprinted the demon with the divine seal. Next, I summoned my godly authority and sent him away to the quarry, to cut stones—which had been brought from across the Arabian Sea and left on the coast—for the temple. However, the demon was afraid to handle iron instruments and begged, "King Solomon, please give me just a degree of freedom, and I will bring all the demons to you." Since the demon did not want to obey me personally, I prayed for Ouriel the archangel to come to my aid. At that moment, Ouriel descended from heaven, into my presence. The angel immediately subjugated Ornias, to do as I had commanded and cut stones for the temple.

The Ring of Power (as Tolkein tells us) carries with it a corrupting influence, and Solomon learns early on that he must submit himself to the yoke of heaven. In order for the demon to obey him completely, Solomon must bombard the divine throne with prayer and supplication. Only with the help of an archangel is he able to compel the demon's complete obedience. So it is with the exercise of our own gifts; all must be submitted to a higher power.

ONE RING TO FIND HIM

We read on:

> Afterwards, I summoned Ornias, took the ring, placed it into his hands, and
> commanded him to find the prince of the demons and bring him to me.

As in Tolkein's epic, the ring conveys unlimited power. But the ring by itself
was insufficient for the task at hand. Solomon was learning how to use the ring,
that it must be coupled with direct intervention from the spiritual realm, hence
his prayer and the dispatching of the angel. Discovering the power within us is a
wonderful thing, but with our power we must learn a dependence on the Divine
Presence. Otherwise, the evil forces we command just might not want to serve
us. But Solomon did something even bolder. He took the ring and placed it in
the hands of the demon, commanding that he summon the chief demon. Clearly
Solomon was prepared to let go of power, to entrust it to someone else, even to a
demon. The challenge is clear. We are called to so trust the transformative power
of good as to place its very emblem and seal into the hands of evil, in the faith that
evil will be transformed. The narrative continues:

> Ornias dutifully bore the ring straight to Beelzebub, declaring, "Come
> this way! Solomon commands that you come to him." Beelzebub replied,
> "Why should I? I do not know who this Solomon is!" At that point
> Ornias threw the ring at Beelzebub's chest, where it lodged. He shouted,
> "King Solomon commands you!" Beelzebub shrieked, as though he had
> been burned with fire. But then he picked himself up and sheepishly
> followed Ornias to me. When I saw Beelzebub coming, I thanked the
> Almighty, for placing even the power of the demons under my authority.
> I proceeded to ask Beelzebub a series of questions. He identified himself
> as the ruler of all the demons. He told me how the demons manifest
> themselves and promised to bring them to me, bound.

ONE RING TO BRING THEM ALL

As the story proceeds, Solomon asks whether female demons exist, and Beelzebub
returns with one named Onoskelis, a woman of great beauty, though her legs are
like those of a mule. She explains that she lives in caves, yet goes about strangling
men and perverting their character. She explains that she came into being via the
echo of a strange voice generated in physical matter. She travels by the energy
of the full moon. But when asked which angel thwarts her, she answers that it is
the angel who resides in King Solomon himself, for she has been subjected to his
power. Solomon, who has now learned to couple the ring with divine power, utters

aloud the ineffable name of the Almighty and puts Onoskelis to work spinning hemp to make ropes for the temple's construction. She is duly sealed by the power of the ring and bound.

Solomon continues his wizardry, summoning additional demons. These include the wicked Asmodeus, who brings evil on newlyweds, marring the beauty of virgins. Solomon puts Asmodeus to work fashioning clay for molding the vessels of the temple. The demon Lix Tetrax is next interrogated by Solomon and commanded to lift up great stones, flinging them to the top of the temple, where the workers set them in place.

Solomon goes on to interrogate seven spirits of wickedness, who appear before him bound together. They announce that they are heavenly bodies and lords of the realm of darkness. Their names are: Deception, Strife, Fate, Distress, Error, Power, and, simply, The Worst. Among the explanations of their deeds, Fate causes people to fight battles rather than make peace. Distress deprives people of moderation and divides them into factions. Power brings down kings but raises up tyrants. And The Worst declares that he will bind Solomon himself.

AND IN THE DARKNESS BIND THEM

But Solomon seals them with the Ring of Divine Power and puts them to work digging the temple foundations. The names of these demons coincide with the worst of human character traits. True to other teachings of the Lost Bible, they are synonymous with the evil inclination—the dark side of our character. It is precisely the evil inclination that is to be transformed into a chariot for God.

Yet more demons are interrogated, bound, and subdued by Solomon, including:

- Murder, a headless monster, who kills and consumes infants through his neck;

- Scepter, who resembles an enormous dog, compelled to retrieve a huge emerald stone, for adorning the temple;

- A lion-shaped demon, who afflicts those who are ill with fatal disease;

- A dragon of three heads, who will be vanquished by the Wonderful Counselor—the Messiah—at the Place of the Skull;

and,

- A lecherous spirit, who kills with the sword and causes people to chew their own flesh—but who is thwarted by the mark of the Savior on the forehead of anyone so sealed.

In the end, however, Solomon's heart is turned away to the worship of pagan deities by one of his many wives, whom he found while touring the kingdom of the Jebusites. The spirit of wisdom subsequently takes leave of the great king, who spends his time building temples to pagan gods instead. His spirit of counsel is darkened, and his words become vain chatter. This is why he has written down his testament—as a warning and admonition, not merely to consider the beginning of a spiritual journey, but also its end.

THE EXCLUSION

Jewish thought has always revered King Solomon, who was the first to be called a true son of God (see I Chronicles 17:13). Solomon was the epitome of wisdom, which itself was personified in later biblical times. But Solomon as a wizard and sorcerer? That was a leap the sages of Israel were not prepared to make.

As we have seen, there was a very ancient tradition in Judaism about Solomon's wizardry and his mystical powers. There is even a reference to Solomon's ring in the writings of the ancient Jewish historian Josephus Flavius:

> God also enabled him to learn that skill which expels demons, which is a science useful to men. He composed such incantations also by which distempers are alleviated. And he left behind him the manner of using exorcisms, by which they drive away demons, so that they never return, and this method of cure is of great force unto this day. For I have seen a certain man of my own country, whose name was Eleazar, releasing people that were demoniacal. . . . The manner of cure was this: He put a ring that had a root of one of those sorts mentioned by Solomon to the nostrils of the demoniac, after which he drew out the demon through his nostrils. (Antiquities, VIII, ii, 5)

If Josephus is to be believed, Solomon was part of the larger trend of Jewish mysticism in late antiquity, which came to be known as Kabbalah. On a philosophical level, Kabbalah involved drawing nearer to the Divine Presence, intimately and personally, through special prayer and meditation. But on a practical level, Kabbalah involved warding off the evil eye using incantations, amulets, and, in the case of Solomon, a ring. While the practice of Kabbalah had throngs of adherents in ancient times, it also had detractors who saw it as a wild esotericism. And among those detractors were the very sages who canonized the Hebrew scriptures. They looked askance at Kabbalah as superstitious and irrational, and they made sure that texts that were too mystical were not included in the sacred canon. Even a book like Daniel appeared too esoteric, too numinous for the rationalistic sages, who included it in the canon only by the barest of margins.

It is likely that while the contents of the Testament of Solomon originated in the ancient world of Judaism, the keepers of the canon had no intention of depicting King Solomon as a Kabbalist. There was certainly no hope of it being preserved, at least in the Jewish canon. As for the text itself, it appears to have been set down between the first and third centuries, C.E., in Greek. The earliest surviving manuscript is in Coptic, from the fourth century. The Testament of Solomon was at some point picked up by early Christians, who added their own interpolations to the text. As with other books of the Lost Bible we are therefore looking at an early Jewish tradition with a later Christian overlay.

Why then was it not included in the Christian canon? The Christians, it seems, had struggled with their own brand of mystics, the Gnostics, whom they repeatedly castigated for seeking a direct communion with God and for de-emphasizing the centrality of Christ. They were terrified that members of the holy flock might start worshiping angels or other intermediaries, and they were certainly not keen on the use of charms, amulets, or signet rings. A book like the Testament of Solomon, even with its overlay of Christian piety, flourished only in Gnostic circles, in Egypt and other parts of the Mediterranean. When it came to inclusion in the formal Christian canon, it did not stand a chance.

WHERE THE SHADOWS LIE

As I sat perched atop the Mount of Olives, my eyes always fell to the single most recognizable landmark in the Holy City. It is the golden-domed shrine known as the Dome of the Rock, the third most sacred site in Islam, after Mecca and Medina. It is the site where, according to Islamic tradition, Abraham ascended into heaven on a ladder of light. It sits in the exact spot once occupied by Solomon's great temple. But alas, Solomon's temple no longer exists. Instead the city is a patchwork of competing religions and ethnicities, none of which get along very well with the others. Will the great temple, whose foundations were laid by Solomon, ever rise again?

During my tenure in Jerusalem, municipal authorities uncovered a plot, hatched by an extreme religious sectarian movement, to dynamite the Dome of Rock, thereby making room for a new temple. Fortunately, those involved were apprehended and subsequently jailed. I remember thinking to myself, "As if the city doesn't already have enough strife and animosity to bring on World War III. We certainly do not need this!" Doubtless, there are more demons in today's Jerusalem than ever before.

There are, nonetheless, other ways of building the temple. The best temples are spiritual temples, built not with human hands but with human hearts. The rabbinic sages of old asked each other why the temple was destroyed. The answer they gave was what they called boundless hatred. Surely, it stands to reason that if the temple were destroyed through boundless hatred, it might be rebuilt through boundless love. When we enter the World of Being, meditatively, we can imagine ourselves being entrusted with a ring bearing the divine image, with all its attendant authority.

THE SECRET

Like King Solomon the wise, we must put that seal—that image—to work, transforming the powers of darkness around us into forces for good. We must all become lords of the ring, finding ways to channel negativity around us into positive directions with God's help. In today's Middle East, the product of centuries of recrimination and strife, it is not such an easy task, but it is possible.

In the mid-1980s, when I found myself working for an American television station in southern Lebanon, one of my duties was to broadcast family-oriented programming throughout the region. I was part of an operation that literally took the power of the airwaves—so often used to convey hatred and animosity—and transformed them as a force for good. The broadcast facility was located smack in the middle of a war zone. I thought of myself as living proof that it is better to light a candle than curse the darkness. As I drove to work each day, wearing a flak jacket, I fancied myself a bearer of King Solomon's ring, and I chuckled.

PART III

THE WORLD OF FEELING (YETZIRAH)

W herever did we get the idea that reason and emotion do not mix? We routinely place our thoughts and our reasoned judgments in one compartment while placing our feelings and emotions in an entirely different box—hermetically sealed and stored away from our rational experience. Perhaps it goes back to the seminal Western philosopher, Rene Descartes, who coined the expression, "I think, therefore I am." Descartes conceived of the body as an elaborate biological mechanism designed to support the reasoned intellect. It is a model that the Western world embraced for centuries. The mind, in Descartes' model, is a machine that reasons. But what if Descartes was wrong? What if reason is itself laced with emotion? What if every thought entertained is predicated on feelings? What if the mind is really just an extension of the heart?

According to another philosopher of the Enlightenment, Baruch Spinoza, feeling is not at odds with reason, but is rather its indispensable accomplice. Truth be told, feelings are in fact nature's way of ensuring survival. The mystics of the Kabbalah grasped this critical role of emotion long before Sigmund Freud thought to probe the human unconscious. The World of Feeling—the emotive world—is not to be shunned or deprecated, but cultivated, so that human beings can fully express their divine calling. To rephrase Descartes, the Kabbalist might say, "I feel, therefore I am."

EMOTION IS THE MOTION OF OUR WORLD

The world of our emotions is a formative world, affecting everything we do. We spend much of our lives in the world of our feelings, or (put another way) our ego. This spirited side of our personality colors and shades every aspect of our life. Our moods, far from being inconsequential, constitute forces that wage many battles within us.

Indeed, the emotive world is a battleground, on which the war of moods, critical to our well-being and our very survival, is fought. It is a war that is waged every day. We may surrender to negativity and acquiesce in the battle or choose to enter the fray and engage each negative emotion with a positive response. It is all a matter of choice. Our greatest challenge is to gird up the loins of our mind (in the words of 1 Peter 1:13 KJV) and charge into combat. We are often beset by a fight-or-flight mentality; sometimes we must choose the fight.

CHAPTER 13

The Unconquerable Job

Out of the night that covers me,
Black as the Pit from pole to pole,
I thank whatever gods may be
For my unconquerable soul.

In the fell clutch of circumstance
I have not winced nor cried aloud.
Under the bludgeonings of chance
My head is bloody, but unbowed.

Beyond this place of wrath and tears
Looms but the Horror of the shade,
And yet the menace of the years
Finds, and shall find, me unafraid.

It matters not how strait the gate,
How charged with punishments the scroll,
I am the master of my fate:
I am the captain of my soul.
—WILLIAM ERNEST HENLEY, *INVICTUS*

In any contest between power and patience bet on patience.
—W. B. PRESCOTT

One of the greatest works of literature ever produced deals with a man who loses everything he has and is plunged into despair. No biblical character is a better expression of this battleground, in the World of Feeling, than the venerable Job, whose life is emblematic of suffering. The Book of Job resonates with universal themes, posing the question: Why do bad things happen to good people? The biblical character of Job curses the day of his birth and raises his complaint to God. He sits in sackcloth and ashes and wallows in self-pity.

There is, however, an alternate account of this man of sorrows, contained in the Lost Bible. I discovered it while sitting in my favorite haunt—the musty old library on a hill in Jerusalem called Mount Zion. It is called the Testament of Job. Here we have a Job who is strikingly different, based on new details missing from the traditional account. This Job will not give in to hopelessness.

THE EXCLUSION

The Testament of Job is quite ancient, having been composed some time between the first century B.C.E. and the first century C.E. Compared with other books of the Hebrew Bible, however, it is a relative newcomer. Based on the date of composition alone, the keepers of the Jewish canon would certainly have wanted its exclusion. Using the tools of modern scholarship, however, we now know that the traditional book of Job is probably no more than a century or two older than the Testament of Job, and therefore may be placed in the same general historical period.

Something else about the Testament of Job must have troubled the sages of revered memory, namely that the original language of composition was not Hebrew, but Greek. The place of composition is equally problematic, most likely Egypt. Notably, the land of Egypt, especially Alexandria, was the locus of a specific type of Judaism—Hellenistic Judaism. Such literary and philosophical giants as Philo Judeus exemplify this syncretistic blend of traditional Jewish thought from the land of Israel and the Greek-style philosophy characteristic of the Mediterranean world. This alternate variety of Judaism was much more tolerant of dualism, the concept of an evil force—call it Satan—at odds with Israel's Deity. As Judaism developed, such dualism was disallowed.

In the traditional book of Job, Satan is depicted simply as one of the angelic messengers in the divine court. He is dispatched by God, but given no power in his own right. In the Testament of Job, however, Satan is far too dominant and independent a character to be tolerated. As with so many other books of the Lost Bible, the keepers of the canon (if they even knew this book existed) had no use for it. It did not stand a chance. But if considered purely on a level of allegory, the Testament of Job advances powerful metaphysical concepts, which should not be ignored.

"OUT OF THE NIGHT THAT COVERS ME"

As the book begins, Job is ill and nearing the end of his life. He gathers his seven sons and three daughters and relates the fantastic tale for which he is famous.

He explains that his real name was Jobab, before it was changed by divine decree to Job. He has lived his entire life near the temple of an idol, causing him to question the very nature of God. His yearnings are answered one evening, when out of the night comes a blinding flash, and the voice of an angel, declaring that the temple is in fact the home of Satan. The angel gives Job authority to destroy the idolatrous shrine, but he adds (in fresh modern paraphrase of the ancient text):

> "If you try to demolish the temple, Satan himself will make war against you. He will not be able to kill you, but he will send plagues on you, taking your possessions as well as your children. However, if you remain patient throughout, you will be remembered forever. All that you lost will be returned in a double portion, and you will rise again at the time of resurrection. But you must be like an athlete, enduring the pain to win the crown."

On hearing those words Job leaps into action. We pick up his narrative, paraphrased from the Lost Bible, as follows:

> I recruited fifty young people, and together we went off to the pagan shrine. We tore down the entire temple. Returning home, I bolted the door securely.

This, then, is why Job is attacked. In the traditional story it is all part of a bet, a wager between God and Satan, to see whether a righteous man who is unjustly afflicted will retain his steadfast faith in God (Job 1:1-12; 2:1-6). But in this account, it is entirely about Satan's vengeance over the destruction of his temple.

Who is Satan? As cartoon character Pogo declares, "We have met the enemy, and he is us." We are our own Satan—the doubts and fears that we entertain. When we are plagued by doubt—about ourselves and our abilities—we allow the Enemy to establish a beachhead on our turf. We allow a pagan shrine to be built right next door, in *our* neighborhood.

Think of it another way, in battle imagery. Allegorically, *defeatism* is idolatrous—a temple occupied by a pagan deity—since it diverts our gaze from the Divine Presence resident in us. In metaphysical combat one cannot afford to lose. The best counsel is to take the offensive. In the World of Feeling, defeat is not an option. Be aggressive; tear down the shrine.

And even so, we will of course be counterattacked. We can expect it.

"BLACK AS THE PIT FROM POLE TO POLE"

As the story progresses, the Evil One disguises himself as a beggar and appears at Job's door. Just as Job instructs his doorkeeper to tell anyone who approaches that he is busy and cannot come to the door, we should be prepared to turn negativity away when it comes knocking. Our negative emotions come like beggars, seeking to feast from our tables. To such parasites we are to show no compassion. When the vagabond returns, demanding bread, Job replies:

> You will not share a single loaf of bread, for we are estranged from each other!

All Job gives to his adversary is a burnt loaf. Satan replies:

> Just as this bread is completely singed, so will I singe your body. In just an hour or so, I will wreak my vengeance on you.

As promised, Satan withdraws to the divine court, where he is given power over Job's possessions. Job relates:

> Then he came and took away all I had.

Courageous resolutions are one thing, but then the battle comes. And it *always* comes to us, just as it did to Job. Notwithstanding his initial piety, the disasters fall swiftly and fast. A plague is unleashed and devastates seven thousand sheep, three thousand camels, five hundred she asses, and five hundred yoke of oxen. Job's own neighbors come and steal away the rest of his flocks, but Job is steadfast.

In the stunning film adaptation of the popular Patrick O'Brien novel, *Master and Commander*, about a British frigate during the Napoleonic Wars, we meet an old sailor, who has tattooed into his knuckles the words: HOLD FAST. Whatever trials and tribulations befall the ship, he stretches out his knuckles to display those two words. When the hapless "Jobian" old sailor receives a massive head wound, and his skull is literally opened—to insert a coin to repair the breach—his knuckles, strapped to his body in front of him, still display those two words: HOLD FAST. That is the main theme—as well as a challenge to the moral relativism of the postmodern age—and it is the means to victory both at sea and in the battleground of emotion. As it happens, those words are biblical as well, appearing prominently in Deuteronomy 11:22 and Job 27:6. When facing the most intractable enemy of all, ourselves, in the World of Feeling, the admonition is simple and direct: HOLD FAST.

Not to be dissuaded, Satan disguises himself as the king of the Persians and gathers a group of bandits before whom he accuses Job (Jobab) of plundering the earth and demolishing the temple of their favorite idol. These rogues demand vengeance, not only on Job, but also on his seven sons and three daughters. Job relates:

> After inciting this mob, Satan knocked down my own house with all of

my children inside, who perished. My own compatriots then descended on the remains of my house and plundered it. When a messenger arrived and showed me the place of devastation, where my children died, I wailed loudly but did not blaspheme. "The Lord gives and the Lord takes away," I said.

Thereafter, Satan is given the power to afflict Job's body. Still, Job holds fast.

"I THANK WHATEVER GODS MAY BE FOR MY UNCONQUERABLE SOUL"

Job relates:

> But still the Evil One had no power over my soul. I was sitting on my seat of honor, where I always sat, though continuing to mourn the death of my children. At that moment Satan became a whirlwind, overturning the massive throne. I was trapped underneath with no escape. I was then stricken with a terrible plague, covering my body. In affliction and torment, I hauled my worm-ridden carcass away from the city, and sat on a dung heap. The ground itself was wet with discharges from my body. Yet, in all of this I remained steadfast.

It doesn't get much worse than this. Of course, in the World of Feeling, there are allies as well as adversaries. In the traditional story of Job, we know very little about Job's wife—only that she taunts him with the words *Barekh Elohim u'met*—literally "Bless God and die" (Job 2:9).[6] But in the Lost Bible she plays a much more prominent role, giving comfort to her husband. For years on end Job sits on his dung heap, immovably defiant. His wife (who, we now learn, is named Sitis) is an active ally in Job's struggle. She becomes a maidservant to a local nobleman, earning bread, which she brings to her afflicted spouse. Her sacrifice has a remarkable effect on Job in the battleground of feeling. He cries:

> How dare this man subject my wife to servitude!

He adds:

> After this took place, I suddenly came to my senses.

When self-pity threatens to consume us—when we are at the brink of despair—the compassion, the caring, and the action of others often helps us regain our perspective. Realizing that we are loved by others makes all the difference in the World of Feeling. When Job quits focusing on himself and begins to worry about his wife Sitis, his mind is restored. Sitis even goes so far as to sell her own hair in order to feed her husband. But alas, even allies can become foes. Satan finally infects Sitis, bringing on her woe-filled admonition: "Blaspheme God, and die!"[7]

Job, however, responds like the fighter that he is. He has never surrendered his soul. Far from letting his emotions defeat him, he summons his feelings, and commands his anger. Indeed, when ego is understood in its proper role, then one need not be reduced to a self-effacing, self-deprecating lackey, which some critics assert is precisely the persona of the traditional Job. By contrast, this first-person account—the Testament of Job—reveals one who has taken charge of his emotions and has wielded them as a weapon against the foe. Job has learned that there is a time to mourn and a time to engage the enemy. In all his righteous might he declares:

> "Look here! For seventeen years my worm-ridden body has suffered plagues, but my soul has never been as depressed as it is right now, after hearing your counsel that I blaspheme the Almighty and perish. We may have lost everything, but why should we be alienated from God, who is our greatest wealth? I know where your words come from, for I see the Evil One standing behind you."

"MY HEAD IS BLOODY, BUT UNBOWED"

Job continues his narration:

> Then I addressed Satan himself: "Come out from behind my wife! Quit hiding! If you are as strong as a lion, come out of your cage. I dare you to fight!"
>
> Satan sheepishly stepped out from behind Sitis, Through his tears, he said: "Listen, Job, I am very tired. Even though I am a spirit, and you are flesh and blood, I must withdraw. While you suffer plagues, I dwell in darkness. You and I are like a couple of wrestlers, one being pinned by the other. The one on top filled the mouth of the one below with sand, shutting him up and bruising him. But the one beneath endured it all and refused to give in. In the end the wrestler on top was defeated. You, Job, are the wrestler pinned below me, suffering plagues. But in spite of my superior strength, you have conquered me! I am defeated."
>
> The shamed Satan departed, leaving me alone.

Surprisingly enough, Job's battle, his wrestling match, is not physical, but emotional. The battle is described as a physical contest, but it consists of nothing more than Job opening his mouth and rebuking both his wife and Satan. In the World of Feeling, physical action is not always required, but fortitude of soul is. We should of course bear in mind that emotional stress can and often does induce physical illness and/or pain. To wrestle emotionally is to feel a physical sickness. To live is to wrestle, and to wrestle is to live.

TONGUES OF ANGELS

As the story concludes, Job is vindicated, given new children, and his fortunes restored. Job counsels his progeny to likewise be patient in whatever befalls them: Hold fast. Afterward, he distributes his property to his sons, but does something even better for his daughters. He brings them multicolored cords, tells each daughter to place one around her breast, and explains that they will thereby magically be able to speak in the language of the angels. No less than three new languages come from the mouths of Job's daughters: the angelic dialect, the dialect of the archons, and the dialect of the cherubim.

Why this emphasis on angels? The Lost Bible has much to say about angels, who are conduits of love to humankind. Why do we need angels? Perhaps it is an angel who must mediate the experience of a heartless universe. But angels are integral to the World of Feeling, perhaps best understood as symbols of forces that operate within every one of us. Some are forces for good, some for evil; some for healing and protection, some for destruction. They are metaphors for our most basic human drives and emotions: love, hate, envy, lust, charity, malice, greed, generosity, cruelty, delusion, vision, despair, fear, and hope. It is our angels of hope that we need to welcome, embrace, and entertain.

THE SECRET

During my residence in Israel I was sponsored to attend Yad Vashem, the international institute for Holocaust study and research. There, in a place devoted to remembering the most terrible genocide in human history, I heard the story of Rabbi Kalimnos Shapiro, a pious Kabbalist who was trapped inside the ghetto in Budapest during the Nazi horror. As the world was falling apart all around him, he composed a diary, which miraculously survived the Holocaust. In it he counseled his holy flock to remember one thing—a divine secret—that the mystical presence of the Almighty (*Shaddai*) resides in every human heart.

You must never surrender to despair, he counseled. You must never give up. You must be steadfast, for if ever you despair, if ever you abandon yourself, you also abandon God. You may feel like Job, or like Abraham's son Isaac, about to be slaughtered, but remember that your emotions are a battleground. You can and you must prevail.

Rabbi Shapiro was murdered at a death camp called Majdanek. But the secret he declared transcends space, time, and the deepest pit into which one may fall: Hold fast, and keep the faith!

CHAPTER 14

Enoch's Travels: Giants in Lilliput

The desire of excessive power caused the angels to fall;
the desire of knowledge caused men to fall.
—FRANCIS BACON

And yet, as angels in some brighter dreams
Call to the soul when man doth sleep,
So some strange thoughts transcend our wonted themes,
And into glory peep.
—HENRY VAUGHAN, ANGLO-WELSH POET, MYSTIC

The topography of the Middle East is a kind of meeting ground between heaven and earth. The barrenness of the limestone hills, the enormous valleys, the desolate canyons, the dried-up river beds known as *wadis*, all seem to pull one's gaze heavenward. It is easy to forget where one is in this world outside of time.

When I sat on my perch on the Mount of Olives, I imagined the armies that had ravaged this eternal city century after century. A few years later, when I lived in northern Galilee, I was all too aware of how this region got its name— Galilee of the gentiles—known for marauding armies who plundered the trade routes, from the Mediterranean Sea to the majestic city of Damascus. One of my favorite lookout points was the Arbel Pass, which afforded a bird's-eye view of the Sea of Galilee, stretched out beneath in the shape of an ancient harp like King David used to play. The tranquility of the lake lay in stark contrast to the cliffs on which I stood, where violence and bloodshed had been the rule of thumb from the days of bronze swords to modern tank warfare. Surely, if God and the angels had ever waged war, the celestial landscape must have looked something like this.

The concept of a war in heaven—involving open rebellion among the angels, many of whom decided that it is better to rule in hell than serve in heaven—has been believed as a primordial fact across the centuries, inspiring (among other works) Milton's *Paradise Lost*. Perhaps, however, it was taken a little too seriously.

Was there really a war in heaven as some ancient sources suggest? Or was there quite a different saga regarding the corruption of the angels? The Lost Bible suggests that the disobedient angels were not cast down to the earth after fierce combat in the celestial sphere, but willingly and voluntarily chose to abandon the height of heaven for the earth below. That story, of how the divine "sons of God" exiled themselves from their celestial abode and lusted after corruptible human flesh, is the subject of a remarkable account purportedly inscribed by the seventh descendant of Adam, the biblical patriarch Enoch.

TREAT YOUR FEELINGS LIKE ANGELS

As most people read it, the first book of Enoch, or I Enoch, is nothing more than legend and folklore, which circulated across the ancient land of Canaan. But read allegorically, it contains a secret: Treat your feelings like angels, and you will learn about the place of self, of individual ego, of personhood in the World of Feeling. How we feel is very much linked to what we desire, and to what we feel we require. King David, in the oft-quoted Twenty-Third Psalm, declares that he lacks nothing—that he has everything he needs. Elsewhere we read, in Psalm 73, David's rhetorical question, "Whom else have I in heaven?" (v. 25, author's translation). In other words, David's desires were spiritual, not earthly.

But according to I Enoch, the disobedient angels were unable to make such a declaration. Instead, their desires were fixed on the women of terra firma. The traditional Bible mentions that angelic beings called the sons of God cohabited with earth women:

> And the sons of God saw that the daughters of men were beautiful, and they took for themselves wives from among all those whom they found pleasing. (Genesis 6:2, author's translation)

Who were the sons of God spoken of here? Tradition says that they were angels, though the term itself could really refer to anyone; we are all children of God. But the interpretation arose that these particular sons of God were the disobedient angels, who descended to earth and made mischief among humankind. These spirit beings manifested themselves in physical form and had sexual relations with earth women. A few modern commentators have gone so far as to suggest that these sons of God may in fact have been space aliens, that the wicked couplings referred to may have amounted to "close encounters of the third kind."

In the final analysis, however, the ancient text may be read in two ways. Either it is a description of ordinary relations between men and women, producing some very unusual offspring, or the Bible is employing code language to describe divine beings who came to earth in search of sex. The Lost Bible's book of I Enoch tells us in no uncertain terms that the latter is the case.

THE FALLEN ONES

Two verses later the Genesis account declares:

> In those days—and afterwards—the *Nephilim* were on the earth, when the sons of God came to the daughters of women and produced offspring. They were the mighty ones, who from days of old were men of renown. (Genesis 6:4, author's translation)

Who were the *Nephilim*? The word means simply "the fallen ones." It is assumed that the "mighty men of old," as they were also known, were giants, which is why the text is sometimes translated, "There were giants in the earth in those days." The Bible itself, however, doesn't necessarily force that conclusion. Only in the Lost Bible are we told this explicitly.

Furthermore, the traditional Bible says little about Enoch, except that he "walked with God; and he was not, for God took him" (Genesis 5:24). But I Enoch (his first-person account) tells us that the heavens were opened to him, whereupon he made a succession of travels to the divine throne and was shown incredible mysteries. We read the following (in contemporary paraphrase) from the earliest fragments of the book, found among the Dead Sea Scrolls:

> A vision of the Holy One of heaven was given to Enoch, who spoke forth his oracles. . . . The Eternal will come down to the earth, treading upon Mount Sinai. The Holy One will be revealed with a mighty army and with great strength from the highest heavens. All of the Watchers will tremble. They will be punished in hidden places, throughout the world.

OF WATCHERS, GIANTS, AND LILLIPUTIANS

Why will the angels—the Watchers, as they are called—be punished? The patriarch Enoch explains it, as follows:

> In those days, while the sons of men multiplied, fair and lovely daughters were born to them. The Watchers—those sons of heaven—were attracted to them and lusted for them. They said to one another, "Let's seek out the daughters of men and rear sons for ourselves." However, their chief,

Shemihazah, spoke up, saying, "I fear that the rest of you will not go through with this plan, in which case only I will be guilty of this great transgression." All of them replied, saying, "All of us will take an oath and swear solemnly that we will not lose heart or abandon this plan until we have carried it out." Afterward, they took the oath, all of them jointly. There were two hundred of them, all together. They descended on the summit of Mount Hermon during the days of Enoch's father Yared.[8]

These acts, according to the Lost Bible, are the very source of the wickedness that proliferated upon the earth, the "original sin" that brought on the great flood in the days of Noah. It wasn't what Adam and Eve did, in eating from the Tree of the Knowledge of Good and Evil. That, as explained earlier, was as much a matter of "falling up" as "falling down," for it brought enlightenment to our species. Here we are told that the angels—the Watchers—rather than starting a war in heaven, did not regard their high estate, but looked down to the earth and coveted the daughters of men. There is a serious warning here about the commingling of spirit and flesh. The angels abandoned their enlightened state, exchanging spiritual reality for the material world. This represents the opposite of the enlightenment prized by the Gnostics and heralded by other books of the Lost Bible.

Enoch continues his account:

They, along with their chieftains, took women for themselves. They chose whomever they desired. They penetrated and defiled them. They taught them witchcraft, magic spells, and how to cut roots and herbs for use in their conjurations.

Interestingly, the Kabbalistic World of Feeling (called *Yetzirah*) is said to be the abode of the angels, who constantly watch over us. This formative world is also linked to various magical spells, incantations, and conjurations to ward off the evil eye. These should perhaps be seen as the righteous use of white magic, to counter the witchcraft taught by the evil Watchers to the daughters of men. The account proceeds, describing a race of giants in a world of "Lilliputians":

The women became pregnant by the Watchers and gave birth to the giants, who grew to be up to three thousand cubits tall. They were born according to the laws of nature and grew up at a constant rate. Moreover, they consumed the produce of the labor of men. None were able to provide for their rapacious appetites. Therefore, the giants (*Nephilim*) conspired to kill the men and eat them. They performed sinful acts—

against all the birds, against the animals of the earth, against the reptiles who crawl on the earth and in the sea and the sky, against the fish of the sea. They ate their flesh and drank their blood. The earth itself condemned these evildoers for everything they had done.

FEEDING THE EGO

The Lost Bible leads us to believe that if these giants had not been destroyed by the flood, they would have devoured all humankind.

Enoch goes on with his narration:

They all started disclosing magical secrets to their wives, as a result of which many people were struck dead. Their cries ascended to heaven. At that time the righteous angels, Michael, Sari'el, Raphael, and Gabriel, looked down from the holy places of the heavens. They saw that much blood had been spilled on the earth, and that the earth was full of evil and violence, which people had perpetrated. The four angels said to each other, "The cries and moans for the annihilation of the sons of earth has ascended to the gates of heaven."

The Eternal replied to Gabriel, "You must return to those illegitimate children of harlotry! You must annihilate the offspring of the Watchers from among humankind. Declare war on them. Their real desire is for life spans of five hundred years, but they are destined not to live much longer." The Eternal replied to Michael, "You must return and tell Shemihazah and all his friends—those who cohabited with women and were made unclean by them—that their offspring will die. Go and bind them in chains in the earth's great valleys, until their judgment day. For soon I will open the windows of heaven."

DESIRE

We are all invested with supernatural, angelic power. We are "little gods." But when, as in I Enoch, spiritual power is mixed with corruptible flesh—desire—the result is not only inflated ego, but destructive behavior. Our feelings, removed from the divine World of Feeling and transposed to the material world below, can become rapacious appetites, which we cannot control. Give in to unbridled desire, and we cause our inner angels to fall from grace; we doom ourselves to destruction.

The battle for our feelings is not to be minimized; it is life-and-death combat. When feelings are negative, laced with raw desire, or consumed with material things, we must annihilate their offspring or they will devour us. We *can* control our feelings by returning our thoughts to their spiritual home.

The Lost Bible admonishes us to fasten our attention on metaphysical reality rather than earthly illusions. In other words, whatever appears to be reality is only illusory; but what appears to be illusion—the World of Feeling—is in fact reality. The first judgment, according to I Enoch, came upon the material world, of earthly preoccupations, by water (the great flood), but another judgment will come, in which the very elements will melt with fire. Nonetheless, declares I Enoch, the ultimate prognosis for humankind is not gloomy, but glorious. We read (in continuing paraphrase):

> All of humanity will become righteous. They will all worship me. All the nations will fall down before me and bless me. All of the world will become clean of defilement and pollution. Never again will I let loose my anger or punish the world's inhabitants.

THE EXCLUSION

Without question, I Enoch was revered as Scripture by many ancient Israelites. Fragments of the book have been found among the Dead Sea Scrolls, in the caves of the wilderness of Judea, which begs the conclusion that it was composed as early as the second century before the Common Era. The scroll fragments are in the Aramaic language, though the original may well have been composed in Hebrew. The book is still considered Holy Writ by the Ethiopian church, which has preserved the book's earliest complete text, from the fourteenth or fifteenth century. Clearly, the ancients believed the claim that the book was communicated by Enoch himself to his descendants, prior to the great flood of Noah.

The text was subsequently preserved on parchment, carefully deposited in wilderness caves by the sect of Essenes. The keepers of the Jewish canon, however, were not impressed. The book's own claim that Enoch wrote it seemed to undercut the supremacy of the most important of all Hebrew Scriptures, the five books of Moses, dictated to the great lawgiver on Mount Sinai.

With regard to the content of I Enoch, there is a famous dictum in the Talmud which states:

> Whoever reflects on four things would be better off having never come into the world, namely, what is above, what is below, what is before, and what is after. (Mishnah Chagigah 2:1)

Clearly, the book thoroughly violates what the Talmudic sages had in mind. It specifically gravitates toward what is above (the realm of God), what is below (the domain of the fallen angels), and what is before (obscure sexual unions in the primordial beginning). The proper concern of human beings, asserted the keepers of the canon, should be ethics and right conduct in the plane of ordinary daily affairs, not vain speculation about the celestial sphere and bizarre events of prehistory, which can be grasped only imperfectly at best.

As for the keepers of the Christian canon, aside from the Ethiopians, they must have been horrified by the book's exploration of the supernatural realm, which they feared would fuel a surge of sectarian Gnosticism. They certainly had no use for it in the Christian Scriptures. But the Lost Bible is unabashed in its aims. After all, knowing what went wrong in prehistory can help us find our own divine nature and avoid the mistakes of the spirits of wickedness.

THE GULLIVER SYNDROME

Decoded, the book of I Enoch is an invaluable aid to self-discovery and spiritual awareness. It is essentially about the individual, on a journey of self-understanding. The giants we encounter in the book are symbols of the progeny of our own spiritual corruption. After all, it is precisely when we do not know who we are spiritually—that the ego swells, and we start suffering from gigantism. The metaphysical message relates to keeping our egos in balance in the World of Feeling. That sometimes means getting above the material world and refusing to allow the commingling of our spiritual selves with the concerns of the flesh.

Living in the land of Israel, I soon learned that the modern Middle Easterners can be just as materialistic as anyone else. Modern Jerusalem is not quite the Holy City that one would imagine. At times I literally had to get away and find myself anew. One of my favorite retreats was a place called Ein Gedi, in the wilderness of Judea.

The oasis of Ein Gedi is a green paradise in an otherwise desolate landscape, where it seems strangely out of place and otherworldly. From the weathered limestone hills and chalky marl cliffs, a gushing stream erupts, snaking its way inexorably toward the Dead Sea far beneath. It cascades over a rocky precipice, as a breathtaking waterfall. It literally brings to life this otherwise barren wasteland, creating what is today a vast nature preserve. I spent days on end getting to know every square inch of that territory, inspecting lush desert fauna and an incredible assortment of wildlife.

The feelings that took hold of me in that place transported me back to Eden. They elevated me above my mundane, worldly existence and made me feel as though I too were an angel in the abode of pure spirit. While Ein Gedi is in close geographical proximity to the Dead Sea, the lowest spot on the face of the earth, I nonetheless felt as though I were on a lofty height far above the material world. I thought to myself: Wouldn't it be nice to live here all the time? Perhaps if I train my mind properly, I can.

THE SECRET

Out there in the desert, I learned the relative unimportance of the material. All we really own is our *feelings*. Ein Gedi was the very spot where young David fled from the wrath of King Saul, who was chasing him. As a homeless, possessionless vagabond, seeking shelter among the caves at Ein Gedi, David turned to writing psalms. He let his feelings go, in some of the most powerful spiritual poetry ever produced. He soared on high, because he refused to descend below. He joined in divine harmony with the heavenly host.

Treat your feelings like angels. That is the secret of I Enoch. If you keep your focus on spiritual reality, you can become, in a sense, ego-less. You can be unfazed by the material cares that would rob you of equilibrium from day to day. It is not merely a matter of rising above the material realm; it is a matter of *staying* above. So, when the cares of materiality press in, focus on higher things. Read a psalm, sing a song. Train your feelings to soar aloft, and you will remain, day by day, in the abode of the angels.

CHAPTER 15

Love Actually: Tobit's Tale

The dew of compassion is a tear.
—LORD BYRON

Compassion is the antitoxin of the soul: where there is compassion even the
most poisonous impulses remain relatively harmless.
—ERIC HOFFER

From my perch atop the Mount of Olives, I stared out across the Kidron Valley, toward the historic eastern gate of old Jerusalem, walled up by the Turkish sultan Suleiman the Magnificent, but rumored to be the very gate through which the Messiah will someday enter. The Messiah will bring peace, so they say. It somehow sounded odd. So many wars have been fought in this land. The centuries bear witness to a seemingly endless cavalcade of battles, conflicts, and crusades. In the Holy Land, there has never been a paucity of hatred and discord. And yet even in the midst of strife-torn Jerusalem, I noticed daily acts of kindness and self-sacrifice. I soon discovered that whenever one has a need, one may simply pound on a neighbor's door, unannounced, no invitation required. There is a sense of community, of caring, of persevering in the face of struggle and hardship, of coming together in ways I had never imagined in the American suburbia of my childhood. Wherever I looked in this enchanted, ancient, yet modern city, I found stories of caring, compassion, and love.

Take for example the Arrivals Gate at Tel-Aviv's Ben Gurion Airport that has witnessed countless tearful reunions of weary travelers and their loved ones, as well as homecomings of Jews returning to their ancient land: massive airlifts, often from places where entire communities have been threatened with persecution or extinction. When bombs would occasionally go off in busy streets, or busses were blown up, there were of course cries of hate and revenge. But, on a deeply personal level, entire neighborhoods came together, rescue workers dashed into action, clinics were jammed with people donating blood.

Whenever I started feeling a bit depressed about the state of the world and the Middle East in particular, I simply reminded myself that love is, actually, all around.

JOB JR.

The Bible itself records a good deal of bloodshed across the centuries, with such graphic detail that many are troubled by it. "Why all the violence in the Bible?" people ask. But notwithstanding the Bible's many tales of war and woe, the Lost Bible gives us a marvelous account of compassion in the World of Feeling. In a book excluded from the formal canon of Scripture, we read about a young man named Tobit, a hapless Israelite who resided in northern Galilee when the kingdom of Israel was conquered by the Syrians in 722 B.C.E. Here (in modern paraphrase) are the words of his account:

> Let me assert that I, Tobit, have always lived a truthful and righteous life, carrying out many deeds of charity on behalf of my people, who were deported along with me to Nineveh, capital of Assyria.

Tobit sounds in his description much like righteous Job, who was ethically upright and deeply pious in his faith. He explains that even though his tribe, Naphtali, was one of the ten tribes that broke away from David's kingdom, including the temple in Jerusalem, he would nonetheless journey to Jerusalem, the holy city, and present his offerings to the priests. He gave a special tithe of all of his income to widows and orphans, and to righteous converts to Judaism. Tobit explains (in continuing paraphrase):

> Though orphaned as a child, when I grew up, I married a woman from our own tribe, named Anna, who bore us a son—Tobiah.

At first Tobit gains favor among his captors. He is made purchasing agent on behalf of King Shalmaneser, but the king is succeeded by the wicked Sennacherib, who, after his abortive attempt to conquer Jerusalem, returns to Assyria enraged, slaying many Israelites as vengeance. Tobit takes it upon himself to bury the dead, as commanded by Israelite law. Tobit continues:

> King Sennacherib, who had no use for Israelite law, was told that I was the one who had buried the dead, and he decreed for me a death sentence. I fled the king and found a hiding place, though everything I had—all of my property—was confiscated.

Tobit is saved by the direct intercession of his nephew, a wise oracle in his own right named Ahiqar, who takes control of the administration of the kingdom upon the assassination of Sennacherib.

THE POWER OF HOPE

It is common to shake our heads and ask why bad things so often happen to good people. But over and over in the book of Tobit we are encouraged to believe that, in spite of catastrophic bad luck, good things happen to good people, resulting quite simply from love, compassion, and hope, in the World of Feeling. Tobit recounts (in contemporary reconstruction):

> And so I came back home, to Anna my wife, and Tobiah my son. We sat down to eat at our festival of rejoicing, called Shavuot, the Feast of Weeks. "But why should we keep our joy to ourselves?" I thought. I sent out my son, Tobiah to find a poor person from among our people and bring him back as our guest, to share in our joy. Tobiah went out, but he came back later, shouting, "Father! One of our people has been strangled to death! His body lies in the street, in the marketplace." I jumped up immediately, rushed out, and found the poor man's corpse. I brought him home, and after eating the meal in sadness, I buried him after sunset.
>
> My neighbors only made fun of me, even as I wept. "Will not he ever learn?" they cackled. "He was already sentenced to death for burying the dead. Now there he goes again!"
>
> Later that night, after bathing myself, I fell sound asleep by the courtyard wall. It was so hot I had not covered my face. Nor was I aware of the birds, who had perched themselves on the wall directly over my head. That night their droppings fell into my eyes. When I woke I could barely see. The doctors I visited told me I had cataracts. They applied various ointments, which only made my vision worse, until I was completely blind. Yet, in all my misfortune, never was compassion lacking. My nephew Ahiqar took care for me for two years, and my wife Anna went to work as a weaver, to help provide for us.

Mrs. Tobit, in her sacrificial service, sounds very much like Sitis—Mrs. Job—as she is presented in the Lost Bible's Testament of Job. She even ends up rebuking her husband, just as Sitis had rebuked Job. She asks rhetorically:

> "What is become of all your good deeds now?"

Tobit only groans, in Jobian fashion, and prays that he might die. Hope nonetheless springs eternal, even for Jobian characters. One of the greatest lessons in life is that hope is a good thing, perhaps even the best of things. And no good thing ever dies. However much we suffer, it is hope that keeps us alive. The disconsolate Tobit still has the audacity to hope, even if for nothing more than a decent and dignified burial. He also has hope for his family—his wife and his son—that they will be well provided for. He then dispatches Tobiah to bring back a great sum of money—the family treasure—which he had previously entrusted to a relative in the land of Media. He says to himself:

> "Why should not I summon Tobiah and tell him about this treasure, before I perish?"

This is the pivotal, turning point of the story. It is where the angelic world enters our own. In spite of the love and compassion of Ahiqar and Anna, if Tobit had remained in motionless despair, he might have gotten his wish and perished. But he does something—he acts—in hope. He dispatches his son, as an agent of hope, declaring:

> "You will be very wealthy, as long as you honor the Eternal."

In turn the Divine Presence (as we shall see) dispatches an angel—Raphael—as an agent of healing.

LOVE HEALS

In the meantime, another family relative, a beautiful young woman named Sarah, has lost seven consecutive husbands, prior to each marriage being consummated. She is accused by her own maid of having murdered them, but she declares that they have in fact been killed by a powerful demon named Asmodeus. Sarah, who is in despair like Tobit, first considers hanging herself, but she doesn't want to bring shame on her father. Like Tobit, she instead prays that she might die:

> "I had rather pass away and live no more than to be insulted like this.
> Why should I go on living, after I have lost seven husbands? Nevertheless,
> O Eternal, if there is any way, please do not end my life! Show me favor
> and mercy, and deliver me from these grave accusations!"

As with Tobit, there is hope in these words, not bitter resignation. The petitions of both are heard on high, and the angel Raphael is commissioned to come to their aid. Raphael's very name is divinely suited to the task. The Hebrew root *rapha* means to heal, and *El* is the Hebrew name for God: thus, "God heals."

The formative World of Feeling (*Yetzirah*), as envisioned by the mystical Kabbalists, is the realm where the angels reside. We may think of angels as literal extensions of the Divine Presence, as messengers from the supernatural world dispatched to perform specific functions in the material world. However, we can also think of the angels as symbolic representations of our own hopes and dreams, our fears and insecurities, our deepest subconscious desires. In this instance, Raphael represents the deepest hopes of our two protagonists, Tobit and Sarah.

The angel disguises himself in human form and meets young Tobiah, who is making active preparations for the long journey to Media. Our paraphrase continues:

> Tobiah went in search of someone to help him navigate the long roads to Media. Not long after he started out, he ran into Raphael, standing by the road, though he did not know he had encountered an angel. Tobiah asked, "Who are you?"
>
> "I am one of your fellow Israelites," the stranger answered. "I have come to this place as a worker."
>
> "Do you know how to get to Media?" asked Tobiah.
>
> "Of course!" answered the stranger. "I have traveled there often, and I know all the roads that lead there."
>
> "Wait right here," Tobiah snapped. "I must go and tell this to my father. I will pay you if you travel along with me as my guide."

GET BUSY LIVING

Studies have shown that motion—taking action—is the best kind of therapy. You either get busy living or get busy dying. In fact, among those who suffer from clinical depression, those who engage in physical activity, such as jogging, recover at roughly the same rate as those who take medication in the form of prescription drugs. The upshot of this research is that our feelings respond to movement and that motion and emotion are linked. As Raphael says to Tobit immediately before he and Tobiah set out:

> "Be courageous, for the Eternal plans to heal you. Buck up!"

The account relates in detail what happens as Tobiah and his angelic companion take to the road:

> The two men traveled on until dusk, camping on the banks of the Tigris River. Young Tobiah stepped into the river to bathe himself, when an enormous fish sprang from the water, trying to bite off his foot. Tobiah shrieked in panic, but Raphael said, "Grab the fish with your hands! Do not let it escape!"

Tobiah did as he was told and dragged the fish to the shore. Next, Raphael commanded, "Slice open the fish, and remove its heart, liver, and gall. Hold on to them at all times. They are good for making medicine. But discard the entrails."

Tobiah is given specific tasks to perform, and he must follow the instructions precisely. From this story we learn that love is hardly a static quality, nor is compassion. For love to be love, it must be given arms and legs.

LOVE'S LIMBS

Raphael and Tobiah continue on their journey, finally reaching Media. As the story progresses, we see that love in action yields divine reward:

After they arrived in Media, Raphael looked at the boy and said, "Listen, Tobiah! Tonight we need to lodge with one of your relatives, named Raguel. His only child is named Sarah. You happen to be her closest living relative, and you are therefore entitled to marry her and to inherit her father's entire estate. Bear in mind, Sarah is full of good sense, courage, and great beauty."

Tobiah's one objection—and a very substantial one—is that he has heard the fate of Sarah's previous husbands, all seven of them. Clearly, the story had gotten around. Undeterred in his purpose, the angelic visitor instructs Tobiah in burning the fish's liver and heart, using the smoke to expel the demon Asmodeus from the premises of the newlyweds:

"When the time comes to enter the bedroom, take the fish's heart and liver with you, and lay them on the embers, to produce incense. Whenever the demons smell the smoke, they will run off and never again trouble her."

Tobiah did as Raphael advised him. He became totally captivated by Sarah and fell madly in love with her.

The lesson is that in seeking to address the needs of someone else, the good son Tobiah has found true love for himself. He and Sarah are blissfully wed. Of course having an angel for a matchmaker never hurt anything.

Thereafter, Tobiah instructs Raphael on how to retrieve the treasure, which was deposited with his father's relative. The angelic tutor now does the bidding of his apprentice and lays claim to the money with a bond that Tobiah has carried with him. Having accomplished his task, Tobiah heads back to Nineveh, his new wife in tow, and bearing the family treasure. The narrative that follows is specially crafted for those who believe in happy endings:

> At that point, Tobiah smeared the fish's gall into his father's eyes. Though it caused them to sting, Tobiah was able to peel away the cataracts. Tobit, on seeing his son again, embraced him. "I see you, my son!" he shouted. "You are my light!"

THE UNVEILING

This is the opportune moment for Raphael to shed his disguise and show forth his identity:

> "My name is Raphael. I am one of seven angels who minister before the Divine Presence."

Mission accomplished, Raphael ascends back into heaven. Before his death, Tobit delivers his final prophetic instruction to his son—to abandon the capital of Nineveh before the city is taken and demolished. But as for Jerusalem, the city that has known so much bloodshed . . .

> "Jerusalem will be rebuilt one day, as the divine throne for eternity. I count it my greatest joy if even a few of my descendants live to see that glory and to give praise to the Eternal."

What do we learn from the book as a whole? Tobit's Tale demonstrates metaphorically how selfless devotion (Tobiah's, for his father) conquers diabolical ill fortune and results in true love. The bottom line is this: How we act affects how we feel. Getting out of the circle of self and opening ourselves to addressing the needs of others results in unexpected blessing—and the accompaniment of angels.

THE EXCLUSION

Not surprisingly, the book of Tobit was a literary "hit" among both Jewish and Christian communities in ancient times. It was composed sometime in the first few centuries B.C.E., and it floated around the Middle East and ancient Mediterranean regions for hundreds of years. Tobit was ultimately incorporated into the Greek translation of the Hebrew Bible, the Septuagint, dating to around 200 B.C.E. Thereafter, it became part of the official Catholic Bible, and tagged Apocrypha. Nonetheless, its original Semitic version (in Hebrew or Aramaic) disappeared, and it was subsequently known only in Greek. Consequently, we can rightly categorize it as part of the Lost Bible.

Amazingly, in the year 1955 fragments of the book of Tobit, in both Hebrew and Aramaic, were found among the manuscripts of the Dead Sea Scrolls. Clearly, many ancient Israelites regarded the book as Holy Writ. Why, then, was its original version allowed to crumble into dust? Why is it conspicuously absent from Jewish Bibles? Why exclude from the canon a book with such a powerful message as the book of Tobit?

The truth is, the keepers of the canon were often more concerned with fine points of theology than with the overall value of a message. In the case of Tobit, the true action hero is not a human being at all, but an angel, Raphael. This must have immediately caused the raising of eyebrows. In the late first century of the Common Era, at the rabbinical Council of Yavne, the Israelite sages were all too aware of pagan influences from Mediterranean lands, which had prompted a great fascination with intermediary forces between the divine world and the physical world.

The end result of this fascination involved endless stories regarding the role of angels in the operation of the universe. "Leave out the intermediaries!" declared the sages. "Let's diminish the role of angels wherever possible. After all, it is ultimately God who heals, not angels." Furthermore, a Johnny-come-lately text like Tobit lacked the literary clout and even the historical believability necessary to merit entrance into the hall of fame of sacred writings. In spite of its inclusion in the Septuagint, the authorized Greek translation of the Hebrew Scriptures, Tobit would be forever exiled from the list of books deemed holy for the Jewish people.

THE SECRET

Love, in all its manifestations, is an eternally popular theme, featured more often than hope. In truth, however, we might want to stress hope even more than love, for it is hope that energizes love, hope that lends love its spirit, hope that transforms despair into healing. As much as love, if not more than love, hope is the emotion that brings forth motion. It is a balm of wellness dispatched on angels' wings.

"Love and desire are the spirit's wings to great deeds," wrote Goethe. But with the help of the Lost Bible, we can make "Love and *hope*" the compound subjects of that sentence. Hope is strength, courage, fortitude. As long as there is hope, there is reason to go on. Tobit might have sat in bitter resignation, reconciled to an inescapable fate, but he did not. As long as we draw breath, there is hope for the future, and hope generates healing. The Lost Bible teaches, through obscure characters named Tobit and his son Tobiah, that there is no adversity that cannot be conquered, as long as we have hope.

Just as important, hope has a dynamic ally in love. "Love conquers all," said Virgil. But when love is combined with hope, the entire angelic world is enlisted on our behalf. Heaven itself is unleashed. Obstacles are flattened; adversaries are neutralized.

Never underestimate either the dynamic of hope, or the power of love. Reach out with your feelings, *move* in consonance with them, and let your spirit soar. You will find that love really is all around.

CHAPTER 16

Good Grief! Barukh the Bemoaner

While grief is fresh, every attempt to divert only irritates. You must wait till it be digested.
—SAMUEL JOHNSON

Even his griefs are a joy long after to one that remembers all that he wrought and endured.
—HOMER

There is a time for everything, the book of Ecclesiastes piously asserts: "A time for birth and a time for dying . . . a time for killing and a time for healing, a time for demolishing and a time for building, a time for crying and a time for laughing, a time for mourning and a time for dancing . . . a time for loving and a time for hating, a time for making war and a time for peace" (Ecclesiastes 3:2-4, 8, author's translation). In the World of Feeling, opposites are linked. That is what the biblical text is telling us. Birth and death, building and demolishing, love and hate, joy and grief. Moreover, nothing in the World of Feeling is more instructive than learning how to mourn. We wouldn't be able to taste the fullness of joy if we had never tasted the tears of sorrow.

Arguably, the one thing we Westerners know least about is mourning. We are trained from earliest childhood to hold back our tears, to retain our composure, to restrain ourselves. Males in our culture are especially reared in the "don't want to show it" syndrome. To be a man certainly means not being allowed to cry. Attending a funeral in the Western world generally involves sitting in a room full of extremely disconsolate people, who aren't allowed to fully express how they feel. The most one will hear is the sound of silence.

But when I lived and worked in the town of Kiryat Shmonah, in northern Galilee, I experienced grief in ways I had never before encountered. There is in Jewish tradition a prescribed period of intense mourning following a person's death. It is termed *Shivah*, meaning "seven," inasmuch as it lasts for a period of seven full days. When the mother of my neighbor and friend Shalom died, I got to witness a *Shivah* Middle Eastern style.

GRIEF IN GALILEE

My friends lived in a modest flat in a typical Galilean apartment complex, constructed of drab, poured concrete, but richly decorated inside with modern Middle Eastern amenities. The family was close-knit, and the extended family all lived in the same town— Kiryat Shmonah—many within walking distance of each other. Like most members of his community, Shalom had maintained an open-door policy. Neighbors and friends were always welcome, without invitation. A mere knock on the door any evening on the week would bring out beer, pretzels, nuts, cakes, and pastries, and the schmoozing would begin, punctuated with humorous stories, laughter, and joy all around.

But during this period of seven doleful days, I found the entire family, literally on the floor, their backs against the wall. They looked perfectly disheveled, unkempt, and unshaven, their clothes rent as a sign of the depth of their sorrow. It was a complete contradiction of the usual tone of that household, and I recalled the words of the ancient prophet: "Clothe yourselves in sackcloth, and roll around in the dust! Mourn deeply . . . wail intensely" (Jeremiah 6:26, author's translation). The weeping, the wails, the moans were all quite demonstrative, in total contrast with more modern, Western ways. The expression of sadness was actively encouraged. The usual dessert delicacies had been replaced by some kind of strong smelling fish, which I preferred not to taste. All mirrors in the house were also covered—another traditional practice of mourning.

My system went into shock at the sight of this spectacle; yet I thought to myself that the ancients who devised such practices were probably quite a bit wiser than we sophisticated moderns. They required by religious law that the family members be together for seven full days, not left to painful solitude. They encouraged the venting of every sentiment, as a kind of emotional purgation. They understood implicitly that grief is only human, and to hold it back is to deny our humanity.

THE SCRIBE ON THE SIDELINES

When we vent our grief, we pave the way, metaphysically, for even greater joy in the future. Little wonder that the Lost Bible should give us several books largely devoted to lamentation. They are attributed to the little-known and underappreciated amanuensis of the prophet Jeremiah, named Barukh.[9] We have all heard of Jeremiah, who lived in ancient Jerusalem and thundered a message of woe against a population so wayward that he deemed it worthy of destruction.

In truth, Jeremiah didn't personally inscribe the words of his famous prophecies. He dictated them to his lieutenant and confidant, Barukh the scribe. Researchers have long known that Barukh was more than just a copyist. He was a master wordsmith who seems to have reworked Jeremiah's prophecies with such literary flair that they were immortalized. Some have even noticed a striking similarity between certain sections of the book of Jeremiah and precise passages from the book of Deuteronomy. Others have gone so far as to suggest that the editor if not the author of the book of Deuteronomy was not Moses, as commonly claimed, but Barukh, the scribe of Jeremiah. But if Barukh were such an important figure in ancient Jerusalem, why did he write no books of his own?

The answer is, he did. The Lost Bible gives us no less than four books to which Barukh's name is appended. As a contemporary of Jeremiah, Barukh witnessed the horrifying devastation of Jerusalem at the hands of the Babylonians in 586 B.C.E. This was the end of the line for the freedom and independence of ancient Judea. It was a turning point for the Israelites as a people. For that terrible year also witnessed the complete destruction of the great temple of Solomon, which prominently occupied a rocky outcropping known as Mount Zion, the most sacred piece of real estate on the planet. Barukh's first book consists of a great lamentation over the fallen shrine. It epitomizes the feelings of a people devastated with grief.

Bear in mind, the destruction of Jerusalem and the holy temple was the equivalent of 9/11 for the Israelites as a nation. The Greek tragedian Euripides wrote, "What greater grief than the loss of one's native land?" Barukh gives vent to a uniquely Israelite expression of grief as only he could. But having vented, he does something more. His lamentation is followed by a hymn, extolling wisdom personified. The hymn is in turn followed by a series of predictions of the future, full of hope and glory.

Clearly, the value of lamentation is that expressing the fullness of grief opens the door for the future. With amazing clarity, Barukh anticipates a time when Jerusalem will be rebuilt, when the foundations of the temple will be established anew, when song and laughter will again be heard in the streets of Jerusalem: "The song of joy, the song of gladness, the song of the bridegroom, the song of the bride." Barukh's prophecy of hope would in fact be fulfilled within a century of his uttering it, for the Israelites, who were carried off into captivity in Babylonia, did in fact return, by special fiat of a new emperor, Cyrus the Great.

They rebuilt the fallen walls of the city. They erected a new temple on the ruins of the old. Mourning was turned into gladness. It is part of the circle of life that new things are built on the ruins of the old, that joy springs forth from the valley of despair.

FAST FORWARD

On May 14, 1948, President Harry Truman announced that the United States would become the first nation to recognize the new nation of Israel, his announcement coming eleven minutes after the new nation was declared. With the possible exception of Jimmy Carter (like Truman, a Baptist), Truman was perhaps the best Bible scholar among all our twentieth-century presidents. At the time he made his decision, he said that perhaps he was the new Cyrus.

David McCullough, in his wonderful biography of Truman, notes that Truman's own secretary of state, the formidable George Marshall, opposed the recognition of Israel and even told Truman he would vote against him in the upcoming election if he recognized the fledgling state. Another advisor, Clark Clifford, took a different tack, and quoted Deuteronomy 1:8: "See, I have set before you this land. Go and take possession of the land which the Eternal swore to your ancestors, to Abraham, to Isaac and to Jacob, to give to them and to their descendants after them" (author's translation). McCullough writes:

> He [Truman] felt great satisfaction in what he had been able to do for the Jewish people, and was deeply moved by their expressions of gratitude, then and for years to come. When the Chief Rabbi of Israel, Isaac Helevi Herzog, called at the White House, he told Truman, "God put you in your mother's womb so you would be the instrument to bring the rebirth of Israel after two thousand years."
>
> "I thought he was overdoing things," remembered David Niles, "but when I looked over at the President, tears were running down his cheeks."[10]

Barukh would admonish: If you run from pain, if you hide from grief, you short-circuit that process. Instead, hold the grief to your bosom. Vent it, write it, even sing it. Then let it go, and that very process will fill your heart with hope. History will deliver its verdict. The book of 2 Barukh likewise memorializes the national grief over the destruction of the temple.

ANGELS OF THE LOST ARK

It not only recounts the grief, it hyperbolizes it, making specific prophecies regarding the sacred temple and the Ark of the Covenant. We read (in modern paraphrase):

> As fate would have it, the Babylonian army encircled and besieged the city of Jerusalem. It was evening time, and I, Barukh, went off by myself. I stood by an oak tree and grieved over the fate of my people, lamenting their enslavement. All of a sudden I felt the presence of a powerful spirit, which literally lifted me up above Jerusalem's walls. I saw four angels with my own eyes. They held fiery torches and stood at the city's four

corners. Then I saw a fifth angel coming down from above and saying, "Don't set fire to the city until I give you the signal; for I have been sent first to prophesy to the whole earth and then to bring upon the world everything that has been ordained." Next, I saw this angel go down into the temple and take away the curtain before the Holy of Holies, along with the Ark of the Covenant, the mercy seat, the two tablets of the Ten Commandments, the sacred priestly garments, the incense altar, and the forty-eight sacred stones worn by the high priest. He carted off the sacred vessels of the tabernacle and shouted with a loud voice: "Listen, O earth, to the words of the Eternal. Accept whatever I entrust to you. Watch over them until the End of Days, until you are given the command to restore them all. No strangers must ever be allowed to possess them, since someday, Jerusalem itself will be restored, to endure forever." When the angel spoke those words, a fissure opened in the earth and swallowed up all of those sacred objects.

It is not coincidental that Barukh's intense grief would be accompanied by some of the most stirring messages of spiritual renewal ever uttered. The idea that the sacred objects of the temple—including the famous Ark of the Covenant—have been stored away, in a cleft in the earth, for some time in the future, when they will be revealed for all humanity, is a notion popularized by Hollywood. But its roots are to be found, not in the biblical text itself, but in the pages of the Lost Bible. It is here that we discover the allegorical significance of the Lost Ark, namely, that the depth of grief opens true vision, to see beyond our situation to the promise of restoration.

In a larger sense the destruction of the temple is a metaphor for grief, both national and personal. In physical time and space, Zion's enemies have besieged her. But on a supernatural plane, it is not some terrible enemy who sets fire to the city; it is the angels themselves. The torches of lamentation are lit by agents of the divine will. How comforting it is to learn that the loss we feel when tragedy strikes is part of a purpose and a plan that we cannot see. To be sure, our character is forged in grief's crucible. Death is universal; the bonds of life are fragile. We are destined to lose those closest to us, but the essence of our lives is delivered to posterity, kept alive in the sacred memories of those who come after us. The ancients believed that our souls, like the temple vessels, are preserved for eternity. The body dies, but the spirit goes on. The Ark of the Covenant, like the human soul, is never really lost. It is merely waiting for a future unveiling. C. S. Lewis wrote, "For this I bless you as the ruin falls. The pains you give me are more precious than all other gains."

THE POETRY OF GRIEF

Barukh declares, "Therefore, my destiny is to mourn for Zion." He is the voice of a people devastated with grief, holding back nothing in the sheer emotional impact of his words. In deeply emotive language, pain is transformed into poetry (presented here in modern paraphrase):

> Happy is the one who was never born
> As well as those who have already died.
> Woe to us who yet survive,
> For we have witnessed the agony of Zion;
> We have seen what has happened to Jerusalem.
> Let me summon the Sirens, to come from the ocean;
> Let me call Lilith, to approach from the desert.
> Let me call the demons and dragons to come from the forests.
> Wake up, and clothe yourselves with grief.
> Chant dirges along with me;
> Lament and mourn with me . . .
> Let the vine produce no more wine;
> For there will be no more offerings in Zion . . .
> Let the sun shine no more;
> Let the moonlight be extinguished.
> Why should any light fall
> When Zion is in darkness?

Does Barukh really mean all of this? The essence of the ancient faith was supposed to be the celebration of life, not a fixation with death. But the exaggeration, the hyperbole, is a necessary part of the grieving process.

The resulting catharsis is liberating. It is the way back to health, encouragement, and level-headedness. But something more results—a firm hope in a new age at the end of days when every wrong will be put right, the Messiah will rule over a world in which sorrow and mourning are no more, and the lion will lie down with the lamb. If it were not for the intense grief experienced by a nation going through a 9/11 trauma, it is doubtful whether the concept of a Messianic Age would have been born at all. We can make a good case that the very word *Messiah* came forth from the crucible of suffering. Grief expressed, therefore, is beneficial, for it has led to the deepest and most powerful spiritual pronouncements in history. As Barukh writes (continuing our paraphrase):

> Above all, don't let your hearts be troubled. Instead, we should all wait
> with expectancy, since all of the promises made to us will surely come to

pass. Don't expect to find present-day pleasure among the nations of our exile; but remember everything promised for the end. The days and the seasons will pass away together, along with all those whose eyes are on the present. But at the end of days, when everyone is judged, a mighty ruler will be revealed. You should fill your hearts with the things you used to believe, so that you are not judged doubly—being taken prisoner in this world and punished in the world to come. For everything that is part of this world—in the present, in the past, and in the future—is adulterated, so that evil doesn't really appear to be evil, and the good doesn't really appear to be good. But the health of this age is becoming diseased, and the strength of this age is becoming weak.

There is no equivocation in these words, no hesitancy or moral relativism. There is strength, clarity, and certainty. Frequently, those who possess the greatest moral clarity (who understand good as good and evil as evil) are also those who best understand suffering and are most acquainted with bitterest grief.

BARUKH, TAKE THREE—THE TEMPLE "UP THERE"

The book of 3 Barukh, like the earlier two, begins with mourning (again, in paraphrase):

> I, Barukh, was grieved in my soul, crying inside, when I thought about my people and about what King Nebuchadnezzar of Babylon did to my city. . . . But an angel came to me and said, "Stop upsetting God! Listen, and I will reveal mysteries to you that you never imagined."

Third Barukh goes a step further than the other accounts, depicting a supernatural temple, already constructed, in the heavenly realm. Many mysteries are shown to the scribe, as he is taken on a supernatural trip through the cosmos:

> The angel came and took me upward into the heavens. In the first level of heaven, he brought me to enormous doors, and said, "Let's go inside!"

Importantly, there is no divine decree that this temple must replace the ruined sanctuary. There is no need for a new temple to be built at all, for the heavenly temple is an even greater reality. What is the message here? Even though the physical temple is gone—destroyed by the Babylonian invaders—it is preserved in the divine realm. In other words, grieve, but let it go; for there is a greater reality beyond. Do not let your grief turn into despair, for there are wonderful things in store for the future, of which you know nothing. Our view of time is limited, so that hope eludes us. But in the larger scheme of things, our present deprivation is only a blip on history's radar screen. This too shall pass; all will be well.

There is one more book attributed to the scribe, 4 Barukh, which depicts the restoration of Jerusalem and the temple sacrifice, not in some distant Messianic Age, but in the here and now. Barukh himself is presented as a kind of mediator between Jeremiah and the Almighty, and is rightly seen on a higher level than even the prophet.

THE EXCLUSION

Why were the books of Barukh not included in the canon of Holy Writ? For one thing, the ancient sages were likely concerned that elevating the writings and the person of Barukh would come at the expense of the prophet Jeremiah. By the time the Scriptures were canonized, Jeremiah had already attained such a presence, such national popularity, that anything perceived as lowering his status would clearly not be in their interest.

But there was another problem, perhaps just as fundamental. Doubtless, the keepers of the canon did not believe that Barukh wrote the books attributed to him. Modern researchers date 1 Barukh no later than 150 B.C.E.. While no firm date has been placed on how early it may have been written, the notion that the historical Barukh (who lived in the five hundreds before the Common Era) was the author is almost universally repudiated. The style and content of the writing seems to reflect a much later time than the precise period of the temple's destruction.

The problem is even more acute when it comes to 2 Barukh, a manuscript originally composed in Hebrew but preserved in Syriac. Here, the depiction of the temple's destruction more closely resembles the destruction of the Second Temple in 70 of the Common Era, than the destruction of the First Temple, in 586 B.C.E. (The Second Temple had been renovated and refurbished by King Herod the Great, so that it was truly one of the wonders of the ancient world.) For this reason, the dominant theory is that the book dates to the early second century of the Common Era. Its real author may in fact have been one of the very rabbinic sages (assembled at the Council of Yavne) who fixed the canon of the Scriptures. Very curious indeed.

In the case of 3 Barukh, we have a Greek composition, dating to sometime between the first and third centuries of the Common Era. The earliest manuscript in existence, however, is from the thirteenth century. As it stands, the book is Christian in its style and in some of its contents. Nevertheless, as with so many other ancient writings, it likely rests on a much earlier Jewish source, stricken from the sacred canon but preserved as a Christian writing. But it never gained enough prominence to merit inclusion in the Christian canon.

Fourth Barukh came down to us in Greek, its earliest manuscript dating from the tenth century, but it was almost certainly a Hebrew writing, composed in the first two centuries of the Common Era. Certainly, the heavy emphasis on Barukh at the expense of Jeremiah was not acceptable to the keepers of the canon, and, as with so many other books, it didn't stand a chance.

BETTER THAN SACRIFICE

In any case, the significance of the Barukh tradition should not be forgotten. The loss of the temple at the hands of Rome's brutal legions was the most devastating blow ever to impact the Israelites as a people. Yet, even in the wake of this most painful of 9/11 moments, the people gained something. The temple was never rebuilt after the Roman destruction. Even to this day it is only a memory. In its place a religion developed which did not need the blood of endless sacrificial animals to make atonement for the people's transgressions. Instead, the very sages who barred Barukh from the sacred canon declared that "acts of lovingkindness" shall atone for the sins of the nation. That important and revolutionary stress on ethics and good deeds, rather than the blood sacrifice of animals, was a direct outgrowth of the worst catastrophe in the nation's history. Not such a bad outcome after all, was it?

In the final analysis, the identity of the author(s) of the books of Barukh doesn't really matter. What matters is the message the books convey—of hope and joy out of the depth of despair, of mourning as a prelude to a brighter day, of the revolutionary benefits of grief.

THE SECRET

As Barukh could testify, learning how to grieve constructively is just as important as learning how to rejoice. Psychology has identified five stages of grief: shock, denial, anger, bargaining, and acceptance. It all begins with shock—a feeling of distress, numbness, even psychological collapse. It is utter trauma. Our eyes become glazed. We have no response at all. There is literally nothing to say.

Next, we enter into denial. We refuse to accept that this is happening. It simply cannot be. It is all some kind of bitter illusion, a bad dream from which we will soon awaken.

As reality begins to set in, we next give expression to anger. We may choose to internalize it—not a very good option—or we may express it, often shaking our fists at the unfeeling universe, pointing an accusing finger even at God.

Fortunately, however, God has been around the block a few times; God can take our anger, and says to us, "It's all right."

We also engage in more than a bit of negotiation, bargaining with God, who has clearly made a mistake in allowing certain things to happen. "If I do this, perhaps God will do that. Perhaps even the unfeeling universe will somehow change its mind, and restore what has been lost."

Finally, we reach the stage of acceptance, the ultimate destination of the process, the place to which our grief inexorably leads us. Our loss is final; the damage is irreparable. And yet we realize, life goes on. There is power in acceptance. Our pain becomes a building block of true character. We grow through our grief and ultimately beyond it.

Grief in the end has positive, transformative value. That is what the books of Barukh underscore. In the words of an old folk song:

> I walked a mile with pleasure,
> She chattered all the way,
> Leaving me none the wiser
> With all she had to say.
>
> I walked a mile with sorrow
> Never a word said she,
> But O, the things I learned from her,
> When sorrow walked with me.

CHAPTER 17

Teach Your Children: Isaac's Living Will

*We need to teach the next generation of children from Day One that they
are responsible for their lives. Mankind's greatest gift, also its greatest curse, is that
we have free choice. We can make our choices built from love or from fear.*
—ELISABETH KUBLER-ROSS, SWISS-AMERICAN PSYCHIATRIST

*You, who are on the road,
Must have a code that you can live by.
And so, become yourself,
Because the past is just a goodbye.
Teach your children well.*
—CROSBY, STILLS, AND NASH

The traditional Bible tells us the story of Isaac, Abraham's son, who, when he grew to be advanced in years, became blind and senile. In his deteriorated condition, he mistakenly conferred his blessing, not upon his firstborn son, Esau, but rather upon the younger Jacob. But as I pored over the musty volumes in that quaint old library atop Mount Zion, I discovered details missing in the standard account, but present in a particular book of the Lost Bible. In a long-forgotten manuscript, I discovered that Isaac was later met by the archangel Michael, who took him on a heavenly journey and restored his sight during the process. It is all part of an incredible document purporting to be the final teaching and instruction of the venerable patriarch. It is called the Testament of Isaac, and it conveys important messages to the descendants of the biblical hero. We might think of it as the quintessential ancient example of a living will. It is all about teaching our children and teaching them well—perhaps the most important task in all of life.

It is often said that the words spoken on the deathbed of a parent or loved one remain forever with those who must go on. In Jewish mysticism, called Kabbalah, it is taught that every single breath is not one that we take but one that is given. The art of breathing, like life itself, is a gift from above. Dying, rather than a grim veil, shrouding us in sadness, may be conceived as God's last kiss, the moment when the breath of life is retrieved by the One who dispatched it, on loan. The dying process need not be lonely, for we leave a living family behind, joined inextricably with the family that has gone before us. Why not, then, use the instrument of a last will and testament, not to spell out, beyond the distribution of assets, the behavior of the heirs? The concept has caught on in modern times, with the development of what is called the ethical or living will. In truth, however, the living will is just about as old as the proverbial hills; and the Testament of Isaac is a prime example.

THE EXCLUSION

Did the great biblical patriarch Isaac, the son of Abraham, born miraculously to his barren wife Sarah, actually write this last will and testament? No, say most researchers. The earliest texts of the book are in Coptic and date from the ninth century, though linguistic clues imbedded in the text suggest that it was most likely originally composed in Greek. The syntax and literary style don't look Hebrew at all, and scholars suggest that the book was probably produced in Egypt, where many writings of a mystical and Gnostic flavor flourished. Egypt was of course an early center of Christian Gnosticism, and one important element of the book as we now have it suggests that it was the product of early Christianity, emerging on the ancient landscape in the second century of the Common Era. We find the following remarkable prophecy in the mouth of Isaac who declares to his son Jacob (in modern paraphrase):

> "One day the Messiah Jesus will be born from one of your descendants,
> a young virgin known as Mary. He will be the incarnation of God."

At this point we need to take a very deep breath and realize that what we have in this passage is either the most astounding prophetic pronouncement ever recorded in human history, or that this prophecy is artfully placed in the mouth of Isaac by a later anonymous Christian writer/editor. As far as modern researchers are concerned, the latter is clearly the case. Certainly, many early Christians sincerely believed that this work was in fact a product of the patriarch Isaac. But the keepers of the Christian canon, struggling as they were with an influx of Gnostic ideas they considered heretical, had no use for one more book out of Gnostic Egypt, whose authorship seemed dubious.

Nevertheless, any serious student of the Lost Bible must put on a detective cap and sort through the pieces of the puzzle, determined to get to the bottom of things and discover the truth about who wrote what, when, and where. The fact is, the Testament of Isaac bears a strong resemblance to the Testament of Abraham, and was likely fashioned on its pattern. Moreover, there is a strong possibility that this testament, like its predecessor, was originally a Jewish work that was later picked up by Christians and edited to reflect the values of early Gnostic Christianity.

Why was the original Jewish version of the Testament of Isaac never accepted in the Hebrew Scriptures? For one thing, it was probably written too late, after the Hebrew canon had already been fixed. Furthermore, even as a Jewish writing, it was probably composed in Greek, as a product of Hellenistic Judaism, which flourished in the Mediterranean regions outside of the land of Israel. Hellenistic Judaism was a syncretistic blend of Jewish and Greek concepts, emphasizing many mystical experiences looked on with a dubious eye by the rationalistic rabbinic sages. But as with other writings of the Lost Bible, we shouldn't dismiss Isaac's last will and testament simply because it is not likely to be the authentic product of Isaac. Truth be told, most modern researchers doubt whether Moses was in fact the author of the first five books of the Bible, Genesis through Deuteronomy. Yet, few would cast doubt on the inspirational value of those books.

THE POWER TO HEAL

All right, so Isaac didn't write it. But the text is nonetheless quite ancient and deserves serious consideration. In fresh, modern paraphrase, the text may be reconstructed as follows:

> Isaac, the patriarch and son of Abraham, composed the following last will and testament, addressing it to his son Jacob and many others who were assembled together. Isaac declared: "Listen, my loved ones, because the teaching I am about to convey is more than instruction. It is medicine, containing the power to heal."

The Lost Bible makes no bones about the fact that words have power. They can inflict great damage, but they can also heal. Isaac's teaching, straight from the World of Feeling, conveys a curative dynamic. He continues:

> "The divine principles are eternal and unchanging. Don't just listen with human ears, but also from the bottom of your hearts. For it is written, 'You have been given a solid teaching about what a person should be like inside. . . .'
>
> "And so it was, when the day approached for me to leave my body and go on to the next world, that the Eternal dispatched Michael, the head of all the angels, the very one who had earlier been sent to Father Abraham. Michael greeted me, saying, 'Peace to you, Isaac, the chosen son.' As I

fell on the ground, I noticed that the angel looked like Father Abraham himself.

"I declared, 'In looking at you, it is as though I have seen the face of the Creator!'

"But the angel replied, 'Dear Isaac, I have been sent from the presence of the Eternal to guide you heavenward, so that you can be with your father and all the departed righteous ones. Abraham has been resting until now, but is waiting for you to join him. You, along with your father Abraham and your son Jacob, shall sit on three thrones in the divine realm, and all the world shall call you patriarchs.'

"I, Isaac, asked in amazement, 'Are you Abraham my father?'

"But the angel answered, 'I am not your father though I am the one who attends to him on high. I am here to tell you to rejoice, for your passing will not be accompanied by sickness. It will be with ease and not pain. Your soul shall move from prison into freedom, to endless light and joy. As for now, you must make up your will and set your affairs in order.' After the angel delivered this message he ascended upward. I, Isaac, just kept staring, deep in meditation. At that moment, Jacob came into my room."

LINE UPON LINE

As the story continues, we are told how word spreads of Isaac's divine encounter. An amazed multitude soon gathers to listen to his teaching and receive his life-giving admonitions. The crowd knows well that Isaac had lost his sight in his old age, a fact related in the traditional Bible. But Isaac now explains that his sight has been restored during his otherworldly experience. Thereafter, Isaac begins his living will. He holds forth, declaring the following, as it were, "principle upon principle, line upon line" (Isaiah 28:10, author's translation):

- If you get angry, don't allow words of slander to come from your mouth.

- Never boast with pride.

- Don't speak with vulgar language.

- Keep your body pure; treat it right, as though it is a holy temple, making sure that you are clean and hygienic.

- Treat your speech seriously, not as sport.

- Never desire things that don't belong to you.

- Make sure you are pure and undefiled before approaching the altar.

- Keep your thoughts separate from the rest of the world.

- Think of yourselves as constantly in the Eternal's presence, at the altar.

- Don't just make offerings, but make peace among all people.

- Don't kill with the tongue (the corollary of killing with the sword).

- Don't remain angry till sunset.

- Don't accept too much praise.

- Don't rejoice at your enemies' downfall.

The assembled multitude gasps in amazement at Isaac's words. They are so simple, yet so profound. And, as the heart of Isaac's last will and testament, they will always be remembered. Make no mistake, the secret of making a better world comes about from the inside out. How will the world be redeemed? Person by person, heart by heart, as we are transformed in the World of Feeling.

FROM THE INSIDE OUT

Soon afterward, we are told, the angel Michael returns and escorts Isaac on high. This is when Isaac is shown the fate of the unrighteous. Granted, the judgments are grisly, perhaps too much so for modern sensibilities. Nevertheless, the Testament of Isaac seizes on a unique concept in the development of religious thought, for the judgments are not depicted as the result of evil deeds per se, as though there is some kind of divine scorecard in heaven, with points added and subtracted on the basis of whether one is naughty or nice. Rather, evil is seen as a direct consequence of bad attitudes and impure thoughts, generated from within and intimately connected with the World of Feeling. Isaac declares:

> "I witnessed a man walking along, among a group of animals. Suddenly, the animals moved away and left the man alone. At that point several lions pounced on him, tearing him to pieces and swallowing him. After they chewed him, they spit him out again, and he came back together. Soon afterwards, another group of mammals descended on him and did the same thing, whereupon he was spat out and returned whole. I asked the angel what he had done to deserve such punishment. The angel answered, 'This person died, having been angry with his neighbor for a period of five hours. Therefore, he must suffer from five persecutors, who punish him for an entire year for each hour he remained angry with his neighbor.'"

The important point is not to understand what hell is like or even whether hell exists. Even if we assume that the only hell is the one we make for ourselves, on earth, we learn from the Testament of Isaac that hell is born from the World of Feeling. The anger we habor within us tends to grow and fester, becoming like a ravenous lion tearing us apart.

Pundits have commented that in today's world we are witnessing a general coarsening of our culture. We exercise the free expression of attitudes and feelings, and what results is a very uncivil society, which inflicts grave emotional harm on its members. We are accustomed to saying, "I can't help what I feel!" But Isaac, in his last will and testament, seems to say, "Oh yes you can! If you nourish the right thoughts, you can even tell yourself what to feel, and thereby avoid the beast of anger."

AT LAST, FATHER ABRAHAM

Finally, Isaac is escorted onward, to meet Abraham, his father. Abraham offers his own discourse, in which he admonishes:

> "Everyone should endeavor to produce their own last will and testament, including their life stories. Whoever does this, and behaves with kindness to others, will be endowed with my strength and with the Divine Presence, for prosperity in this world."

This advice, coming from the greatest patriarch of all, is down to earth and practical. Beyond leaving a will, write a living will, and include the story of your life. After all, there is no greater lesson for children than the example of the parents. That example—that testimony—begotten in the World of Feeling, shapes the lives of your descendants for generations to come. It makes all the difference between living in heaven and living in hell.

IMAGINE . . .

Is there a hell? Is there a heaven, such as shown to Isaac? I can only recount my own experience when I first laid eyes on the terrain due east of Jerusalem, known as the Wilderness of Judea. This landscape, nestled in the great Jordan River Rift Valley, is breathtaking in its aspect. I often thought of it as a meeting place between heaven and earth. I could not help but believe that some unseen hand must have fashioned this terrain—from its terraced limestone cliffs to its deep ravines and canyons—to elevate us from our mundane existence, to hear the voice of the Eternal. That more than anything is the essence of heaven. It is hardly coincidental that this was where the ancient Essenes made their abode, on the northwest shore of this bitter lake. I readily understood why they spent their days copying, not only the Bible, but the Lost Bible as well.

But as I drove south along the Dead Sea, to the most southern appendage of this ancient lake, the landscape took on a distinctly different appearance. The floor of the valley was literally covered with deposits of salt, sometimes forming pillars, which remind the visitor of how Lot's wife was turned into a pillar of salt for looking back at Sodom (Genesis 19:23-26). The heat was stifling; the air was filled with the pungent smell of sulfur. Somewhere in this location, we are told, the ancient cities of perdition, Sodom and Gomorrah, were destroyed by fire and brimstone (vv. 23-25). In that merciless environment I distinctly remember thinking to myself: Hell is no illusion; I'm looking at it.

John Lennon once admonished:

> Imagine there's no heaven;
> It's easy if you try.
> No hell below us
> Above us only sky.

By contrast the Lost Bible declares, with bold audacity, just the opposite. There is much more than sky up there, for our ancestors look down upon us continually, to see whether we have heeded their words. Imagine . . . what the world would be like if we paid attention.

THE SECRET

Feelings are elusive movements of energy; they arise from mental constructs. Why then should we worry about our emotions, or how we feel toward others? After all, aren't there more important considerations in life, like making a buck? Or so we think. In point of fact, our feelings do interfere by imposing themselves onto our every relationship and transaction. There is an important principle here: Every action, good or bad, begins with an attitude. Feelings are like fire, both our friend and our enemy, and we must understand them in order to put them to their best and most productive uses. We must master them, and not let them master us.

The Testament of Isaac invites us to imagine our ancestors or departed loved ones looking down on us from the hereafter. Imagine the kind of thoughts, feelings, and attitudes they would like us to harbor. Recall the negative feelings we have toward others and how we might transform them, allowing them to rise, but then letting them pass. We can visualize negativity as a vacuum, waiting to be filled with positive attitudes. We can imagine . . . a door on high being opened to those attitudes, and imagine them flowing into our deepest being. Finally, we can imagine . . . the great patriarchs, looking down upon us, and smiling.

PART IV

THE WORLD OF DOING (ASIYAH)

A Hero's Tale

The mid-1980s found me in a small metropolis in northern Galilee called Kiryat Shmona, nestled in a valley between a broad range of hills to the west and the northern tributaries of the Jordan River to the east. Kiryat Shmona had for years suffered the ignominy of being the target of periodic rocket attacks, launched from just over the Lebanese border to the north and the west. As I have noted, my residence in Israel in those days was explained by the fact that I had been hired to work for a ragtag American television station located in a little town, Marjayoun, in southern Lebanon. My daily routine involved commuting over a hostile border, sporting a flak jacket, into what in those days amounted to a war zone. The mission: to broadcast family-oriented television programming from all our brave little stations, across the troubled landscape of Lebanon, Syria, and northern Israel, as far as Cyprus.

Working the night shift, it fell to me to broadcast a variety of sports events, old movies, and American Westerns. I liked to boast that I was the man who brought *Bonanza* to the Middle East. These were difficult times. The Israeli army, which had been engaged in combat all the way to Beirut, was now steadily withdrawing toward its own borders, while the situation all around slowly deteriorated. The specter of terror was omnipresent, and driving along the dilapidated roads of the Lebanese countryside, I never knew what kind of threat might be lurking around the next corner.

There were frequent electrical outages, plunging our small broadcast facility into darkness. Since there was no one else on duty, I would have to grab my flashlight, rush out to the tool shed in the back, and crank up an enormous electrical generator. It made a frightfully deafening sound, as though it were going to explode, but it got the broadcast system up and running, and it got Hoss Cartwright back in the saddle again.

Fortunately, those of us on staff received valuable assistance on occasion, from an American named Bill, who lived not far from us in Marjayoun, Lebanon. Bill had acquired technical and engineering experience with TV broadcasting back in the States, and whenever our technological glitches became more than we could handle—an almost daily occurrence—one of us would grab a walkie-talkie and holler at Bill. Whatever the problem, he always seemed to come up with an instant fix.

Bill was not an official member of our staff, however. He had other fish to fry. He had been working back in the American Midwest when he kept hearing and reading about the Lebanese civil war and all the children who had been orphaned during years of relentless fighting. But shaking his head, shedding a tear, and saying a prayer wasn't enough for him. He had to act. He entered the World of Doing.

He talked it over with his family, packed up his household, and brought his wife and children to Lebanon. Property in this battered country could be had for a song, and Bill managed to buy up a sprawling residence, turning it into his own private orphanage. He began inviting little Lebanese children who had lost both parents to come and live with him and his family. It was barely a dent in the humanitarian crisis that had developed in Lebanon, but to those orphaned children he made all the difference in the world. He was doing his part to change the planet, one child at a time. While deeply admiring what he had done, many of us were incredulous as to how he could make such a sacrifice. "In the Bible it says, 'Go ye!'" Bill used to say. "Nowhere does it say 'Come back.'"

In time Bill started getting death threats from local terrorists, alleging that he was somehow establishing a foreign outpost on Lebanese soil. Bill just laughed them off. Back in America he had lived for himself. Now, for the first time in his life, he was doing something for others. One evening during devotions, a knock came at the door. When Bill answered, several armed terrorists forced their way in, brandishing weapons and shouting curses. They grabbed Bill's wife and all the children and shoved them into one of the bedrooms, proceeding to bind them hand and foot. They grabbed Bill at gunpoint, pushing him down the hall and shoving him into the bathroom. One of the terrorists took aim and fired at point-blank range. He put one bullet into Bill's back and another in his neck, then deposited his lifeless body in the bathtub, in a pool of his own blood.

I could hardly believe my eyes the next day, as the international scoop played out on our TV screens. CNN picked it up first. There was the International Red Cross, carrying Bill out of his front door in a body bag. He had paid the ultimate price for entering the World of Doing, but the impact he made on the lives of those orphans will never be forgotten. What of the orphanage? What Bill started could not be extinguished so easily. His wife stayed on, and the work continued. In the final analysis there is no substitute for action.

CHAPTER 18

Oh, Susanna! . . . and Her Hero/Rescuer

POLARITY, or action and reaction, we meet in every part of nature.
—RALPH WALDO EMERSON

"Courage!" he said, and pointed toward the land,
"This mounting wave will roll us shoreward soon."
—ALFRED, LORD TENNYSON, *THE LOTUS-EATERS*

T he Lost Bible teaches that empowerment begins with action. There is a power in the universe, a force (called *ruakh*[11]) which courses through all of nature and everything in it (animate and inanimate) energizing creation. Acting in accordance with this force—identifying its rhythms and moving in concert with them—enables one to discover the momentum of any given situation and to use it for maximum effect. Think of a surfer, out on the beach, trying to find the perfect wave. The surfer can't create a wave. Even the best of surfers is subject to the natural forces operating on any given day—the tide, the current, or the undertow. One needs to know exactly when to mount the board, so as to tap into the energy of the rushing water.

The mystics taught that events are not random; the universe is alive with divine power. Instead of struggling against obstacles, one must learn to take advantage of universal principles in every situation, moving consistently with the inner force and power of the universe. Learn to surf the momentum of each situation. Make it a point to ride the wave.

USE THE FORCE!

Of course a lot depends on how you look at the world around you—your own particular worldview. In a universe of utter randomness, might makes right. The only measure of good or evil comes from the power of the sword. But the Lost Bible tells us stories of a people in captivity who have lost the power of the sword, who have been conquered by foreign despots, and who must seek help and deliverance from an unseen power. It is an energy field that inhabits the whole of creation and that delivers immeasurable power to the one who is wise enough to tap into it.

The ancient stories remind us that no problem lacks a solution. It only lacks actors on the scene, those who know when to move, when to be still, and how to align themselves with the *ruakh* of the universe. In the Lost Bible the greatest accolades are reserved for those who have attained true knowledge, and that knowledge usually involves knowing when, where, and how to act. It requires no special strength or power; action taken deliberately and consistently can transform the most ordinary soul into a hero or heroine of considerable stature. Nevertheless, knowledge of the *ruakh* is required to know how to act effectively, and that action involves a superb sense of timing.

The Lost Bible relates the incredible tale of a young woman made famous by ancient lore, named Susanna. We read (in modern paraphrase) the following:

> Long ago, when the people were exiled in Babylonia, there was a very wealthy Israelite named Joakim. He was married to a very beautiful and righteous woman, whose name was Susanna. Susanna's parents were upright and pious, raising her to observe the laws of Moses. Adjacent to Joakim's house was a lavish garden, where many Israelite guests would gather to hear this most eminent citizen.

As with so much drama, wherever we find beautiful women, we also find lusty ne'er-do-wells, eager to concoct wicked schemes:

> Two leading citizens were made judges at that time; though their character was dubious. They spent most of their time at Joakim's house, so that whoever wanted their cases decided had to come there as well.

The two lusty Israelite judges spy on Susanna in her garden and seek to seduce her:

> As it happened, the two wicked judges noticed Susanna every day, as she walked through the garden after the crowd had left. They burned for her with perverted passion, and were utterly smitten. But they were too embarrassed to tell each other that they desired her sexually. Nevertheless, they anxiously waited each day just to catch a glimpse of her. When they finally admitted their lust to one another, they decided to stalk her until she was alone.

HERE COME THE JUDGES

The narrative goes on to explain that on a very hot day, Susanna decides to take a bath in the garden. After she dispatches her servants for olive oil and soap, the two judges, who had been lying in wait, suddenly appear. They exclaim (in continuing paraphrase):

> Look, the garden doors are closed, and nobody knows we are here. We are burning with desire for you; so just say yes, and sleep with us. If you refuse, we will deliver testimony that you were together with a young man, and this was why you sent your servants away.

Of course Susanna promptly rejects the lewd proposition of the judges and screams loudly, alerting the entire household that something has happened. The next day, when the crowd gathers (as is their custom), Joakim hears the evidence. The two wicked judges come forward and summon Susanna, commanding that her veil be removed in order to face her accusers. In actuality the judges simply want to gawk at her beauty, even as she weeps and looks heavenward for deliverance. The judges proceed to accuse her of having sex with a young man in the garden in broad daylight. As fickle fate would have it, the tribunal believes the accusers and decrees death for Susanna.

In a genuine double standard, biblical law allows a man to have as many wives as he pleases, while a woman may have only one man, her husband. Susanna is convicted of the crime of adultery against her husband, Joakim. In the nick of time a hero arises—a young man of no special rank or privilege, of neither royal nor priestly stock, yet destined for fame, eternally, as a heroic prototype. His very name, Daniel, is the secret key to unlocking the story, for it means, "God is my judge." This of course is the same Daniel who appears in the biblical book by this name—who is miraculously delivered from a fiery furnace and from the jaws of lions. Daniel knows that God is indeed the only true judge, enthroned above any human magistrate. It is God who judges the judges, as it were, who in turn are impotent before the Divine Presence.

INSIGHT VERSUS INSTITUTIONS

The idea that judges are not autonomous agents but are themselves subject to a higher authority is still controversial in modern society. After all, it is argued, judges don't make the law. They are not omniscient dispensers of power, gifted with a kind of judicial infallibility. The judiciary may seem imperial, an institution determining willy-nilly what the law says and how it is to be applied. In truth a judge has no authority save what has been given to him by a higher power. Young

Daniel, the insightful hero, knows this instinctively. He is no kin of this woman and has no stake in the matter, save the desire to see justice—true justice—done. He stands in the midst of the assembly and holds forth:

> "You fools!" he shouted. "You have convicted an innocent woman without evaluation of the evidence. She deserves a new trial, because she is a victim of false testimony."
>
> The leaders of the tribunal responded, "Why don't you sit on the panel, Daniel? It is the will of the Eternal, who has privileged you."

The elders seem aware of something that modern jurisprudence has forgotten, that a higher power is in operation. But Daniel is himself no judge. What can he do, realistically, to prove false the testimony of men respected as much as the two wicked judges? Daniel, at home in the World of Doing, has an idea, which he now sets into motion. He calls for the wicked judges and asks each of them, independently, "Under which tree in the garden did you see the alleged act of fornication take place?"

The first judge answers, "Under a mastic tree." The second declares, "Under a live oak tree." Touché! They have just been caught in the act of bearing false witness against their neighbor. Immediately, all of the people assembled before the tribunal leap upon the judges and tear them limb from limb. They who plotted murder against an innocent daughter of Israel are themselves killed without mercy. Perhaps someone should have let them in on yet another secret of the Lost Bible: what goes around comes around. Susanna is thereafter praised for her refusal to compromise with immoral behavior; and Daniel from that day forth is highly honored among all the people.

Notice, however, what Daniel doesn't do. He doesn't take the law into his own hands. He doesn't organize a vigilante mob. He acts decisively, but he acts through insight, which is his secret weapon and sacred ally. Thus, the World of Doing comes full-circle, back to the World of Knowing, from which true enlightenment is born. The story is meticulously crafted to combine action with insight. Its success is apparent, for those who read it, from generation to generation, are moved to tears.

THE EXCLUSION

The date of composition of the book of Susanna, which appears in the Apocrypha, is hard to estimate. While many researchers trace it to the first century before the Common Era, the story itself may go back as far as the period when Persia controlled the entire Near East—the fifth century, B.C.E. While the earliest texts are Greek, linguistic clues suggest that the composition was originally Semitic, most likely Hebrew, and that it was written in the land of Israel itself.

Why was a book with such a profound message, which has been called a literary masterpiece, barred from the canon of Holy Writ? The book was indeed included in the Greek translation of the Hebrew Bible, the Septuagint. It appears immediately in front of the traditional book of Daniel, though it was ultimately rejected by the rabbinic sages at the Council of Yavne.

Recall that the entire book of Daniel was very nearly tossed out by those same sages, who deemed it unhistorical and quite possibly a clever contrivance. Better to err on the side of caution, thought the sages, and not sanctify a text that had probably been written centuries after its claimed date of composition. Furthermore, the book's explicitly erotic content, and the denigration of the very type who sat upon the council that decided the content of the canon, helped doom it.

But in striking Susanna, the sages inadvertently struck some of the most important secrets the Lost Bible has to offer, namely, how to stand up for right, even when the judges are wrong, how insight can triumph over institutions, and how to be a rescuer in the World of Doing.

In the final analysis, I would ask, if you are bold enough to believe that the book of Daniel is genuine, authentic, and historical, then why not the book of Susanna?

PORTRAIT OF A RESCUER

There is a powerful irony in the fact that Israel's ancient religion was deepest and strongest, not in the days of King David or Solomon, or even Moses, but long afterward, when Jerusalem and its great temple lay in ruins, and when the people had been taken away into foreign captivity. Something happened during those dark years that "morphed" what had been nothing more than one more religious cult in a sea of ancient cults into a transcendent faith of universal ethics and morality, capable of transforming the world. Perhaps there is something about oppression and captivity that brings out the best in people and converts otherwise obscure characters like Daniel into heroes of everlasting fame.

Why are we so drawn to characters like Daniel? Perhaps it is because in Daniel we find a prototype for the true action hero, who rescues the proverbial damsel in distress. Of course if the damsel happens to be a close friend, colleague, or relative, rescue makes eminent sense. But what if there is no special relationship, familial or otherwise? What if the rescue is undertaken merely for its own sake, because it is the right thing to do? Such was the case when Daniel rescued Susanna.

The question of rescue came to the fore during the Second World War, when the Jews of Europe faced certain annihilation at the hands of Adolf Hitler and his Nazi minions. Most citizens of continental Europe stood by silently and did nothing to aid the innocent victims of the genocidal terror. They became phlegmatic witnesses of the most shocking crimes ever perpetrated on the planet. But there were a few—very few—who moved, who acted, who risked everything, including their own lives, to save at least a handful of Europe's Jewish population from certain destruction. Such people hid Jews in cellars and secret hiding places, falsified documents for them, hustled them to neutral countries, and did whatever was required to protect them with almost superhuman determination. They were true rescuers, modern-day Daniels.

THE SECRET

Many such rescuers were interviewed after the war years and asked why they did what they did. The expectation was that some great ethical, moral, or political principles would be cited, that the rescuers would reveal themselves as crusaders for a cause, boldly laying it all on the line for what they truly believed in. What was found, to the contrary, was that in almost every case, the rescuers simply recognized human need, close at hand, and responded in a natural and unassuming fashion. Even in history's darkest hour, they engendered hope for humanity. They demonstrated the heroic power of love. In the final analysis, we find that ordinary people become heroic by simply responding to situations where needs present themselves. The lesson—and the secret—is simple: Get out of yourself for a change. Take notice of situations of human need around every corner, all the time. Stop, observe, and act. Always ask what you can do to make a difference. "Ride the good wave," and the rest will be history.

CHAPTER 19

Judith, the Feminist Heroine

Actions are the seed of Fate; Deeds grow into Destiny.
—A. L. LINALL, JR., AMERICAN LITERARY EDITOR

All human strength and force comes from faith in things unseen. One who
believes is strong; one who doubts is weak. Strong convictions precede great actions.
—JAMES FREEMAN CLARKE, THEOLOGIAN, AUTHOR

The World of Doing is all about riding the wave, identifying forces inherent in a given situation and acting in consort with them. Bear in mind, the better part of riding the wave is a degree of *chutzpah*—brazen gall that sometimes appears as raw nerve. The Lost Bible is full of action heroes. As allegory, it hails the deeds of people who make a difference in every age. How do you make a difference today? Not by pondering what to do, but by doing what you already know is the right thing. When you align yourself with natural forces in a situation, you take advantage of the unseen force in the universe.

The Lost Bible, in an incredible book known as Judith, tells the story of an Israelite woman who saves her people from a bloodthirsty Babylonian general. In an otherwise desperate situation, she comes forward as a cross between Wonder Woman and *Star War*'s Princess Leah.

LONG AGO, IN AN EMPIRE FAR AWAY . . .

We are told that in the days of King Nebuchadnezzar, the evil emperor who subjugated the land of Israel in 586 B.C.E., a mighty general named Holofernes is engaged to do the bidding of the evil empire. He has at his disposal an army of 120,000 foot soldiers and 12,000 cavalrymen.

The king becomes involved in a military campaign against the Medes, next door to Persia, and demands help from across his realm. The subject peoples of the west, however, don't share the emperor's zeal. Word spreads that a rebel alliance has been at work, frustrating the emperor's plans to rule a vast empire. Of course such resistance is clandestine. We read (in fresh, modern paraphrase):

Nebuchadnezzar's request was ignored far and wide, since the people didn't think the war could be won. Instead, they made fools of his emissaries, sending them back to the king with nothing. Nebuchadnezzar became violently angry, swearing vengeance upon them all. He determined to execute everyone who lived in the lands stretching from the Mediterranean coast to the Persian Gulf.

The emperor specifically dispatches his general:

> "I hereby send you, Holofernes, to march before me, taking control of this entire region. If their soldiers submit without a fight, keep them prisoner until my arrival; for I will mete out punishment. If they will not surrender, kill all of them and plunder the whole area. This is what I have sworn to do, by my life and by my throne, and I will surely carry it out. You must fulfill my commands, for I am the emperor!"

The general, we are told, goes about systematically crushing the rebels, destroying any pathetic militia that dares muster against him. Panic sets in. Many are terrified into surrendering. They declare:

> "We serve you loyally, King Nebuchadnezzar, and we will do whatever you tell us. Everything we have belongs to you: our homes, our land and fields, the grazing animals, and even our tents. Do with them as you will. We ourselves will become your slaves."

In the ancient Near East, the price of submission is the worship of the emperor, in this case Nebuchadnezzar himself. One group of rebels, however, continues stubbornly to resist—the tribes of Israel. Holofernes's army pauses to regroup and collect supplies before making a final advance on a narrow, Thermopylae-like pass called Bethulia. That is when the rebels' mysterious, charismatic high priest, dressed in fine white raiment, goes into action organizing a resistance movement. The high priest Joakim calls his people together and begins serious fasting and deep meditative prayer, calling on Israel's Deity:

> At that time everyone in Jerusalem, men, women, and children, fell prostrate before the temple, where the Divine Presence was known to hover. They sat there in sackcloth and ashes, entreating the Eternal to spare them.

In the meantime, the king of the Ammonites, Akhior, delivers some military intelligence and friendly advice to Holofernes. He knows that spiritual power—the *ruakh*—is strong among the Israelite warriors. The high priest Joakim is particularly attuned to this power. The Israelites are not, therefore, to be underestimated. They do have a weakness, however. When they forget what the Deity has taught them, when they look to themselves and forget their spiritual disciplines, they can stumble. They can even fall prey to the evil inclination. They have done so at various times in their long history, which is why they were at first subjugated by Nebuchadnezzar. However, when they appropriate the dynamic of the *ruakh*, they become incredibly powerful, even invincible. No army can defeat them then, not even Holofernes's. No power can conquer them, as long as they properly inhabit the World of Doing.

Holofernes's own advisers declare:

> "Should we be fearful of Israel? After all, they are helpless, incapable of mounting a defense. We should attack, for our army can easily annihilate them."

The great general responds to Akhior with a prophecy of his own:

> "You sniveling Ammonite! On my life, you will not see my face again till I have wreaked vengeance on these Israelites, who migrated up from Egypt."

Akhior is sent as a miserable captive to dwell among the Israelites at Bethulia, until Holofernes arrives to slay them all. But as fate will have it, such arrogance will not stand.

THE REBEL BASE

Soon thereafter, Holofernes besieges Bethulia, and despair grips the rebel base. The Israelite warriors even contemplate surrendering if their situation does not improve over the next five days. This is when a wealthy widow named Judith enters the scene. She is indisputably beautiful, and she realizes that she can use her attractiveness to good advantage. The situation presents itself for her to become a leader, and she rises to the occasion. A proto-feminist of sorts, she steps forward to take the helm of the resistance—not by heredity or privilege, but by sheer competence and power of command. She admonishes everyone not to put Deity to the test with an ultimatum demanding deliverance in a few days, but to tap into the *ruakh*. She declares, with the spirit of an ancient Braveheart:

> "Our surrender as slaves won't bring us honor, but disgrace. Instead, we must be an example for our people, since they rely on us with their lives. Even our temple and the sacred altar depend on us alone."

Judith hatches a daring plan. She combs her hair, crowns herself with a tiara, and dresses in her finest clothing:

> She wore the best sandals and adorned herself with jewelry—bracelets, anklets, rings, and earrings, so that all the men who saw her would be allured by her beauty.

She and her maid stealthily make their way into enemy territory. The military patrol that meets Judith is amazed and bedazzled by her beauty. She relates:

> "I have a message for General Holofernes. I know of how he may subdue the entire hill country without taking any casualties, either killed or captured."

The soldiers suspect that their commander will want Judith for himself, and they take her to Holofernes in his tent. Sure enough, the great general is so utterly taken with her that he tries to seduce her. He invites her to a lavish banquet, arranging for all the guests to depart at a prescribed hour, leaving the two of them alone. This might have been the time for him to make his move, but he has poured so much liquor down his throat that he is thoroughly intoxicated and lies down on his bed.

OFF WITH HIS HEAD!

There they are, the powerful Holofernes, second-in-command to the emperor himself, and the lovely Judith, adorned like a princess, though in actuality a leader of the rebel alliance. In an instant, our heroine taps into the *ruakh* and acts. Judith aligns herself with the natural forces inherent in the situation. She first says a little prayer to herself:

> "O Eternal, you are the One who possesses all power. Please show favor on what I am about to do, because it is for the sake of oppressed Jerusalem. This is the moment when your people need help. Therefore, let my actions succeed, to defeat the enemies who seek to destroy us."

Extending her hand to the bedpost, she instinctively grabs the general's own sword and wields it with a mighty stroke that catches him in the neck and completely severs his head. The scene is grisly beyond depiction, as the decapitated Holofernes lies lifeless on the floor. Adding insult to injury, Judith hands the severed head to her maid, who stuffs it into her food sack—the ancient version of a doggie bag—in this case used to bring kosher food to the banquet. One can only imagine the ancient audience laughing hysterically at such a bawdy tale.

"Princess Judith," accompanied by her maid, leaves the enemy camp, carrying the doggie bag to the gates of Bethulia. Taking the severed head out of the bag, she exclaims:

"Behold, the head of Holofernes, general of the Assyrian army!"

In an odd twist of fate, Holofernes is seen again, just as he had prophesied to Akhior—though hardly in the way he had imagined. The townspeople and the elders are astonished that a valiant woman has prevailed over a mighty general. This is the turning point for the rebel cause. With Holofernes out of the picture, the forces of the evil empire panic and flee. The Israelites completely rout them, plundering their camp and bestowing Holofernes's possessions on Princess Judith. Having led her people to victory, she becomes one of history's most effective, though little-acknowledged, feminist heroines. As for Akhior, he formally joins the house of Israel, throwing in his lot with the other faithful Israelites. We are left with a sense of celebration, straight from the World of Doing.

FAITH IS *CHUTZPAH*

In sum we have here an ancient account of a woman who takes strategic, effective action. A massive problem is met with focused energy and sheer *chutzpah*. Problem solved.

The book of Judith presents us with a true proto-feminist in the World of Doing. It is tempting to suppose that the farther we go back in history, the more sexist and patriarchal things were. It took the spirit of modernism to bring about the feminist revolution. Or so we think. We assume that women were to be silent and submissive, homemakers who sat on the sidelines, quietly in awe of the men in their lives. Not a few modern religionists go as far as to insist that this was the divine order, an eternal pattern for gender relations. The biblical world is seen as a man's world, where faith is equated with patriarchy. But the Lost Bible gives us, in the book of Judith, a startling example to the contrary.

Here we see faith, wielded as a weapon by a woman in the World of Doing. We can almost imagine her crooning the lyric line of Helen Reddy's classic hit, "I am strong, I am invincible, I am woman." Judith doesn't let circumstances control her; she controls the circumstances. While the mighty general, Holofernes, may appear to be the one with power, she knows that men are in fact the weaker sex. Often ruled by sight and the lust of their own eyes, they succumb easily to temptation. That is in fact the natural order of things.

Judith's challenge is to identify the natural order working in a situation, utilize it, and turn it to her advantage. She allows the momentum of the situation to work on her behalf, keeping her own power in reserve until it is needed. She is by no means a sex object, but she is not embarrassed to use her sexuality to good purpose, in this case the deliverance of her people from a foe of vastly superior military strength.

THE EXCLUSION

Why would the keepers of the canon toss out a book with such a triumphant message as Judith? As with several other books of the Apocrypha (subsequently included in Catholic Bibles), Judith first appeared prominently in the Septuagint, the Greek translation of the Hebrew Scriptures which came together in Alexandria in the third century B.C.E. The original language was most likely Hebrew, though no Semitic version has survived. There was in antiquity a sizable Jewish population in Egypt, and Alexandria in particular produced some of the greatest thinkers, scholars, and philosophers ever to grace the Jewish world. If the Alexandrian community considered the book of Judith to be Holy Writ, how dare anyone exclude it from the sacred canon? Yet, subsequent generations of sages did just that, and the book was not included in the canonical list that grew out of the Council of Yavne.

Perhaps the feminist overtones of the text were too strident for the patriarchal minded sages of the day. This, however, seems unlikely, because other biblical books contain their own proto-feminist stories. The book of Esther, for example, tells the story of an Israelite woman who saves her people through a similar act of *chutzpah*. There was also Deborah, the Israelite judge who inspired her outnumbered forces to victory over the Canaanite general Sisera, and Yael, who slew Sisera by driving a tent peg through his skull. Doubtless, there was room among the ancients for feminist tales, and it is hard to imagine that Judith would have been "axed" for this reason.

There was, however, another problem with the book. The Council of Yavne clearly wanted to believe that every text to which they "gave the nod" was not only inspired, but historical. Any story related in Holy Writ must actually have transpired in space and time. The sages were literalists, who constrained themselves to believe that every book of Scripture must have been literal fact. The book of Judith, by contrast, begins with a glaring inconsistency. It states, "When King Nebuchadnezzar of Assyria ruled from his capital in Nineveh . . ."

The fact is, Nebuchadnezzar was king of Babylon, not of Assyria. It would be like asserting that George Washington was the king of France. This literary *faux pas* invalidated the book on its face, and the sages, who knew better, clearly had no use for it. Once again, however, the sages seem to have thrown out the proverbial baby with the bath water. They failed to consider that the text might be clueing the reader deliberately to the fact that it is in essence a parable—a mythological account, which was never intended to be taken literally. Another possibility is that a scribal error simply inserted the name Nebuchadnezzar where it didn't belong. If a copyist's error had produced the incongruity, then the book might in fact be conveying historical events. But whether or not the book is historical, it nonetheless teaches eternal lessons: of faith, action, and *chutzpah*. Wouldn't it have been nice if the sages had simply allowed the text to stand on its own, and let the people decide?

THE SECRET

Winston Churchill once declared, "An appeaser is one who feeds a crocodile, hoping it will eat him last." The lesson is simple. Surrender is not an option: Not then. Not now. Not ever. The message is also contained in the book of Numbers. The Israelites are wandering around in the desert, and Moses sends out a dozen scouts to determine whether the strength of their enemies is sufficient to prevent them from entering the Promised Land. Ten of the scouts come back saying, "We saw the Nephilim there—the sons of Anak from among the Nephilim [another reference to the Lost Bible]; and we seemed in our own eyes like grasshoppers, and so we must have seemed in theirs." (Numbers 13:33, author's translation). They advise against invasion. Two of the spies, Caleb and Joshua, advise the Israelites to attack—claiming that they will prevail. The Israelites take the advice of the ten, and the Jews continue to wander around in the Sinai for forty years.

On another level, the book of Ecclesiastes comments, "The race is not won by the speedy, nor the battle by the mighty . . . for time and misfortune befall everyone" (Ecclesiastes 9:11, author's translation). Therefore, when you do decide to act, bide your time, wait for your chance. Know that the perfect moment of action will come. Whether you are a brazen feminist, a traditionalist, or even a member of the weaker sex—a male—you can be a hero if you find your foe's Achilles' heel and let the momentum of the situation work on your behalf. There is a simple acronym that well suits the World of Doing: STOP. Broken down, it amounts to four principles:

Stop. Several times in the text, Judith stops and offers a prayer, openly or simply to herself. Quit flailing about in your own strength, and do nothing at all until the time presents itself.

Think. Employing the *ruakh* does not mean that you disconnect your reason. Put your brain to work, and the course of action will become clear.

Observe. You will never know what to do if you don't look keenly at what is going on around you. Open your eyes. Be aware.

Plan. Formulate a course of action, flexible enough to survive contact with reality, yet unbending in its goal. Don't be sidetracked, and don't be dissuaded. Determination will get you there. Remember, faith is *chutzpah*—in action.

CHAPTER 20

The Mighty Maccabees

A good history covers not only what was done, but the thought that went into the action. You can read the history of a country through its actions.
—BENJAMIN L. HOOKS, AMERICAN EDUCATOR

A human action becomes genuinely important when it springs from the soil of a clear-sighted awareness of the temporality and the ephemerality of everything human. It is only this awareness that can breathe any greatness into an action.
—VACLAV HAVEL, CZECH PLAYWRIGHT, POET, POLITICIAN

I sat in a darkened movie house in downtown Chicago and stared in bewildered awe at the fantastic events transpiring on the silver screen. A wooden chest, completely covered with solid gold, was the object of a desperate and frenetic chase—by nefarious Nazis on the one hand, and by a renegade archaeologist with a penchant for adventure on the other. The chest had been fashioned by ancient Israelites for the purpose of containing two stone tablets, delivered into the hands of Moses on Mount Sinai. It was the Ark of the Covenant. When the armies of Israel carried that chest in front of them into battle, they were invincible. So the story goes. In just two hours of cinematic magic, the entire biblical world was brought front-and-center into the modern psyche, invading the minds of the movie-going public.

Like so many others, something entered me that evening that wouldn't let go. For the first time I realized that the traditions of the biblical past amount to a lot more than Sunday school trivia. In fact I discovered to my amazement that there are not a few modern adventurers in search of the sacred Ark, and that they have in fact spawned a whole new science. Call it (forgive me) "Ark-eology." Within a year of watching Hollywood's depiction of the lost Ark, I found myself on my life's first journey to the Middle East. I was not seeking material remains from the ancient past, but merely knowledge.

I knew that the sacred Ark was said to have rested deep within Solomon's great temple in the heart of ancient Jerusalem. I also knew that it disappeared somewhere in the mists of antiquity. But what became of it? Was it destroyed along with the temple, at the hands of the Babylonians? Or did it miraculously survive? The Bible itself is ominously silent. But there, in my favorite little library, occupying an inconspicuous corner of Mount Zion, I pored over the text of that other Bible—the Lost Bible—the books excluded from the sacred canon. That was when I discovered a clue I had never seen before. It was hidden among the four books that bear the name Maccabees.

THE TEMPLE OF DOOM

The Second Book of the Maccabees relates how the city of Jerusalem is sacked and burned by the ferocious Babylonians. The temple is torched and leveled. However, the Ark of the Covenant survives, along with the sacred tent and altar of incense. The prophet Jeremiah organizes an expedition to a mountain in Transjordan. This is the exact place where Moses had died, after he beheld (but did not enter) the Promised Land.

Jeremiah finds a cave in the vicinity, brings the sacred utensils into it, and blocks up the door. We read (in modern paraphrase):

> It is written in the record books that the prophet Jeremiah commanded those being deported from Israel to Babylon to take some fire with them. . . . It is recorded in the same record books that Jeremiah received an oracle from on high, and promptly commanded that the sacred tent and the Ark of the Covenant should be brought along with him. After these things, he journeyed forth to the mountain Moses had long ago ascended, when he looked into the Promised Land. Having come this far, Jeremiah found a cave, to which he brought the sacred tent, the Ark of the Covenant, and the altar of incense. After depositing them there, he sealed up its entrance forever.

Many who follow Jeremiah look for the cave. The account (transposed to contemporary style) continues:

> Some of the people volunteered to come along to mark the way, but they couldn't find it. When the prophet Jeremiah heard of this, he sternly rebuked them, declaring, "This place will be unknown until the time when the Eternal brings our people together again, revealing divine mercy. At that time all these things will be unveiled, and the Divine Presence, along with the pillar of cloud will be seen, just as they were seen long ago in the days of Moses, and in accordance with King Solomon's request that the Eternal's dwelling place should be specially sanctified."

Is this in fact what happened to the Ark of the Covenant? Is it still somewhere in Transjordan, tucked away in a cave, waiting to be found? While theories on the whereabouts of the Ark abound, and place it anywhere from a Coptic church in Ethiopia to any number of secret tunnels underneath Jerusalem's Temple Mount, the account in 2 Maccabees is in fact a written record, preserved, at least ostensibly, as a historical document. Perhaps someone following the footsteps of Lawrence of Arabia may be lucky enough to have a metal detector handy, and may someday stumble upon the actual chest containing the Ten Commandments.

But even if the Ark is never found, even if this account is mere allegory, it certainly teaches us something we cannot afford to ignore. Consider the underlying message. By withdrawing from the Holy City when things were going badly, the prophet preserved the source of the Israelites' power. Allegorically, there are times when you need to withdraw, when choosing *not* to confront is the wise decision. Choose your battles carefully. In retreating you wait out the time of trouble, until the time comes when the Divine Presence is revealed. As a skilled surfer knows, every trough anticipates another wave.

THE SECRET

According to the Lost Bible, the ancient prophet Jeremiah knew how to align himself with the *ruakh*. When the situation is going well, ride the wave. When things are going badly, withdraw—another form (paradoxically) of action.

It is a lesson well appropriated in modern times by the Chinese students who demonstrated in Tiananmen Square, in the heart of Beijing, in the late 1980s. The crackdown on their budding movement involved overwhelming force, against which they had no chance. They chose to withdraw, to end their demonstrations and slither away in melancholy fashion. Many in the West watched in despair as their movement for freedom of thought and expression foundered under the weight of tyrannical oppression. But all is not lost. Those students and their ideas may have withdrawn for the moment (not unlike Jeremiah, as he hauled away the sacred Ark), but they have not disappeared. They may have "hunkered down" for the time being, but the source of their power remains. They are patiently waiting (a very non-Western trait) for their time to come. And most assuredly, it will.

DESPAIR AND DELIVERANCE

The flip side of withdrawal is engagement. The books of Maccabees go on to relate the most stirring of action stories. Though the Ark itself is never found, the time does indeed come for its spiritual dynamism to inspire not just individual deeds, but an entire revolution. It comes in response to a dark shadow that descends upon the land in the second century before the Common Era. For a maniacal king rises in Syria in the second century B.C.E., whose eccentricity is matched only by his cruelty. His name is Antiochus IV, though he takes for himself the infamous surname Epiphanes, meaning manifestation, for he thinks himself to be the incarnation of a god.

He goes forth as a conqueror, stretching the borders of his kingdom beyond the land of Israel, all the way to Egypt. The writings of the ancient historian Josephus complement the book of 1 Maccabees to fill in the details. Antiochus besieges the city of Alexandria and prepares to make his final assault. At that point, however, he is unexpectedly met by a Roman legate, an emissary from the great empire to the west with which Egypt has formed an alliance. Rome will not allow Antiochus Epiphanes to subjugate its client state. The legate demands that the Syrian withdraw his army. Antiochus realizes that he is faced with a vastly superior force, but he desperately wants to save face. He asks the legate for time, so that he can "decide the matter." The legate takes out a long stick, draws a circle in the sand, completely surrounding the befuddled king, and directs him to "decide before leaving this circle."

Shamed and embarrassed, the Syrian potentate withdraws his forces and begins a humiliating retreat up the coast. Meanwhile, back in Jerusalem, word has spread that the army of the dreaded emperor is withdrawing. Rumor has it that Antiochus is in fact dead. Stirred by this news, a faction of the population, headed by the high priest, begins a revolt. Unfortunately for the Judeans, however, rumors of Antiochus's death are greatly exaggerated.

Humiliated in Egypt, the king now unleashes his fury on the Jerusalemites with a vengeance. Advancing on Judea's capital, he not only crushes the revolt, he unleashes history's first genuine religious persecution. Over the course of time (some two years after his defeat in Egypt), Antiochus commands that the sacred temple (burned to ashes centuries before by the Babylonians but rebuilt some seventy years later, in the days of the high priest Ezra), be ritually defiled:

> With great arrogance he went into the holy sanctuary and seized the golden altar. . . . He also confiscated the silver, the gold, and the priceless vessels. He even took the hidden treasures that he found there. Having looted all of them, he returned to his own land. He committed many murderous acts, speaking arrogantly all the while.

The orders are given for a swine to be slaughtered upon the holy altar, as a mock sacrifice. The most sacred site in the entire nation is thereby rendered unclean and desecrated.

THE ABOMINATION OF DESOLATION

A curious footnote to history is the fact that the Ark of the Covenant is not there. It is still secreted away in the cave were Jeremiah had hid it. But the sacred precincts have nonetheless been desecrated in the most abominable fashion. Beyond this, King Antiochus commands that an idol (presumably of Zeus) be sculpted and brought into the sacred precincts, in utter mockery of the most important of the Israelite commandments: "You must not fashion for yourselves a chiseled statue" (Exodus 20:4, author's translation). This is idolatry in the clearest of terms.

Adding insult to injury, there is a subtle, twisted irony in the placement of the statue. It comes to rest on the very altar that had been defiled. The ancient texts append a terrible designation to the fearsome image: the Abomination of Desolation. We read (in continuing paraphrase):

> Every community in Judea went into shock and mourning. The leaders and the elders moaned. The young men and the maidens became faint-hearted, and the blush of beauty departed from the women. The bridegrooms turned to lamentation, and the brides, sitting in their bridal chambers, only mourned. The land itself trembled on behalf of its inhabitants, and all the descendants of Jacob were filled with shame.

It is the most horrible series of events ever to befall the Holy City and its sacred shrine. Handwritten scrolls of the books of Moses are seized and destroyed. The fearful narrative continues (in paraphrase):

> In accordance with the decree, they executed the women who circumcised their children. They killed entire families of those who practiced circumcision, along with those who performed the ritual. They even hung the circumcised infants from their mothers' necks.

The Jewish faith is literally driven underground, its adherents meeting in secret behind closed doors. The pious among the people flee for safety into the desert.

Meanwhile, emissaries from King Antiochus are dispatched to cities and hamlets across the length and breadth of Judea. Their charge is simple. Every single Judean is to renounce the ancient faith of Abraham, and they are to prove it by consuming a piece of swine's flesh, in deliberate violation of the laws of Moses.

It comes to pass that in a little town on the border of Samaria, called Modiin, a certain Israelite is ordered by a Syrian emissary to pick up a swine and carry it to slaughter. The Israelite complies, but the episode is observed from a distance by a wise old man—a priest named Mattathias—with the fear of God in his eyes.

There is a time to withdraw, as the prophet Jeremiah knew when he brought the Ark of the Covenant out of Jerusalem to a secret hiding place. There is a time to retreat, as the pious knew when they fled into the desert. There is also a time to act. Mattathias and his sons know that this is no time for equivocation and appeasement. The old man grabs a spear close at hand, and in a moment of unparalleled spiritual dynamism, impales the young Israelite as well as the Syrian emissary upon the very altar where mock sacrifice was to be offered. He calls his five sons to his side and raises a standard of revolt. He cries out to the whole town:

> "Let all those who are fervent for the Law and faithful to the Covenant follow me!"

They head off into the hills, to fast, to pray, and to wait for the inevitable engagement with the enemy. The first religious persecution in history is met with the first guerilla war.

In the twentieth century, when civilization was faced with another kind of persecution—the threat of Nazi fascism—there were those who responded with appeasement and those who (like Mattathias) stood firm. When British prime minister Neville Chamberlain returned from Munich, having signed an agreement with Hitler to dismember helpless Czechoslovakia, he was widely hailed for having achieved, in his words, "Peace in our time." Winston Churchill thought otherwise: "You had a choice between war and dishonor. You chose dishonor, and you shall have war."

THE HAMMER

Soon after the events in Modiin, the old patriarch Mattathias dies, passing the torch to his sons. He never sees the liberation of his people, which he so desperately desired. But like Moses before him, he had gone to the mountaintop, looked over, and seen the Promised Land. In the worldview of the ancients, progress is generational. Step by step, generation by generation, the world is to be made better, perfected, redeemed by our own labors in the World of Doing, brought back to Edenic innocence, inching ever closer to the Messianic Age.

The message has been transmitted across the centuries, being picked up by the likes of Mahatma Gandhi and echoed by Martin Luther King, who also dreamed of freedom and who declared on the night he was shot:

> "I just want to do God's will. And He's allowed me to go up to the mountain. And I've looked over. And I've seen the promised land. I may not get there with you. But I want you to know tonight, that we, as a

people, will get to the promised land. And I'm happy tonight. I'm not worried about anything. I'm not fearing any man."[12]

As for the budding revolution of the sons of Mattathias, the eldest of the five, named Judah, now takes up the sword on behalf of his oppressed people.

A massive Syrian army, commanded by the infamous Apollonius, musters against the Judean renegades. Marching in fine columns, their armor gleaming under a brilliant sun, the Syrians are attacked from out of nowhere by the sons of Mattathias, who have organized a militia of freedom fighters. The Syrians are cut to ribbons. Apollonius's sword is taken up by Judah, who now wields it as a symbol of defiance, pursuing the fight for the liberation of Jerusalem.

In response, the head of the entire Syrian army, Seron, heads south toward Judea to crush the resistance. Judah's troops tremble at the strength of their foes. Our paraphrase continues:

> When they looked out and saw the vast army coming against them, they cried out to Judah, "How can we, so few in number, stand up against such a great and mighty force? Furthermore, we feel faint, since we haven't eaten anything today." Judah responded, "It is easier than you think for a great army to be surrounded by only a few, since in the eyes of heaven, there is no difference between salvation by a multitude and salvation by only a few. It is not how big the army is that insures victory in battle, but the power that comes from above. They attack us in their pride and their lawlessness, seeking to annihilate us, along with our wives and children. They fight to plunder us, but we fight for our lives and for our laws. Mark my words, the Eternal will defeat them before us! I tell you, don't be afraid of them at all." After he uttered these words, he rushed into battle against Seron and his army, who were utterly routed before the Israelites.

Antiochus Epiphanes is furious and dispatches an additional force. At its helm is another crack general, Nicanor, who engages the Maccabee brothers in fierce combat. Second Maccabees tells us, in cryptic language, that just before the battle, Judah has a dream-vision, in which the prophet Jeremiah makes a return visit to his beleaguered people:

> Suddenly a figure appeared, whose gray hair distinguished him with dignity. He possessed an aura of majesty and power. . . . This man, Jeremiah the prophet, extended his right hand and delivered to me a golden sword. He said, "Accept this holy sword as a gift from on high. Use it to slay your foes!"

The dream is prophetic. Jeremiah well knows the power of the sacred Ark, even in its hiding place in the desert. The fate of Nicanor's army is the same as the first army. Nicanor himself is slain, and his troops flee in blind panic. The account spells it out in detail:

> At that point the Judeans confiscated the spoils of war and the plunder. They severed Nicanor's head, along with his right hand, which he used to stretch out in arrogance. They brought them back and put them on display just beyond the walls of Jerusalem. All the people rejoiced that day and celebrated it as a day of great deliverance. Thereafter, the land enjoyed rest for few days.

Judah comes to be known as the Maccabee, parroting an ancient Hebrew word meaning hammer, for he struck hammer blows into the flanks of the Syrian forces.

Of course tyrants are not accustomed to giving up so easily. Antiochus sends yet another army, which meets a similar fate:

> The foreign invaders were annihilated, their remnants fleeing into the plain. All the troops who stayed in the rear were slain.

After four grueling years of battle, in 165 B.C.E., the ragtag army of the Maccabees marches into the city of Jerusalem. A cry of freedom goes up that has not been heard since the days when Moses led the people out of Egypt.

THE INEXTINGUISHABLE FLAME: RAIDING THE LOST ARK

Nevertheless, not all is as it should be. The temple lay in dismal disrepair, its altar defiled by the juice of a swine. Slowly the Judeans begin the laborious task of putting things right:

> Therefore they dismantled the altar, taking the stones and piling them in a designated location on the Temple Mount, until some future time, when a "true prophet" will come and direct them what to do with them.

A new altar is then erected in its place. The writings of the later rabbinic sages add some additional details. Inside the temple itself, says the Talmud, the eternal flame, a seven-branched candelabrum that symbolizes the divine presence, had been extinguished long ago. A small amount of oil is found, but only enough to light the menorah for a single day. The task of making new oil would take eight days.

The menorah is therefore lit with such oil as is on hand, leaving the rest in God's hands. Miraculously, the flame does not go out. The menorah continues to burn for eight full days until the new oil is ready. In commemoration of these events, a great festival is organized in Jerusalem. Lasting for eight days, it is known henceforth as Hanukkah, the Festival of Lights. Today, in every synagogue a replica of an oil lamp hangs above the Ark where the Torah is kept. Though it is fueled by electricity rather than oil, it is always lit, for it represents the everlasting light of the *ruakh*.

But in spite of the restoration of the menorah, an essential piece of furniture was still missing from the temple. Consider the fact that the whereabouts of the Ark of the Covenant was still unknown in those days. Nevertheless, its presence, its spirit, its power, had energized the Maccabees and enabled a guerilla band to triumph over insurmountable odds. In every age, the energy of the Ark is still there, in the universe, lacking only willing souls to tap into it. It is a reservoir of strength for the downtrodden, the oppressed . . . or for any individual who seeks power in his or her life. It is a divine gift for the World of Doing.

It wasn't hard to apply the lessons of the Maccabees in my own life, residing and working in the Middle East. Whenever I hopped into my jeep and headed down the road, from Galilee into war-torn Lebanon, I thought about what I was doing at that little television facility, working to bring a message of hope to a troubled region, via the airwaves. Could broadcasting family-oriented programming, in a war zone (from *Bonanza* to *The Waltons* to *Little House on the Prairie*) really make a difference? From the response of our viewers, we all knew it did. I might not be Judah Maccabee, but somehow, in my own small way, I was carrying his sword.

THE EXCLUSION

The four books of Maccabees, like a number of other books of the Lost Bible, are included in the Septuagint, the Greek version of the Hebrew Scriptures, and subsequently in the Apocryphal portion of Catholic Bibles. Clearly, the ancient Jewish community of Alexandria revered these books and considered them divinely inspired. Carrying as they do the triumphant message of deliverance, they have served as a beacon for the ages to those who cherish freedom from oppression: from William Wallace—Braveheart—in his courageous struggle against England's tyrannical king, Longshanks, to the patriots of the American Revolution.

Why did the sages at the Council of Yavne bar the testimony of these books from the sacred canon? The reasons were multiple, ranging from doubt about these books' historicity to misgivings about their political messages. On one level, it was evident that the books of Maccabees were guilty of exaggeration of the facts. Notably, the books depicted vast armies of tens of thousands doing battle across the landscape of Judea. In truth, the engagements consisted of skirmishes involving much more modest numbers. The keepers of the canon were not about to endorse a group of texts containing such serious inaccuracies.

But there is another reason behind the exclusion, much more serious and politically charged. The sages knew that, historically, once the Maccabees had won their revolution, they spawned a new Judean dynasty, a monarchy of their own, which came to be known as the Hasmoneans. It was a dynasty that began in the spirit of liberation, seeking to ensure the independence of Jerusalem from foreign domination. But as time passed, the motives of the Hasmoneans became less spiritual and far more temporal. They sought power and dominion, becoming in time virtually as corrupt as the foreign viceroys they had successfully overthrown.

One Hasmonean ruler, named Alexander Yannai, was so hated by the pious sages of his day that the Pharisees staged an open revolt against him. The revolt failed, and the tyranny continued until the year 63 B.C.E., when independent Judea was conquered by the legions of Rome, under a general named Pompey. The liberation sought by the Maccabees vanished in an instant. The sages at Yavne were certainly aware of the sad legacy of the Hasmonean dynasty, and they decided to "de-Hasmonize" history, by striking from the canon all reference to the genesis of the Hasmoneans. Interestingly, the miracle story of the oil and the menorah is not to be found in the books of Maccabees themselves, but is instead contained in the writings of the rabbinic sages centuries later, collectively known as the Talmud. The story is a clever substitution for the books they deliberately barred.

THE SECRET

In striking the books of Maccabees, the sages also eliminated one of the most important messages of the Lost Bible—that spirit can prevail over brute force, that might does not make right, that well-timed action in the World of Doing, even on the part of a single individual such as the aged priest Mattathias, can in fact change the world. There is a verse from a famous hymn sung at the time of Hanukkah that could not better express the underlying message and meaning of these books of deliverance:

> Children of the Maccabees,
> Whether free or fettered,
> Wake the echoes of your songs,
> Where you may be scattered.
> Yours the message cheering,
> That the time is nearing,
> Which will see all men free,
> Tyrants disappearing!

CHAPTER 21

The Fate of a Prophet

A good action is never lost; it is a treasure laid up and guarded for the doer's need.
—PEDRO CALDERON DE LA BARCA, SPANISH DRAMATIST, POET

*The difference between a man who faces death for the sake of an idea and an imitator
who goes in search of martyrdom is that the former expresses his idea most fully
in death while the latter really enjoys the bitterness of failure.*
—SOREN KIERKEGAARD, DANISH PHILOSOPHER, WRITER

Just down the side of the hill from my perch atop Jerusalem's Mount of Olives
are some very ancient tombs, meticulously chiseled into the barren limestone.
I visited them not infrequently as a young student in the Middle East, and years
later, escorting groups of my own students to important archaeological sites in
old Jerusalem. The tombs are dim, dank, and musty, though at least in tradition
their significance is astounding. They are purported to be the tombs of the biblical
prophets Haggai, Malachi, and Zechariah who, in the sixth century before the
Common Era, thundered messages of encouragement and hope to a people who had
suffered ignominious exile but returned to rebuild their devastated homeland.

Their prophetic oracles have inspired generations of the faithful as well as
subsequent prophets through the centuries. Their tombs are barren now; the
perpendicular niches cut in the limestone walls are empty, without a trace of
human remains. Most authorities doubt that the tombs are authentic, but the
place nonetheless contains an aura of sorts, stirring me from deep within. Many
true believers still hold the conviction that the path to heaven is the shortest and
most direct from this location. After all, it is said in hoary Jewish tradition (see
Zechariah 14:3-5) that the general resurrection of the dead will begin at this
place—the Mount of Olives.

But all of the folklore notwithstanding, the tomb of my favorite prophet,
arguably the greatest prophet who ever lived—Isaiah—is curiously missing. Other
prophets were rightly hallowed in death; but what of Isaiah? Has he no tomb? It
was not until I looked into the books of the Lost Bible that I realized that there is
in fact a tradition regarding the death of the "prince of the prophets." He didn't

just die; he was murdered. There it was, in a dusty volume I pulled from the shelf in the library on Mount Zion. I thought of history's many martyrs, who, even in their deaths, have helped to make the world a better place for all of us.

"I may not get there with you," said Martin Luther King. "But we as a people will get to the Promised Land." The fact is, great leaders don't always get to see the fruit of their efforts. True visionaries are often cut off in their prime. I wondered to myself, what happens when things don't work out as they did for the mighty Maccabees? When instead of victory, the end of the struggle is defeat and even ignominious death?

TROUBLEMAKER AT THE TEMPLE

A composite book widely circulated in the ancient world but stricken from the biblical canon, known as the Martyrdom (and/or Ascension) of Isaiah, tells of how the prophet Isaiah—after a lifetime of sometimes controversial action—finds himself in trouble for his *chutzpah* and actually predicts his own demise.

We really shouldn't be surprised that Isaiah ran into trouble. After all, the role of a prophet—a true prophet—is to stir things up. Ancient Israel was unique in that sense. Other ancient civilizations had their soothsayers and their shamans, their oracles and their wisdom teachers. Fortunetellers were as ubiquitous in antiquity as psychics are today. You might go to the Greek isle of Delphi, for example, to see the great Oracle. You would be required to bring the appropriate offering—a goat—that would be ritually sprinkled with water. If the goat shivered, it meant that a prophecy was about to come forth from Apollo. Of course a fee would have to be paid, whereupon a spirit-possessed woman would hold forth in a great babble of words, which were in turn translated by priests.

These oracles commanded an enormous following in ancient society, but the Israelite prophets were in a class by themselves. They actually changed society. They proclaimed social justice for the downtrodden and excoriated the wealthy elite class who oppressed the poor. In the traditional book of Isaiah we read of the prophet's great vision, in which he sees the Eternal "high and uplifted" the mystical Divine Presence filling the temple (Isaiah 6:1-13). This is more than a spiritual fireworks show; it is Isaiah's commission, the driving force of his life, which makes him utterly different from any oracle preaching enlightenment. His divine encounter instead brings forth pain and anguish. His burden is to wrestle with his own culture—including the priggish temple priesthood—creating a counterculture movement that will energize the World of Doing. He is to wake his slumbering people from their complacency.

In the name of God he cries out, "An ox knows its owner, and an ass knows its master's feeding trough. But Israel does not know; my people are without understanding!" (Isaiah 1:3, author's translation). He decrees defeat and catastrophe for the nation, including its king, Hezekiah. Fortunately, Hezekiah is a humble king, who personally repents and tries to woo his nation back to the right path. But Isaiah's honeymoon with the monarchy will not last. Hezekiah's successor, Manasseh, will turn on the prophet, on the theory that if you cannot silence the message, then silence the messenger. Like Martin Luther King after him, Isaiah senses that his time is short. The justice he seeks will not come about in his own lifetime, but (as has been noted) progress, in the worldview of the ancients, is generational, and a better day will someday dawn. The Lost Bible fills in the gaps in his life—and his death—with the following account (reworked in modern paraphrase):

> King Hezekiah of Judah summoned his only son, Manasseh, along with the prophet Isaiah and his son Josab. With Josab nearby, but beyond earshot of Manasseh, Isaiah said the following to Hezekiah:
>
> "As the Eternal lives, and as the divine *ruakh* which speaks to me lives, all of your commandments and good words will be nullified by your son Manasseh. His destiny is to torture me, after which I will depart this world."

Isaiah possesses an amazing degree of personal peace and tranquility. According to the text he knows that he will be persecuted and killed, but his true strength is internal. He accepts what he sees as a divine decree without protest. What will be will be. The traditional book of Isaiah contains a famous passage in the fifty-third chapter, describing some mysterious individual whose fate is death:

> He was despised and rejected; a person of suffering, accustomed to sickness. As one who hid his countenance from us, he was despised, and we did not regard him. He was bearing our sickness and suffering our pain. We considered him stricken, beaten and tortured by God. But he was wounded because of our transgressions and beaten down because of our sins. The chastisement that made us whole was upon him, and by his wounds we were healed. . . . Surely, he was cut off from the land of the living. (Isaiah 53:3-5,8, author's translation)

The passage reminds modern readers of Jesus of Nazareth, but researchers are quick to point out that when it was first composed, the passage was probably describing the prophet himself: *Isaiah* was the suffering servant who would lay down his life as a sacrifice. The New Testament itself hints that this was a common interpretation, in the account of a certain Ethiopian eunuch, traveling along the road to Gaza, who finds himself reading Isaiah 53. He is met by the apostle Philip, whom he asks pointedly, "About whom is the prophet speaking, about *himself* or some other person?" (Acts 8:34, author's translation, italics added). Philip of course takes the opportunity to speak of Jesus, but it is likely that most of the population in those days were strongly influenced by the Lost Bible's tradition of the Martyrdom of Isaiah.

We can certainly think of Isaiah as an ancient Martin Luther King, prepared to suffer and die for the cause of social justice. It is axiomatic that standing up and making one's voice heard, in a committed way, generally involves paying the price of commitment. Each of us must ask, as we enter the World of Doing, are we ready to pay that price?

IN COLD BLOOD

Back in King Hezekiah's court, Isaiah continues his dire prediction:

> "King Manasseh will do as he pleases. Instead of following my teachings, he will devote himself to Belial. He will provoke the Jerusalemites and Judeans to forsake the truth. Belial will live in Manasseh's heart, so that he seizes me and has me sawn in two."
>
> When King Hezekiah heard this, he began to weep, rending his clothes.

Isaiah, however, takes the occasion to correct the king, even in his sympathy:

> "Your will shall not come to pass, for I have been predestined to this fate."

It is not as though Isaiah has some dark, melancholic desire to die. He has no morbid death wish, and he therefore decides that this might be the opportune time to "get out of Dodge." Winston Churchill once quipped, "Although prepared for martyrdom, I *prefer* that it be postponed." Doubtless, the ancient prophet feels similarly. He forthwith withdraws, during what is clearly a time of trouble. Our paraphrased account relates:

> Isaiah realized that the people of Jerusalem had turned away from the Law and had taken up satanic worship without restraint. In response he abandoned Jerusalem entirely. He lived for a time in Bethlehem, in Judea, but he saw so much apostasy there that he retreated to a mountain out in the desert. He was soon joined by the prophets Micaiah, Joel, and Habakkuk, as well as his son Josab and many people of faith. They

all wore hairy garments and owned nothing at all. They all mourned bitterly over the people's great waywardness. All they ate were wild herbs that grew on the mountainsides. . . . They all lived together on the mountains and hillsides for the next two years.

Nevertheless, fate will not allow Isaiah and his band of "merry men" to remain unmolested. A false prophet named Belkhirah (possessed by the evil spirit Belial) accuses Isaiah of treason:

> Belkhira, a devotee of Manasseh, was well acquainted with the hideout of Isaiah and his band of prophets, since he lived in the area of Bethlehem. He uttered false prophesies in Jerusalem, and though he was a Samaritan, he gained many adherents among the people. . . .
>
> Belkhira brought charges against Isaiah and his fellow prophets, declaring, "Isaiah and his accomplices have prophesied that Jerusalem and the cities of Judea will be devastated, and that the inhabitants of Benjamin and Judah will be taken captive. They have even prophesied against you, O king, that you will be taken away with hooks and chains. Nevertheless, their prophecies are false! Isaiah has boasted, 'I have better vision than our greatest prophet, Moses.' But it was Moses who said, 'No one can see God and survive.' Isaiah says, 'I have seen God and, look, I still live!' He even compared Jerusalem with Sodom, and its princes with the people of Gomorrah. But, O king, Isaiah is lying!" Belkhira brought many more charges against the prophet and his acquaintances.

BRAVEHEART

In life's great chess game, one should not expect evil to remain passive. The Lost Bible indicates that malevolent power also exists in the World of Doing, and that we should brace for it. Isaiah expects what is coming. In the end he is not only apprehended, he is gruesomely sawn in two with a wooden saw. As the blade begins its fearsome task, the wicked Belkhira offers the prophet one last chance. He will yet be spared if he declares openly that Belkhira and Manasseh are upright and blameless. Isaiah's answer is unequivocal:

> "As long as there is a breath in my body I will say this: May you, your entire household and the power you wield be cursed and damned! All you can take away from me is my flesh, nothing more!"

Obviously, Belkhira is not pleased, and Isaiah's fate is sealed. We read:

As Isaiah was being executed, Belkhira arose and made more accusations. The other false prophets rose as well, laughing at Isaiah and rejoicing at his death. . . .

As the evildoers were sawing Isaiah in two, he didn't cry in pain or weep, but he uttered his words with the power of the *ruakh,* until his body was severed.

Two additions to the text, known as the Testament of Hezekiah and the Vision of Isaiah, complete the account. As the soul of the murdered prophet ascends, he is shown the seven heavens, each with its own angel. He glimpses departed souls, from righteous Abel to Enoch, and ultimately has an audience with God. The Lost Bible teaches that even death loses its power when people hold on to their conviction that there is life beyond life. By encountering those who had gone on before him, Isaiah reminds us that progress is indeed generational. We can each say, "I may not get there with you, but we as a people will get to the Promised Land." Fear is banished.

THE EXCLUSION

Modern researchers do not accept the proposition that this text goes back to the days of the prophet Isaiah himself. Isaiah of Jerusalem is a real historical character who lived in the eighth century before the Common Era. But this tale of his martyrdom has all the earmarks of being a text of the second century B.C.E., since it deals with a subject very pertinent to Israel at the time of the great persecution of Antiochus Epiphanies—martyrdom. An account of the execution of the greatest of the prophets would certainly stir the heart of the pious of those days, many of whom laid down their lives, making the ultimate sacrifice for their faith.

While the text came down to us in Greek (along with a complete Ethiopic text and fragments in Latin and Coptic), the original language of the martyrdom account, based on internal linguistic clues, was certainly Hebrew, having been composed on location in ancient Judea. Nevertheless, the subsequent rabbinic sages were not fooled by the text's lack of historical credibility, and they barred it from the canon.

It is theorized that the text was originally an Essene composition, due to the stark dualism that pervades it, including an emphasis on Satan and Belial. The term Belial, as a euphemism for the incarnation of Satan, is common among the Dead Sea Scrolls and thrived among sectarian circles in ancient Judea. Since the Martyrdom of Isaiah preserves a sectarian flavor, the mainstream sages wanted nothing to do with it. The Judeo-Christian sect, however, clearly revered it and may have accepted this pseudepigraphal text as Holy Writ.

The account was ultimately taken over by the Christians, who turned it into a tripartite composite work, appending the so-called Testament of Hezekiah and the third section, the Vision of Isaiah. These additions add material that is highly theological, conveying a Christian spin.

The clearest evidence of the book's popularity among Christians is found in the New Testament's epistle to the Hebrews, which, without mentioning Isaiah by name, makes stunning reference to the details of his martyrdom. In a famous passage about heroes of the faith we read:

> They were stoned to death. They were tried. They were sawn in two. They were murdered with the sword. They wandered around in sheepskins and goatskins. They were needy. They were afflicted. They were mistreated. The world was not worthy of them. They wandered through deserts, over mountains, in caves and in holes in the ground. . . . Therefore, since we have such a great cloud of witnesses encircling us . . . let us patiently run the race that is set before us. (Hebrews 11:37-38, 12:1, author's translation)

As was the case with other books of the Lost Bible, the sages appeared to have been influenced by an all-or-nothing approach. If there were any doubt about a text's historicity, or if a text carried any concepts that didn't quite mesh with prevailing theological norms, they tossed it out. A book had to be deemed inerrant, or it was worthless, with no shades of gray allowed. In this case the keepers of the canon failed to consider the fact that there was a long-established tradition in ancient Judea that Isaiah really was martyred. The traditional book of Isaiah provides no details as to the prophet's ultimate fate, and this pseudepigraphal work is the only independent testimony we have.

Even more perplexing is the question of why the Martyrdom of Isaiah never found its way into the Christian canon. After all, for early Christians it was important to point out that Isaiah had been cruelly executed, just as Jesus had been crucified. Perhaps the developing Christian church simply didn't know where to place the book in its canon. It clearly didn't belong with other New Testament books, since it was about Isaiah, not Jesus or the apostles. And since it had been stricken from the Hebrew canon, and did not even appear in the Septuagint, it was simply ignored. Thus, a tantalizing puzzle piece in the worldview of the earliest Christians was neglected, forgotten, and lost.

THE SECRET

What do we learn from the testimony of this little-known text? Perhaps we ought to learn the universal lesson that the suffering of great individuals on the world stage is really little different from our own, as we struggle to get by on a daily basis. In a sense we are all castaways, like Isaiah and his prophetic band, hiding on a mountain in the desert.

Sometimes life seems to be a continual mêlée, and we long for enlightenment— Nirvana—a state of tranquility, without struggle and turmoil. Yet the message of Isaiah and his fellow prophets is to embrace the struggle and the turmoil, because change invariably involves pain. Perhaps it is not death that we fear as much as the attendant pain. Yet, it is only through pain, like birth pangs, that we can bring forth a better life for ourselves and our posterity.

Living and dying are functions of one another. As the dean of science fiction writers, Robert Heinlein, said, "The supreme irony of life is that hardly anyone gets out of it alive." Some people fear dying so much that they are afraid to live. Others are afraid of living and actually prefer death. Still others are afraid of both living and dying. Only a small minority is sufficiently wise to accept both life and death with equanimity, whereupon they are free to enjoy the ongoing waltz of the corporeal experience.

There is physical death, and there are other kinds of death as well. What happens when our dreams die? When our world is suddenly turned upside down and unexpected reversals knock us off our feet? The Martyrdom/Ascension of Isaiah reminds us that ascent stems from descent, as rebirth follows death. It is all part of the circle of life. Emerson wrote: "Justice is not postponed. A perfect equity adjusts its balance in all parts of life."

CHAPTER 22

Wisdom from the Patriarchs: The Lost Bible's Twelve Apostles

A man is the sum of his actions, of what he has done, of what he can do. Nothing else.
—MAHATMA GANDHI

Our principles are the springs of our actions. Our actions, the springs of our happiness or misery. Too much care, therefore, cannot be taken in forming our principles.
—RED SKELTON

He has told you, O man, what is good. And what does the Eternal demand of you? Only to do justice, to practice loving-kindness, and to walk in humility with your God.
—MICAH 6:8, AUTHOR'S TRANSLATION

S itting on my perch atop the Mount of Olives, looking down at the tranquil city below, I nonetheless acknowledged that living in the land of Israel is anything but tranquil. The holiness of the terrain itself can only inspire. Why, then, has this been home to such a legacy of violence, from the days when King David conquered the city from the pagan Jebusites to modern times, when it has become the focal point of an international conflict gripping the entire Middle East? With religion omnipresent and on every street corner, how could there yet be so much aggression, bloodshed, and murder?

When I grew tired of looking down on the city, I would cast a glance upward, asking the Ruler of the universe to give me a clue. I never received an answer on the Mount of Olives. It came instead from a surprising location. While meeting a group of tourists one day at Tel-Aviv's Ben Gurion Airport, I spotted a little sign placed there by a sect of Orthodox Jews. It said: "Looking for God? Go home!"

I knew instantly what was meant. Throngs of tourists from around the world come regularly to see the Holy Land, many convinced that exposure to this sacred turf will somehow bring a solution to their deepest problems. But the answers are already out there, in black and white, in a library of books from the ancient past.

Go home and read them! The Divine Presence spoke to me that day. It wasn't long before I found myself back "home" in Jerusalem, in my favorite musty library, inconspicuously situated on Mount Zion. I sat at a long table, the ancient hills glowing gold in the distance, and opened the books.

GO DO THE RIGHT THING

The ancients were very practical. They didn't just preach pious maxims; through their stories they conveyed no-nonsense advice on what to do and what not to do on a daily basis. Unlike a good deal of modern metaphysics, they didn't leave their readers rudderless, nor were they particularly interested in conveying warm fuzzies. The ancient library of the Dead Sea Scrolls, for example, contains lists of virtues and vices, do's and don'ts. In a document unknown to the world until its sudden discovery in the desert in 1947—the Manual of Discipline—we read of two ways and two spirits of human conduct:

> The spirit of unrighteousness brings forth the following: avarice, slug-gishness in doing righteous deeds, evil lying, pride, arrogance, falsehood, and cruel deceit. . . .
>
> And these are the ways in the earth to enlighten human hearts and make plain before them all the ways of righteousness . . . a spirit of humility, of longsuffering, of abundant mercy, of everlasting goodness, of intelligence, of understanding, of mighty wisdom, trusting in all the works of God. (Manual of Discipline, Column 4, author's translation)

Could there be a more important thing to convey to one's descendants than a list of behavior patterns to be emulated and those to be shunned? As trite as it may sound, what parent does not want to tell his or her children, "Don't repeat my mistakes"? As we have learned, the concept of a living will was very important among the ancients. Instruction conveyed on one's deathbed frequently amounted to the accumulated wisdom and insight of a lifetime. The text of the traditional Bible records in detail the last words of Jacob, whose name was changed to Israel and who became the progenitor of the twelve tribes. But what about Jacob's sons, the patriarchs of the twelve tribes themselves? Did they not convey similar testimony as they approached the end of their lives?

An important book of the Lost Bible says *yes*. It is called the Testaments of the Twelve Patriarchs, and it appears to have been one of the most popular pieces of literature in the ancient Near East. There are of course a dozen different deathbed exhortations (or, if you will, testimonies), each uttered by one of Jacob's sons. While these testimonies cover various subjects, as one would expect, their overarching message is summed up in a single statement: Go do the right thing.

In these texts and others, the sages who wrote the Lost Bible taught that experience reveals two roads, two ways. One leads to life, the other to destruction. Moreover, the greatest gift bestowed upon human beings is the power of choice. It is incumbent upon each individual to choose for himself or herself which path to embrace. To that extent the Lost Bible is not a map for the Holy Land; it is a guidebook for the wilderness. Life is lived in the outback, and we need, above all, road signs in the desert. We need moral clarity and singleness of vision. The sages of the Lost Bible would counsel us not to try to be all things to all people, but rather to stand for something, and to put what we stand for into action.

OF VICE AND MEN

At the beginning of each of the twelve testimonies, we find a statement relating to a particular vice or virtue, followed by practical commentary. The first is of Reuben, Jacob's eldest son. His testimony tells us at the outset that it relates to lustful desire, which in turn leads to fornication. In an expanded account of what is alluded to only briefly in the traditional Bible, Reuben remorsefully recounts how he slept with his father Jacob's concubine, Bilhah. It is an important affair, since we are told that for this reason, Reuben's status as the eldest son is officially revoked.

Bear in mind that concubinage was in ancient times just a step beneath marriage, so that an illicit relationship with a concubine was akin to adultery. Reuben appears in stark contrast with righteous Joseph, the brother who was sold into slavery in Egypt, only to be approached seductively by the wife of a rich and powerful man named Potiphar. Whereas Joseph spurns the woman's advances, Reuben confesses that he sought out Bilhah, whom he spied while she was bathing.

Reuben goes on to warn his descendants about the wiles of women. It was women who, according to another account in the Lost Bible, charmed the heavenly Watchers in the days before the great flood of Noah—a detail that hardly resonates well with modern readers. But we shouldn't let ourselves be put off of this important text because of it. Consider what Reuben is really saying. There is a deeper problem involved here. A simple glance leads to thought, and the thought, when entertained, leads to action. In other words, fornication is something more than physical. It frequently involves being disingenuous and deceptive, ruled by raw, selfish desire. According to Reuben, if the action is unchaste, it amounts to nothing less than idolatry. The truly wise person, by contrast, needs nothing, lacks nothing, desires nothing, and like Joseph, is capable of confirming inner strength concretely in the World of Doing. We read (in modern paraphrase):

> Seven spirits are given to human beings, by which all action is accomplished: Life, Seeing (along with Desire), Hearing (with attendant Instruction), Smell (along with Breathing), Speech (with Knowledge following), Taste (which brings eating and thereby Strength), and Procreation (with attendant indulgence and error).

The Buddha taught that desire is at the heart of human error. One must therefore learn to conquer it. Reuben would heartily agree.

JEALOUSY IS INSECURITY

The second of Jacob's twelve sons is Simeon, who delivers his own deathbed testimony. He relates (in paraphrase):

> Let me tell you what is on my heart. I am the second son of my father Jacob and my mother Leah. I was named Simeon because the prayer of my mother was heard on high. In my youth I was extremely strong. I never hesitated to act. I was fearless and lionhearted, possessing great courage and dispassionate emotions.

However, something goes awry over the course of his life. Simeon's chief concern and admonition relates to his downfall—envy. Jealousy of course is never really about the other person; it's always about us—the fact that we are not really comfortable inside our own skin. At its core, jealousy is insecurity. Get beyond it, and we will have built a cathedral for our soul.

Returning to Joseph, a favorite character in Israelite lore, Simeon admits that he was so jealous of his brother that at one point he actually plotted to kill him. Left alone, envy consumes us, takes over our personhood, to the point of inspiring murder. Again, simple thought leads to disastrous action in the World of Doing. The text reads (in contemporary style):

> If you purge yourselves of envy and hard-heartedness, my very bones will revive like a rose in bloom. My flesh will blossom like a lily. . . . The whole world will find rest from its troubles, and all the inhabitants of the earth will be delivered from war.

The constant theme of these testimonies is that the descendants should learn important lessons from the patriarchs, that wise action should be emulated and foolish action shunned.

ARROGANCE: THE PERIL OF POWER

The Testament of Levi represents the centerpiece of the entire series of texts. Its theme concerns the sin of arrogance, as it relates to the temple priesthood. This son of Jacob recounts two separate visions. First, an angel escorts him up to heaven, where the priesthood is conferred upon him and his descendants for all eternity. Secondly, Levi has a supernatural audience with his grandfather Isaac, who relates that the priesthood will someday be corrupted by the priests themselves.

The fact is, the Jerusalem priesthood was not only religiously influential in antiquity; it was incredibly wealthy and politically powerful as well. It was this very elite status that led to its corruption. English historian Lord John Dalberg Acton once said, "Power tends to corrupt, and absolute power corrupts absolutely." To which scientist and novelist David Brin retorted, "It's said that power corrupts, but actually it's more true that power attracts the corruptible." The lesson here is that spiritual reality is unimportant to the materially minded, even if they happen to be priests. Levi is shown a vision of the divine realm, including the supernatural temple and the attendant angels. Nevertheless, we are told (continuing our paraphrase):

> The sons of men are unconcerned and keep transgressing. . . . Someday the rocks themselves will dissolve. The sun will go out. The waters will evaporate. Even the invisible spirits will disappear, and hell will open its mouth at the command of the Most High. Yet, unbelievably, human beings will continue to do wrong.

The Testament of Levi gives us a clear warning from antiquity regarding the peril of power. Moreover, when religious power is fused with political power, the menace is particularly acute. The lesson of this testimony is that true service should come about through an attitude of humility. Let those who lead do so by force of character, not force of arms.

OF COURAGE AND KINGS

The Testament of Judah focuses on the triple themes of courage, avarice (lusting after money), and fornication (lusting after the flesh). The first section of this testimony—the first nine chapters to be precise—recounts Judah's early years, which were filled with personal bravery. He shares how his father had in fact declared him to be a king, a stunning proclamation in a society that prided itself on having no king but God. Judah demonstrates his worthiness for such office by fending off wild animals, as well as by being victorious in battle. Courage, in the World of Doing, amounts to the willingness to act, to get moving, relying on divine providence as one's ultimate source. C. S. Lewis once poetically observed, "Safety, ease, rest, are good, not best."

Judah, in his younger years well understands that motion is at the heart of courage, and that courage is the attribute that, perhaps more than any other, epitomizes the World of Doing. Unfortunately, Judah's character takes a turn for the worse, along the road of life. He enters a marriage with a non-Israelite woman named Bathshua. Worse still, he sleeps with his daughter-in-law, Tamar, who, in a clever ruse, had dressed like a harlot by the side of the road. While the traditional Bible's account of these events is marked by brevity, the Lost Bible fills in the salacious details, revealing, for example, Judah's proclivity to strong drink, which motivated his untoward behavior.

It is his drinking that leads Judah to commit another foible, namely divulging divine secrets and mysteries to pagan women, which ultimately reveals him to be unworthy of the royal status bestowed upon him. The good news is that the promise of kingship will not be revoked, in spite of Judah's copious errors. Though Judah's descendants are warned not to follow his example, the conclusion of his testimony reveals the image of yet another king, the Messiah to come, in whose days the general resurrection of the dead will occur.

The lesson for the contemporary world is profound. Each of us has been given authority and dominion—a kingship. It is a trust bestowed upon us that is capable of bringing forth a Messianic Age. While God acts, in our world and in the universe at large, the Divine Presence does not act alone. The divine will needs human beings to bring to fruition the divine desire. Judah declares (in contemporary paraphrase):

> Dear children, I want you to know that two spirits are seeking to infiltrate humanity. One is the Spirit of Truth, the other the Spirit of Error. The conscience of the mind is caught between the two, choosing according to its own inclination.

In the final analysis, anything that impedes us, that inhibits the expression of our spiritual nature, from substance abuse to lustful foibles, also impedes God. Choice is an awesome gift in the World of Doing; we must use it wisely.

THE TAO OF ISSACHAR

Another example of virtue in the World of Doing can be found in the Testament of Issachar, which is devoted largely to the theme of simplicity. It describes the simple agricultural existence of a farmer—quite the converse of the action hero we find in Judah.

Action, however, can take many forms. While the World of Doing presents a way of action, it is a way that can also be simple and unassuming. Issachar may be contrasted, not only with his brothers, but also with the typical modern corporate executive, upwardly mobile and successful, but whose accomplishment is matched by attendant stress and misery. Issachar is not trying to get ahead. He simply works the fields. The secret of Issachar's life is not unlike Taoist philosophy, which relates a fundamental paradox: The way up is down, and true happiness results not from rising higher, but in staying where one is.

Increasingly popular in the West, the Tao (which in translation means the way) suggests a self-revealing path, expressed in the heart of nature. Not surprisingly, those who till the soil are the ones most intimately familiar with this natural way, who hear its mundane intonations, in the plants that sprout, the leaves and blossoms, and the earth itself. Leave off all the machinations of polite society. Retreat to the countryside, to the wilderness, if need be. Return to nature; return to yourself.

The teachings of the great Taoist sage, Lao Tzu, are echoed in the testimony of Issachar. Seek the simplicity of solitude rather than the complexity of society. The most noble state is being connected to the earth. Returning to the Garden of Eden, the traditional Bible depicts Adam's life after the fall as cursed, inasmuch as he must work the fields by the sweat of his brow. But in Issachar's testimony we see the redemptive side of hard labor. For joy is perfected in simplicity. Issachar declares (in paraphrase):

> Dear children, pay attention and live with integrity. . . . A person who is authentic doesn't desire gold and never defrauds anyone else, doesn't live on a fancy diet, and doesn't need fine clothing. Such a person doesn't make plans for life, but waits on the divine will. The Spirit of Error has no power over such a person.

As Thoreau would later write while sitting on the shores of Walden Pond, "Simplify, simplify, simplify." Issachar is no Thoreau, but he would certainly agree that "the mass of men lead lives of quiet desperation." He also knows, as we moderns are only now discovering, that simplicity breeds contentment.

HOLY JOE

Another contented character of the Lost Bible is Joseph, whose testimony says much about the way virtue was perceived by the ancients. Joseph is the quintessential model of chastity, an attribute that has fallen out of favor in modern times. Approached seductively by the wife of Potiphar, a wealthy Egyptian known for jealous rage, the righteous Joseph rebuffs the unwelcome advances, only to be accused by the outraged woman of attempted rape. As noted, chastity represents more than mere sexual abstinence. It suggests plainness and simplicity of style. As practical advice for the World of Doing, Joseph's testimony is all about being simple and direct, open and honest. He is quintessentially ingenuous, not worldly experienced, but remarkably innocent. He relates (in continuing paraphrase):

> Dear brothers and children, . . . I have witnessed envy and death in my lifetime, but I have not veered from the path. . . . I was sold into slavery, but the Most High released me. . . . I was hungry, but the Eternal fed me; alone, but the Eternal visited me; weak, but the Eternal cared for me; in prison, but the Savior acted in mercy toward me; in bonds, but set free.

In a hauntingly similar passage in the New Testament book of Matthew, we read:

> For I was famished and you gave me food to eat. I thirsted and you gave drink to me. I was a stranger and you sheltered me. I was naked and you clothed me. I was sick and you visited me. I was in prison and you came to me. (Matthew 25:35-36, author's translation)

Moreover, Joseph's life is distinguished, not so much by what he does, but by what he doesn't do. This is seen in various details regarding the seductive behavior of Potiphar's wife, absent in traditional Bibles.

She threatens to have Joseph tortured if he does not lie with her. Nonetheless, he does not consent. She employs overwhelming flattery, asserting that she will worship his God, yet he does not consent. She employs a magic potion known to be an aphrodisiac; still, he does not consent. Instead, he neutralizes the potion. She declares that she will have Potiphar murdered, so as to marry Joseph. Still, he does not consent. In desperation she warns that she will kill herself; still he does not consent. Moreover, throughout his ordeal, Joseph remains silent with regard to his eleven treacherous brothers, who had sold him into slavery in Egypt to begin with. He knows that he will be vindicated in the end, but he doesn't know how. He does not know that Pharaoh himself will have a dream and that he will be called upon to interpret it, after which he will be elevated to Pharaoh's second-in-command.

There is a Taoist principle which states that the most effective action is inaction. When in doubt, take no action at all. Rather than ranting and raving, flailing about madly, or shaking your fist at the universe, step back. Withdraw. Preserve your energy. Wait for an opportune moment when the time will be right to ride nature's great wave. This, more than anything, is what sets Joseph apart, what distinguishes him from all his brothers and makes him a true warrior in the World of Doing.

THE EXCLUSION

Why bar these important testimonies from the accepted list of holy books? This we know: the Testaments of the Twelve Patriarchs are quite ancient, dating back as far as 250 B.C.E. While the earliest texts are in Greek, from the Middle Ages, they were certainly copied from an earlier Semitic work, written in either Hebrew or Aramaic. Furthermore, the Testaments show signs of having been composed by a single hand, one author, who likely relied on yet earlier sources, either oral or written. Importantly, the Testaments most likely derive from the land of Israel itself, which alone should lend them a certain weight of authority.

All of this notwithstanding, the sages who gathered at Yavne were not impressed. The keepers of the canon were quintessentially conservative, quite prepared to ban any book about which they had serious reservations. How could they really be sure that these words came from the patriarchs themselves? How did they know that these texts were anything more than folklore, which had evolved through centuries of retelling?

Moreover, they shied away from the whole doctrine of the two ways, which had grown in popularity among sectarian groups such as the Essenes. They could accept one way—the way of God—but they could not accept an opposing way, dominated by an evil power. While the Dead Sea Scrolls and even the New Testament mention a satanic figure called Belial, there would be no place for this figure in the worldview of the rabbinic sages.

Highlighting the popularity of these texts among so-called sectarian groups is an incredible fragment found among the Dead Sea Scrolls, bearing striking resemblance to the Testament of Levi. Known among researchers as the Aramaic Levi Document, it may in fact represent an early version of what ultimately became the Testament of Levi. It proves beyond a doubt that the concepts and even the language of the Testaments of the Twelve Patriarchs floated around Judea for centuries, prior to being incorporated into the version that came down to us in Greek. But the fact that the Testaments carried a sectarian tone and sectarian concepts made them, at the very least, highly suspect among the keepers of the canon.

Having been excluded from the Jewish canon, the Testaments were picked up by the early Christians, who edited them to include their own theological convictions. The brief Testament of Asher, for example, appears to have been reworked with the following Christological message placed in the patriarch's mouth:

> You will be dispersed across the whole world, denigrated and persecuted. But someday the Most High will pay a visit to the earth, coming in the form of a man, who will drink and dine with other humans. He will crush the head of the dragon in water, saving Israel and all of humanity, speaking God's words as a man.

From such evidence it is clear that the Testaments were popular among early Christians and adopted by them. Why, then, did they not make their way into Christian Bibles? As Christianity developed, it appears to have made a sharp distinction between the so-called Old Testament (the Hebrew Bible) and the New Testament. Since the Testaments of the Twelve Patriarchs appeared in no Jewish Bibles, including the Septuagint, the texts could not be considered Old Testament. And since they represent neither a gospel nor an epistle, they hardly belong with the genres of the New Testament books. The Testaments were therefore relegated to a literary dustbin, occasionally copied as curiosities but rarely read or studied.

Thus, an important literary voice from Israel's sacred past was silenced. But their message, of responsible action and, if need be, refraining from action, has never been more important. In a world of narcissistic self-absorption, of experience junkies whose moral fiber is incapable of just saying no, the lonely voice of the patriarchs whispers to us all from across the millennia: Go do the right thing!

SUMMING UP

Another word for *messenger* is *apostle,* and, regardless of whether these texts are genuine or clever contrivances, we can think of the sons of Jacob as apostles to modern society. What do we learn from the twelve apostles of the Lost Bible? We have already seen some major themes developed and issues addressed:

> Reuben—Desire
> Simeon—Jealousy
> Levi—Arrogance
> Judah—Courage
> Issachar—Simplicity
> Joseph—Chastity

Some additional themes from the twelve patriarchs, scattered among the rest of the texts, include:

> Zebulun—Mercy and Compassion
> Dan—Anger
> Naphtali—Orderliness
> Gad—Hatred
> Asher—Single-mindedness and Duplicity
> Benjamin—Imitation of Goodness

THE SECRET

This last concept, imitation, is crucial to our self-identification and to our behavior in the World of Doing. Each of us must find his or her way through life, navigating through obstacles. While modern technological society has blessed us in ways unimaginable to our forebears, it has also left us with a sense of growing alienation. We are cut off from our roots. We have lost the sense that progress is intergenerational; nor can we find a sense of continuity with generations gone by. We live in an age when contemporary heroes have virtually vanished, when public figures are routinely sullied, when the very notion of a code of honor is passé.

If the ancients could counsel us today, they would probably advise us to seek out parents or elders, and ask them to relate their own life stories, to recount their mistakes as well as their triumphs, to tell us what they have learned along the way, so that we might imitate their goodness and avoid their mistakes. Those we approach will probably be shocked to find that we are even interested, but they will also share with us a treasury of life experience that we could never acquire on our own.

In the middle of the last century, a generation of young men went off to war, decisively entering the World of Doing. They refused to be labeled as heroes, yet they obediently marched into the fray and liberated our planet from fascist tyrannies that would otherwise have enslaved us all. They are dying now, but these silver-haired saints, members of what has been called the greatest generation, still have stories to tell. All they lack is ears that are willing to listen and voices that ask.

Despite all the wisdom we have discovered and explored in these chapters, we don't necessarily have to search among lost manuscripts and ancient texts to find what we are looking for. That was one important lesson I brought home with me after my long and eventful residence in the holy city of Jerusalem. Granted, I still pore through lost manuscripts and ancient texts, but I know something important about the secrets I have so diligently sought. They have been with us all along. Let me conclude our journey with this nugget from the World of Doing, the greatest secret of all: the Golden Rule, as related by the great sage, Hillel the Elder:

A certain heathen came to a teacher named Shammai and said to him, "Make me a proselyte, on condition that you teach me the whole Torah while I stand on one foot." Thereupon he repulsed him with the rod that was in his hand. When he went to Hillel, the sage said to him, "What is hateful to you, do not do to your neighbor: that is the whole Torah; all the rest of it is commentary; go and learn." (Talmud, Shabbat 31a)

Epilogue

*The person who has wishes seeks possibilities; the person who has
no wishes seeks only explanations.*
—RUSSIAN PROVERB

T urning my back on the weathered, walled city of Jerusalem, I walked over
the ridge at the very summit of the Mount of Olives and gazed east. It was
the very contradiction of my view to the west. There was nothing out there, just
an empty wasteland. The low rolling hills dropped away beneath me, extending
toward the Jordan River Rift Valley and the Dead Sea, off in the distance. The
chalky dust was lifeless and barren, interrupted only by a hint of green, where an
occasional desert shrub was clinging to life. Yet east was the favorite direction of
the ancients. It is no accident that ancient maps were oriented toward the east,
with this direction on top and west on the bottom. It is believed that one day the
Messiah will come from the east, as surely as the sun peeks above the horizon
and illumines the land with its life-giving rays. As I turned around and trudged
westward once again, I noticed, far below, the main gate of the Old City—the
Eastern Gate—perfectly aligned to catch the light of the morning sun.

It is almost as dominant a feature of Old Jerusalem as the golden Dome of
the Rock itself. Having been built as part of the city walls, under the Ottoman
sultan, Suleiman the Magnificent, in 1517, the Eastern Gate sits directly on top
of an earlier gate, dating from the first century before the Common Era. It was
long held that the Anointed One, who will reestablish the throne of King David,
will enter through this gate. For that very reason, Suleiman gave orders that it be
walled up, forever preventing his entrance. So it is today, a massive, double-arched
gate with no entrance, completely covered in stone.

Much folklore has arisen about when and if the Eastern Gate will ever be
opened, and much of the speculation is, as we might well expect, overly literal.
Will there really be some kind of seismic disturbance, possibly an earthquake,
that will open the gate before the Holy One? I wouldn't hold my breath. But I
would think of the walled-up gate in another way, metaphysically, as a symbol
of our blocked-up souls, crusty and impenetrable. The gate is emblematic of the
religious dogmas and brittle ideologies that have separated people of faith from
time immemorial. Dogma rarely serves to enlighten, only to wall us off from one
another and keep the Messiah out.

WALLING OUT THE BOOKS

As I continued to stare at the Eastern Gate, I also thought of the sacred canon, the authoritative list of holy books, circumscribed by a wall of theological defense mechanisms and impervious to assault. But in walling off the list of inspired books, the sages and religionists (from the rabbis at Yavne to the bishops of the church councils) also closed off themselves and their flocks from important spiritual ideas, concepts, and insights. Sadly, those insights, such as contained in that other Bible—the Lost Bible—just might have revealed the syncretism inherent in the great faith traditions, bridging the centuries of misunderstanding among religionists, their disciples, and the cultures that sprang from them. The world of faith should never have become a closed system, shut off from all contradictory ideas, but an open book, intimately approachable, hiding nothing.

As I trudged my way back to Mount Zion, to my favorite little library, I asked myself several important questions, which I felt should have been in the minds of the religious leaders all along. Why require a canon at all? Why not just allow the books to be out there, letting people decide for themselves what speaks to them, what messages seem geared for their lives? After all, texts consist only of words on parchment, papyrus, and paper. Isn't God bigger than a book? Doesn't the entire concept of a canon force frail mortals, in their councils and conventions, with all of their religious baggage, to make decisions about what is in and what is out? Isn't such a process flawed on its face?

In the final analysis, there is no one book or set of books that define God. Moreover, even books that are fundamentally flawed can still deliver profound spiritual truth to the individual heart, which is after all the true cathedral of faith. The United States has its Constitution, but that doesn't preclude its citizens from reading the Federalist Papers, or Jefferson's writings, or any number of other works from the Founding Fathers. The desire for a set of recognized documents as a framework for a religious establishment is certainly understandable, but it was equally clear to me that in ancient Judea, the canon was left officially open. There was no authoritative list until around 90 of the Common Era. It took a council of sages at Yavne to wall off the canon, close and seal it.

Aren't there other options? A community of faith can say, "These are our principles, this is what we hold," without baptizing one book or set of books, and some religious traditions are in fact just that ecumenical. In a world where people still kill each other over questions of faith, I thought to myself: What a breath of fresh air!

THE QUEST OF THE SPIRIT—SEEKING POSSIBILITIES

Sitting once again in my favorite library, the weathered hills of Judea in the distance, I resorted to a little meditation. I pensively considered what the books banned from the Scriptures actually mean, as a whole. With a little help from the mystics, who pioneered the Kabbalah, I came to the realization that the books of the Lost Bible are more than just a collection of esoteric trivia from the ancients. They open to us moderns the minds and worldview of the people at large in the days when the Bible was edited and finalized. Furthermore, they dovetail with four major areas of life about which the Kabbalistic masters were trying to teach us. The principles are simple, and the possibilities they present are awesome:

- Know who you are,

- Be true to yourself and the divine image that is in you,

- Reach out authentically with your feelings, and

- Dare to do great things.

I asked myself: What is it that propels people's spiritual quest? Wishes, hopes, desires and dreams, the need to be connected with transcendent reality, above and beyond our finite selves. It is all about the desire to be something greater than what we already are, and it is that upward motion that makes us fully spiritual, and fully human. As long as that remains our motivation, we need not fear being corrupted by the contents of a book.

From the dusty pages of those books, the voice of Wisdom speaks to us still.

Notes

1. Edmund Wilson, *To the Finland Station: A Study in the Writing and Acting of History* (New York: New York Review Books Classics, 2003).
2. See C.S. Lewis, *The Problem of Pain* (New York: Simon & Schuster, 1996).
3. San Francisco Zen Center, Dean of Buddhist Studies Michael Wenger, *US News & World Report*, "Mysteries of Faith," Special Collector's Edition, 2003, p. 15.
4. This is an electronic version of The Holy Qur'an, translated by M. H. Shakir and published by Tahrike Tarsile Qur'an, Inc., in 1983. The text was provided by the Online Book Initiative and subsequently marked up at the HTI in SGML.
5. Lyrics of "Superman" by Five for Fighting.
6. The Hebrew phrase *Barekh Elohim v'mut* ("Bless God and die") has traditionally been translated "Curse (or blaspheme) God and die," since it is assumed that this must have been the original intent of the author.
7. The Greek writer has chosen to mimic the wording of the Septuagint (Greek) version of Job, which renders "Bless God and die" as "Curse the Lord and die": *"Epon ti remah eis kurion kai teleuta."*
8. *Yared* means descend in Hebrew/Aramaic.
9. Note that the standard spelling of this biblical name is Baruch. I have spelled it with the letters "kh" to avoid the mispronunciation of the back-of-the-throat sound as an English "ch," as in "brooch." At such slaughter of the Hebrew, the real Barukh would be offended!
10. David McCullough, *Truman* (New York: Simon & Schuster, © 1992 by David McCullough), p. 620. Rabbi Herzog's statement is quoted in Alfred Steinberg: *The Man from Missouri: The Life and Times of Harry S. Truman* (New York: Putnam's, 1962).
11. As with Barukh, I have preferred the "kh" spelling, to mimic a back-of-the-throat sound, so as not to confuse this beautiful Hebrew word with something that sounds akin to "roach"!
12. Permission to use granted by the manager of Dr. Kings' estate: Intellectual Properties Management, 1579-F Monroe Drive, Suite 235, Atlanta, GA 30324.

Lost Bible Time Line

400 B.C.E.	Song of Solomon 1 Chronicles
	2 Chronicles Ezra-Nehemiah
300 B.C.E.	
	Ecclesiastes Septuagint Testaments of the Twelve Patriarchs
200 B.C.E.	Tobit Susanna/ Judith Daniel/ Bel and the Dragon/ 1 Barukh 1-2 Enoch/ Jubilees Judith 1 Maccabees/ Martyrdom of Isaiah
100 B.C.E.	
	2 Maccabees Apocalypse of Zephaniah 3 Maccabees Testament of Job
1 C.E.	Apocalypse 4 Maccabees Life of Adam and Eve Gospel of Thomas History of the Rechabites
100 C.E.	Testament of Abraham/ 2 Barukh 3-4 Barukh Testament of Isaac Infancy Gospel of Thomas
200 C.E.	Testament of Solomon
300 C.E.	

The Books in Brief

KNOWING

Life of Adam and Eve
Language of composition: Hebrew (?)
Language of translation/preservation: Greek and Latin
Era of composition: First century, C.E. (?)
Place of composition: Land of Israel
Genre: Pseudepigrapha
Probable reason for exclusion: Dualism—belief in two competing forces
The Secret: Don't bemoan your "fallen" condition; embrace knowledge, accept the reality of pain, and experience divine compassion.

Gospel of Thomas
Language of composition: Greek
Language of translation/preservation: Coptic
Era of composition: First century, C.E.(?)
Place of composition: Uncertain
Date and location of discovery: 1945, Nag Hammadi, Egypt
Genre: New Testament Pseudepigrapha
Probable reason for exclusion: Gnostic flavor
The Secret: We are all "light-bearers." Know that the things you seek have been in you all along.

Apocalypse of Zephaniah
Language of composition: Greek
Language of translation/preservation: Coptic
Era of composition: First century, B.C.E. (?)
Place of composition: Egypt
Genre: Pseudepigrapha
Probable reason for exclusion: Similarities with "pagan" traditions
The Secret: Believe in your own goodness and purity, whatever hellish experiences you encounter.

Bel and the Dragon
Language of composition: Aramaic (?)
Language of translation/preservation: Greek
Era of composition: Third century, B.C.E. (?)

Place of composition: Land of Israel (?)

Genre: Apocrypha

Probable reason for exclusion: Account seemed "far-fetched"

The Secret: Seek "organized knowledge" and "organized life," and calm will appear in the midst of any storm.

I Enoch

Language of composition: Hebrew, Aramaic (?)

Language of translation/preservation: Greek/Ethiopic

Era of composition: Second century, B.C.E. (?)

Place of composition: Land of Israel

Genre: Pseudepigrapha

Probable reason for exclusion: Mystical speculation

The Secret: Accept the fact that nothing is permanent. Seize the day!

BEING

Jubilees

Language of composition: Hebrew

Language of translation/preservation: Greek/Ethiopic, Latin

Era of composition: Second century, B.C.E.

Place of composition: Land of Israel

Genre: Pseudepigrapha

Probable reason for exclusion: Focus on angels, and a solar calendar

The Secret: Don't surrender to doubt or despair. Become aware of the larger pattern, and of "fate." Don't just do something; sit there!

2 Enoch

Language of composition: Hebrew, Aramaic (?)

Language of translation/preservation: Slavonic

Era of composition: Second century, B.C.E. (?)

Place of composition: Land of Israel

Genre: Pseudepigrapha

Probable reason for exclusion: Gnostic speculation

The Secret: You are not a mere copy of the divine image; you are that image.

Life of Adam and Eve

Language of composition: Hebrew (?)

Language of translation/preservation: Greek and Latin

Era of composition: First century, C.E.

Place of composition: Land of Israel
Genre: Pseudepigrapha
Additional reason for exclusion: Too exalted a view of humanity
The Secret: Recognize the divine fullness in yourself, others, and in the natural world around you.

Alphabet of Ben Sira
Language of composition: Hebrew
Era of composition: Seventh century, C.E.—eleventh century, C.E.
Place of composition: Uncertain
Genre: Biblical commentary
Probable reason for exclusion of Lilith account: Challenges male superiority
The Secret: When conflicts arise, hold your fire. Remember: what goes around comes around.

Testament of Abraham
Language of composition: Hebrew or Aramaic
Language of preservation: Greek
Era of composition: First century, C.E.—second century, C.E.
Place of composition: Egypt (?)
Genre: Pseudepigrapha
Probable reason for exclusion: Seemed "far-fetched"; theologically troublesome
The Secret: Cultivate a "God's-eye view" of your world, a higher perspective that will help you make the right choices.

Infancy Gospel of Thomas
Language of composition: Greek
Language of translation/preservation: Latin
Era of composition: Second century, C.E.
Place of composition: Land of Israel (?)
Genre: New Testament Pseudepigrapha
Probable reason for exclusion: Diminished the "holiness" of Jesus
The Secret: There's a hero hiding in each of us. We can all be transformed, from mischief to "messiah."

History of the Rechabites
Language of composition: Uncertain
Language of translation/preservation: Syriac
Era of composition: First century, C.E. (?)

Place of composition: Land of Israel (?)
Genre: Pseudepigrapha
Probable reason for exclusion: "Far-fetched"; theologically troublesome
The Secret: The accumulation of "stuff" never satisfies.

Testament of Solomon
Language of composition: Greek
Language of translation/preservation: Coptic
Era of composition: First century, C.E.—third century, C.E.
Place of composition: Egypt
Genre: Pseudepigrapha
Probable reason for exclusion: Elements of "magic"/"sorcery"
The Secret: Become a "ring-bearer," channeling the negativity of life situations in positive directions.

FEELING

Testament of Job
Language of composition: Greek
Language of translation/preservation: Coptic
Era of composition: First century, B.C.E.—first century, C.E.
Place of composition: Egypt
Genre: Pseudepigrapha
Probable reason for exclusion: Dualism
The Secret: Your emotions are a battleground; never surrender to despair.

I Enoch
Language of composition: Hebrew, Aramaic (?)
Language of translation/preservation: Greek/Ethiopic
Era of composition: Second century, B.C.E. (?)
Place of composition: Land of Israel
Genre: Pseudepigrapha
Probable reason for exclusion: Mystical speculation
The Secret: Treat your feelings like angels; let them soar, and don't look down!

Tobit
Language of composition: Hebrew, Aramaic (?)
Language of translation/preservation: Greek
Era of composition: Third century, B.C.E. (?)

Place of composition: Land of Israel
Genre: Apocrypha
Probable reason for exclusion: Focus on angelic intermediaries
The Secret: Let hope energize love and actualize deeds as you move in consonance with your feelings.

Letters of Barukh
Language of composition: Hebrew, Greek
Language of translation/preservation: Greek, Syriac
Era of composition: Second century, B.C.E.—first century, C.E. (?)
Place of composition: Land of Israel
Genre: 1 Barukh—Apocrypha; 2-4 Barukh—Pseudepigrapha
Probable reason for exclusion: Written too late; diminishes Jeremiah
The Secret: Let your pain be transformed into the building blocks of character.

Testament of Isaac
Language of composition: Greek (?)
Language of translation/preservation: Coptic
Era of composition: Second century, C.E.
Place of composition: Egypt
Genre: Pseudepigrapha
Probable reason for exclusion: Written too late; overly mystical
The Secret: Harbor attitudes that would make your ancestors proud.

DOING

Susanna
Language of composition: Hebrew
Language of translation/preservation: Greek
Era of composition: First century, B.C.E. (?)
Place of composition: Land of Israel
Genre: Apocrypha
Probable reason for exclusion: Authenticity doubted; erotic content that denigrates "elders"
The Secret: Where needs present themselves, let the hero in you find expression.

Judith
Language of composition: Hebrew (?)
Language of translation/preservation: Greek
Era of composition: Second century, B.C.E.?

Place of composition: Land of Israel
Genre: Apocrypha
Probable reason for exclusion: Contains historical inaccuracy
The Secret: Discover the "momentum" in any situation. Stop. Think. Observe. Plan.

Books of Maccabees
Language of composition: Hebrew, Greek
Language of translation/preservation: Greek
Era of composition: Second century, B.C.E.—first century, C.E.
Place of composition: Land of Israel, Egypt?
Genre: 1-2 Maccabees—Apocrypha; 3-4 Maccabees—Pseudepigrapha
Probable reason for exclusion: Politically "incorrect"
The Secret: Well-timed action in the World of Doing, even by a single person, can change the world.

Martyrdom of Isaiah
Language of composition: Hebrew
Language of translation/preservation: Greek/Ethiopic, Latin, Coptic
Era of composition: Second century, B.C.E.
Place of composition: Land of Israel
Genre: Pseudepigrapha
Probable reason for exclusion: "Sectarian" flavor
The Secret: Embrace struggle and turmoil, as part of living.

Testaments of the Twelve Patriarchs
Language of composition: Hebrew or Aramaic
Language of translation/preservation: Greek
Era of composition: c. 250 B.C.E.
Place of composition: Land of Israel
Genre: Pseudepigrapha
Probable reason for exclusion: Historicity doubted; doctrine of "two ways" shunned
The Secret: Imitate the virtues and shun the vices of previous generations.

ACKNOWLEDGMENTS

The author wishes to acknowledge the following publications as valuable resource material in producing this volume:

Charlesworth, James, *The Old Testament Pseudepigrapha*, Vols. 1-2, Garden City, New York, Doubleday Books, 1985.

Goodspeed, Edgar, *The Apocrypha: An American Translation*, New York, Vintage Books, 1989.

Porter, J. R., *The Lost Bible: Forgotten Scriptures Revealed*, Chicago, University of Chicago Press, 1989.

INDEX